W9-DES-476

JOHNSON & WALES UNIVERSIT...

3 5154 00082915 4

MATHEMATICS IN THE PRIMARY SCHOOL

A Sense of Progression

Edited by

Christine Hopkins, Susan Gifford and Sandy Pepperell

CME
Centre for Mathematics Education

This book has been written by the team of tutors at the Centre for Mathematics Education, Roehampton Institute London

Contributors: Kathy Goodman, Richard Harrison, Shirley Lee, Rosanne Posner, Geraldine Wood

Kathy Goodman is currently Deputy Head at The Mead County First School, Surrey. Geraldine Wood is currently Deputy Head at Bolingbroke Primary School, Wandsworth

David Fulton Publishers
London

Published in association with the Roehampton Institute London

David Fulton Publishers Ltd
2 Barbon Close, London WC1N 3JX

First published in Great Britain by David Fulton Publishers 1996

Note: The right of Christine Hopkins, Susan Gifford and Sandy Pepperell to be identified as the editors of this work has been asserted by them in accordance with the Copyright, Design and Patents Act 1988.

Copyright © David Fulton Publishers Ltd

British Library Cataloguing in Publication Data

A catalogue record for this book is available from the British Library

ISBN 1-85346-384-1

All rights reserved. No part of this publication may be reproduced, stored in a retrieval system or transmitted, in any form, or by any means, electronic, mechanical, photocopying, recording or otherwise, without the prior permission of the publishers.

Typeset by The Harrington Consultancy Ltd
Printed in Great Britain by the Cromwell Pres Ltd, Melksham.

Contents

Acknowledgements

We thank all the teachers, children and students who have contributed ideas and material to this book, and in particular the teachers and children at: All Saints' Church of England First School, Merton; Abelour House, Banffshire; Bishop Gilpin school, Wandsworth; Charles Dickens School, Southwark; Cypress Infant School, Croydon; Fairchildes Primary School, Croydon; Kingsley Infant School, Croydon; Sheringdale School, Wandsworth; St. Mark's Church of England Primary School, Kingston; St. Matthew's Church of England Primary School, Kingston; Surbiton Hill Nursery School, Kingston. Further material contributed by Suzanne Cowan, Jon Kurta, Penny Latham and Valerie Newman.

Preface

An expert teacher working with a class of children can make teaching look easy, but the background preparation needed to reach this stage is substantial. Not only does the primary teacher need to have a grasp of the general principles of children's learning and of the content of a range of National Curriculum subjects but also of the approaches and emphases which will make those subjects come alive. All teachers know that events in the classroom do not always turn out as they expect and that constant reflection and adaptation is required to provide appropriate learning experiences for the children.

This book is concerned with just one aspect of the primary curriculum: mathematics. We have tried to identify important principles which might inform mathematics teaching and hope that this will be useful both to students preparing to be teachers and also to teachers re-examining their approach to mathematics teaching as a part of the continual process of professional updating.

It is not uncommon for mathematics to be treated very differently from other aspects of the curriculum. The learning experience of children can, in some cases, consist almost exclusively of working through a series of textbooks. This approach would horrify if applied across the curriculum to subjects such as English, music, geography and science – yet it is considered normal for mathematics. It is worth examining how this situation came about, what sustains it and whether there are realistic alternatives. One of the earliest schemes, Mathematics for Schools (Fletcher), was introduced during the 1970s with the aim of broadening the primary mathematics curriculum, of ensuring that children who had been following a very restricted arithmetic diet encountered more varied topics and more practical approaches. At the time initial teacher education did not prepare for this more varied approach and so the scheme was designed to operate to some extent independently of the teacher. In many schools scheme-dominated work became the norm.

There are reasons to suppose that the time is ripe for a move from a mathematics curriculum which is 'scheme-dominated' to one which might be described as 'scheme-as-resource'. There are four main reasons for this:

1. The National Curriculum makes explicit a structure for the mathematics curriculum which includes elements of practical work, exploratory work and requirements to help children develop communication skills which clearly cannot be fulfilled solely by individual written work.

2. Through in-service training, particularly '20-day courses', and initial teacher education courses with increased time allocation for the study of mathematics, knowledge about more varied approaches to primary mathematics is spreading.

3. There are now some schemes which assume that the teacher will exercise more control, will organise group and whole-class work. These schemes used in

conjunction with their teacher guides encourage a diversity of approaches.

4. Increased emphasis on the role of curriculum co-ordinators, school development plans and a commitment by headteachers to review and monitor the curriculum on a school basis are resulting in more team planning, drawing on the skills of all the teachers on the staff.

This last trend of school curriculum review can have a particularly positive effect on mathematics because it can highlight the range of experiences to which children are entitled in all areas of the curriculum. It can stimulate discussion as to why some subjects become 'ghetto areas' with only a limited range of experiences for children. Analogies between different areas can be fruitful: for example, if children are required to be creative when writing, why are they not required to be creative when doing mathematics?; and if children are required to communicate clearly their reasoning in science, why are are they not required to communicate their reasoning in mathematics?

These positive trends within schools receive, unfortunately, less external support than previously due to the reduction in the numbers of advisory teachers and teachers' centres so perhaps the above analysis is an optimistic one.

The 'scheme-as-resource' approach requires the teacher, in the context of school planning, to have an overview of the mathematics curriculum and a sense of the important strands and significant activities within that curriculum. The teacher then draws on the detailed activities devised by the authors of schemes and a variety of other resources to make manageable the task of planning, but not to replace it; the scheme is seen as just one part of the children's experience rather than most of it; and the full range of activities suggested by the authors of the scheme is used, not just the pupil books. In practice this means that the teacher's handbook is on the teacher's desk rather than in the cupboard together with a file of teacher-planned activities. If the teacher, not the published scheme, is to be in control the teacher will need:

- a range of teaching approaches to support and sustain the children's learning;
- supportive group planning within the school encouraged by the Headteacher and the Mathematics Co-ordinator;
- a broad overview of the mathematics curriculum identifying important themes, such as decision-making, communicating and reasoning.

We hope that this book will support the professional development needed to implement confidently such an approach to primary mathematics.

Christine Hopkins, Susan Gifford and Sandy Pepperell
Roehampton, April 1996

Section 1: Using and Applying Mathematics

WHY DO CHILDREN LEARN MATHEMATICS IN SCHOOL?

Responses to this question usually include:

- the need to solve practical everyday problems;
- to use mathematics in other areas of learning;
- to learn to reason logically;
- to gain some satisfaction and enjoyment from exploring this area of human knowledge.

These basic reasons lead naturally to an emphasis on using and applying mathematics. It is of little use if a child can correctly complete pages and pages of sums but doesn't know how to get started when faced with an unfamiliar problem or a task presented in a practical rather than a written form. It is harder for children to relate the mathematics they do in one situation to that required by another than is sometimes assumed. We need to be encouraging children to generalise and abstract from particular situations and experiences, so they can move from concrete to abstract and back again. This relates to the essential nature of mathematics as the discovery and application of numerical and spatial relationships. Generalising is therefore involved both in the process of abstraction and in the transfer of mathematical ideas from one context to another.

A separate section of the National Curriculum entitled Using and applying mathematics' identifies an approach to the teaching and learning of mathematics which develops the skills needed to tackle unfamiliar problems and the processes used in mathematics. It divides these into three strands:

1. mathematical decision making;

2. communicating;

3. reasoning mathematically.

The last of these, *reasoning mathematically*, is the most central because it focuses on generalising mathematical relationships and is perhaps the most difficult to develop. Because of this, it is the one we concentrate on most in this section and a recurring theme throughout the book. The other two strands support it: *mathematical decision making* involves seeing a problem as not just allied to one method of solution, and making links between contexts. *Communicating* is about encouraging children to articulate their thinking and to move towards using more abstract language, symbols and representations.

Using and applying mathematics in the National Curriculum refers to all the other attainment targets: to Number, to Shape, Space and Measures and to Handling Data. It is an important element of any mathematical activity.

IMPLICATIONS FOR THE TEACHER

Using the above conceptual framework, we can say that children are using and applying their mathematics when they are given opportunities for the following:

- *Mathematical decision making:*
  - making their own decisions about appropriate mathematical content and/or materials (e.g. number line, calculator, cubes, squared paper) for a task;
  - drawing upon a variety of strategies;
  - making links between different aspects of mathematics and between mathematics and other subjects.

- *Communicating mathematically:*
  - talking about the mathematics:
      listening, reflecting and responding;
      explaining why a method works;
  - posing their own mathematical questions;
  - using mathematical language/terminology;
  - using a range of representational forms.

- *Reasoning mathematically:*
  - searching for patterns and relationships within their mathematical work;
  - moving from particular examples to general statements about mathematical ideas and vice versa;
  - thinking logically in a mathematical situation.

When planning children's work, these three themes can act as a checklist for judging the value of the activities in which the children will engage.

Having set up opportunities for the children, the teacher's role is to develop and sustain the children's thinking. Case studies are used throughout the book to give some indication of how the teaching principles identified might influence classroom practice. The case studies are in different schools with children of different ages, but it will become apparent that similar questions are used to extend the children's thinking.

Key questions

The thoughtful use of certain key questions by the teacher can encourage mathematical reasoning by the children. In practice it is not the questions alone which support the problem-solving but all aspects of the verbal and non-verbal interaction between the teacher and the children. By showing interest, puzzled looks and body language the teacher sustains the children's thinking, while the tone of voice in which the questions are posed shows the teacher's involvement with the problem. If the teacher poses these questions in many different situations, then the children have the opportunity to internalise the questions and develop as independent thinkers.

The questions serve to encourage different ways of reasoning:

- **Looking for patterns and relationships:**
  What's your prediction...?
  How many different...?
  What will happen if....?

- **Moving to general statements:**
  Are they the same...?
  Is it true that...?

- **Thinking logically:**
  What makes you think that?
  How do you know that...?
  How can you be sure...?
  Why doesn't it work...?

- **Drawing conclusions and testing them out:**
  So that means that...
  If we are right then...
  If that's true then what about....

CASE STUDIES

How can we develop reasoning at Key Stage 1?

Here is a 'Maths Morning' in a Year 1 class, where the majority of the children are 5 years old. By looking closely at the activities in which the children are involved, we can identify teaching strategies for promoting the children's mathematical reasoning. This can be developed by giving the children opportunities to:

> use and apply mathematics in practical tasks, in real-life problems and within mathematics itself;
> explain their thinking to support the development of their reasoning.
> (Mathematics National Curriculum, KS 1)

So what might this look like in the Year 1 classroom? At first sight, it looks like a typical group work session with different groups working on different tasks set up by the teacher. However, all the tasks are related in that they have arisen from the theme of 'Pairs', taken from the HBJ Mathematics scheme (Kerslake *et al.*, 1992). This is a commercially published scheme in which the activities are related to cross-curricular themes.

The morning begins with 'Maths Talk Time', where the teacher sits with the whole class gathered together on the carpet and encourages them to work out how many children are in their class today. This is a small example of a *real life problem*, in the context of completing the register. The numbers are entered by the teacher in the dinner register in full view of the children. She also shows them and comments on the day and the date displayed on the class calendar board, so there is an expectation that mathematical ideas can be the subjects of discussion. *'Twenty-*

seven children are here today,' Misha points out. Asking Misha to explain to everyone *how* she worked that out is one way of supporting the development of her mathematical reasoning.

When the teacher introduces the class to their tasks for the morning, she asks them if they think they have enough sky and water yet in the Noah's Ark role play area that they are creating by painting and building in one corner of the room. (This is to be their 'boat corner' where the animals will go in two by two!)

Asking the children this as well as how much more they think they need to paint encourages them to make a decision about a practical problem involving measuring and estimating. Getting children to think about the purpose of their work gives them a focus for their reasoning. Sharing with them clear expectations for how they will work and what they will have achieved by the end of the time available also supports their attempts at reasoning by showing them the parameters within which they can make their own decisions about the problems to be solved.

Some children are playing the 'Sock Game'. This entails moving counters around a sock-shaped board, and then covering the small sock pictures they land on with any matching sock cards that they are holding. The use of a spinner with numbers on it tells the players how many spaces to move their counters. The aim of the game is to be the first to place all your cards on the board. The children have to start by checking that they each have the same number of cards to ensure that the game will be fair. As in many board or card games, the children may start to predict, and the teacher can encourage this prediction using questions such as *'What will happen if you spin a four on your next go?'* The children are beginning to think about issues of probability and are being encouraged to consider different possible outcomes. These are early examples of reasoning in the form of prediction, which is important because it involves thinking ahead and is related to the beginnings of abstract thought. Later, the children pass on the instructions for how to play the game to other children, which ensures that they articulate the thinking involved.

Another group are exploring whether their own feet are the same size or different sizes. Kayleigh says that she does not think that hers are the same size. This prompts her teacher to ask *'What makes you think that?'* in order to explore the child's reasoning. Kayleigh then tests her estimation by measuring. The teacher has put out a selection of materials for the group to use, including string, scissors, rulers, plain and squared paper. *'What do you think your feet will measure?'* the teacher asks them. One child uses the markings on a ruler to count without reading the actual numbers. Others count squares to compare the area of each foot. Asking them why they have chosen these particular materials and methods gives the children another opportunity to explain their reasoning.

At the end of the morning, the teacher gathers the whole class back onto the carpet. Adam reports to the other children, *'When I was doing my foot work, I measured to see if my feet were the same...'.* His group have been testing predictions about the size of their feet, and now they are explaining their reasoning to other children who have been engaged in other activities. The teacher shows genuine interest in the children's thinking to encourage them to share what is going on in their heads. She can ask further prompting and probing questions such as

'Why?' or 'How do you know that?' This gives high status to the mathematical reasoning that has been going on and helps to build an atmosphere of mathematical curiosity in the room.

As far as the development of mathematical reasoning is concerned, we have seen that the Mathematics National Curriculum (KS 1) is being implemented in this Year 1 classroom in many different ways. The children have been using and applying mathematical ideas in practical tasks, in relevant and realistic problem-solving situations, and to investigate within mathematics itself. They have also had opportunities to explain their thinking which will support the development of their reasoning.

The teacher helped to make this happen by:

- Setting up interesting and rich *activities*.
- Providing access to appropriate *resources*.
- Using the classroom *space* effectively.
- Using *time* creatively and efficiently.
- *Grouping* and re-grouping the children flexibly.
- *Intervening* skilfully and supportively, mainly through the use of prompting and probing questions.

How can we develop reasoning at Key Stage 2?

An afternoon in a Year 6 class reveals more of the using and applying of mathematics and, in particular, opportunities for developing the children's mathematical reasoning. The Mathematics National Curriculum (KS 2) states that pupils between the ages of 7 and 11 should be taught to:

(a) understand and investigate general statements;
(b) search for pattern in their results;
(c) make general statements of their own, based on evidence they have produced;
(d) explain their reasoning.

In this Year 6 classroom, we can see in the following account how the children are reasoning mathematically, and how this reflects the Mathematics National Curriculum. Some of them (Tammy, Della, Billy, Lorraine, Michelle and Emma) are working on an exploration called 'Using weights' from the HBJ Mathematics scheme's 'True or false?' theme (Figure 1.1):

> There are five weights:
> 1 ounce, 2 ounces, 4 ounces, 8 ounces and 16 ounces (or 1lb).
> Is it true that these could be used to weigh any item up to 31 ounces?
> What if there is also a 32 ounce weight? What weights could be made with these? What weights could not be made?

The following snippets of conversation both between the children seated around the table and with their teacher show not only how the pupils are explaining their reasoning but also how the teacher is prompting and probing their thinking by observing closely, listening carefully and intervening skilfully. As we shall see, she even uses a tactical 'no response' as one of her strategies.

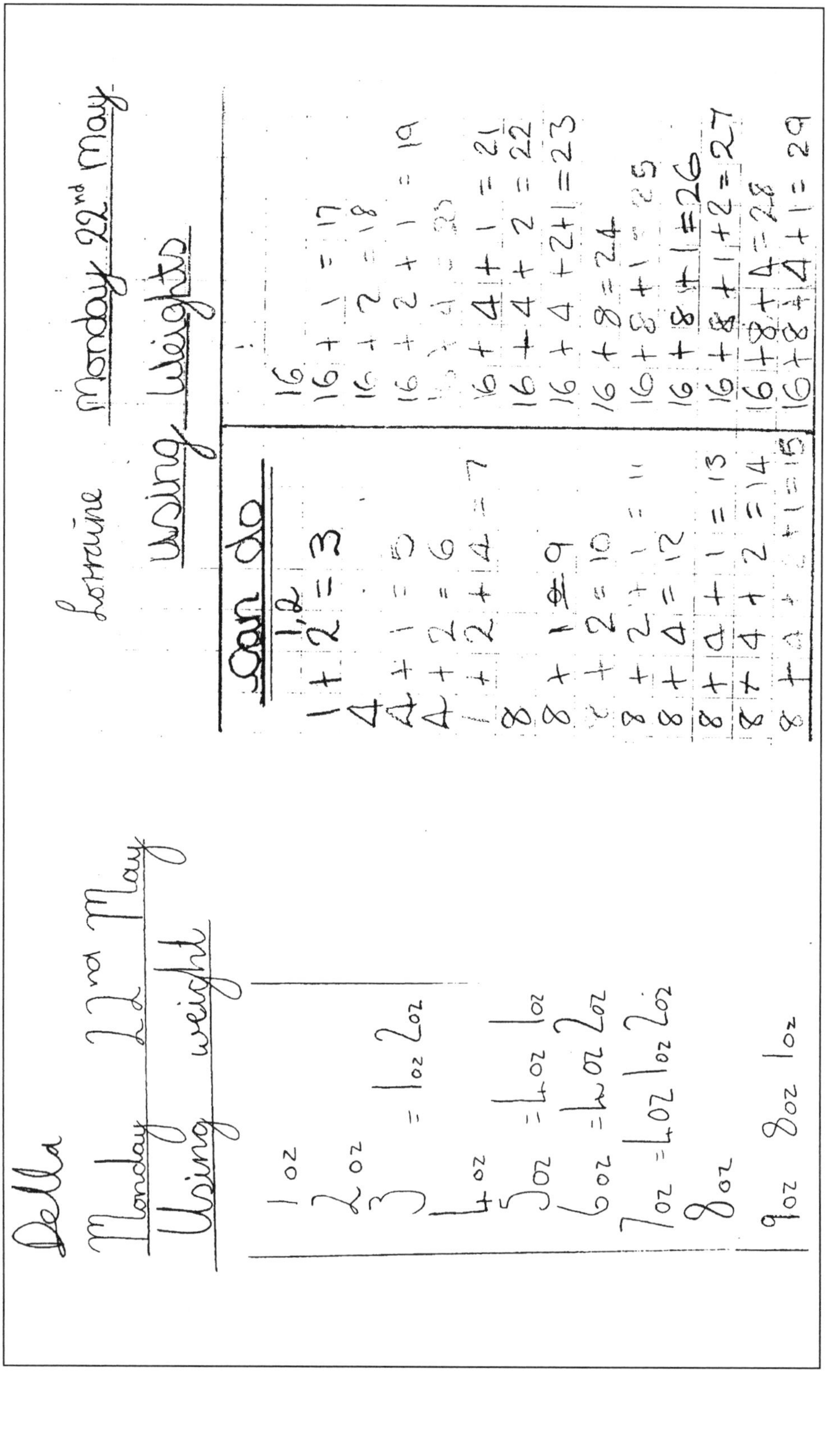

Della

Monday 22nd May
Using weight

1 oz
2 oz
3 = 1 oz 2 oz
4 oz
5 oz = 4 oz 1 oz
6 oz = 4 oz 2 oz
7 oz = 4 oz 1 oz 2 oz
8 oz
9 oz 8 oz 1 oz

Lorraine   Monday 22nd May

Using weights

Can do
1, 2
1 + 2 = 3
4
4 + 1 = 5
4 + 2 = 6
4 + 2 + 4 = 7
8
8 + 1 = 9
8 + 2 = 10
8 + 2 + 1 = 11
8 + 4 = 12
8 + 4 + 1 = 13
8 + 4 + 2 = 14
8 + 4 + 2 + 1 = 15

16
16 + 1 = 17
16 + 2 = 18
16 + 2 + 1 = 19
16 + 4 = 20
16 + 4 + 1 = 21
16 + 4 + 2 = 22
16 + 4 + 2 + 1 = 23
16 + 8 = 24
16 + 8 + 1 = 25
16 + 8 + 1 = 26
16 + 8 + 1 + 2 = 27
16 + 8 + 4 = 28
16 + 8 + 4 + 1 = 29

Figure 1.1 Della and Lorraine's work on the 'Using weights' problem

The children embark on their exploration into the possible ways of combining the values of the five weights by making (and recording) an initial prediction that can then be tested:

Teacher: *What's your prediction?*
Child:　*Is a prediction like an estimate, Miss?*

For the teacher, this is an opportunity to discuss the meaning of some mathematical terminology with the child. Billy does not believe that it is possible to make up all the other weights using those provided. He is happy to venture his opinion because he knows the teacher will not scold him if it turns out to be inaccurate. Indeed, she positively encourages a questioning and conjecturing atmosphere by her reassuring yet thought-provoking interactions with the class.

The children are used to working in an investigative way and they set about the task with noticeable commitment, diligently exploring the possibilities for combining the weights and systematically recording their results. With no prompting from their teacher, they begin to add the values of the weights together effortlessly in order to investigate the *'Is it true that...?'* statement in the wording of the exploration.

Emma:　*Miss Sandell, can you do take-aways?*
Child:　*Don't be so stupid, of course you can't!*

The teacher appears to let this go unnoticed but she has made a mental note of Emma's question. Undaunted, Emma continues creating the addition sums that are enabling her and the others to proceed with their exploration.

Child:　*Once you get past sixteen you use sixteen all the time.*

This child is searching for a pattern in the results, as is the next one.

Child:　(looking perplexed): *It should go 'one plus one equals two, two plus two equals four...'*

Teacher: *Why doesn't it do that?*

Child:　*Because you can't do any one of them twice.*

This is an example of children explaining reasons and of mathematical reasoning itself, prompted by the teacher's skilful use of questioning.

Child:　*You could make sixty-three if you added a thirty-two ounce weight.*

We know that this child is predicting and conjecturing (speculating) because she is thinking aloud about a possibility that has not yet been tried.

Teacher: *Is that all? Are there any other possibilities?*
Child:　*Yes.*
Teacher: *How do you know that there are?*

The teacher is probing the child's thinking here to prompt further reasoning.

After working on the task for a while, one child makes a general statement while looking at the results already obtained:

Child: *If you had the numbers one to ten you could go on forever.*
Teacher: *You would need to work it out, perhaps by recording it systematically, in order to prove this.*
Child: (with a look of excitement on his face): *Can you do forty-seven?*
Child: *You can't do it.*
Teacher: *What exactly is it that you can't do?*

Here the teacher is probing the child's thinking to provoke him into identifying for himself where the obstacle he perceives lies and what form it takes. This is instead of blocking the child's thinking by telling him that he is either right or wrong.

On another occasion, a child searches for and spots a pattern in the results:

Child: *So when you get to 47 you start using the number 16 in the middle instead of at the beginning.*

Earlier, Emma had asked if they could do 'take-aways' (as well as adding), so later, the teacher re-joins the group to demonstrate the use of balance scales to get the children thinking about the numerical differences between the values of the weights. The teacher encourages the children to work out the results there and then, so there is a great deal of quick calculation in the form of mental, finger and pencil and paper methods happening. The teacher is also able to discuss with the children the special meaning in mathematical language of a term like 'difference between' in a context where it matters to them.

The group can now make up weights in new ways because they can use the differences as well as the totals. For example, a 12 ounce parcel can be weighed by placing a 4 ounce weight alongside the parcel and a 16 ounce weight on the other side.

Following the discussion about using the differences between the values of the weights as a method of weighing more items than have been possible before, an interesting thought occurs to one of the children:

Child: *What if you timesed them now, Miss Sandell?*

This child's idea of changing the operation involved shows that responsibility is being taken for extending the task by suggesting an alternative method. Unfortunately, classroom time is running out by this stage, but the child is left with an intriguing self-made puzzle to take away and mull over.

The afternoon ends with these children reporting their exploratory work to another group which has not been involved in this particular activity. This has the effect of consolidating their recent mathematical reasoning by making them re-present their ideas explicitly to communicate effectively with a new audience. Opportunities for them to receive and answer questions from the listeners serves to extend their reasoning even further.

The exploratory nature of this activity, in which the children are required to make decisions for themselves, provides many opportunities for the using and applying of mathematics and for mathematical reasoning in particular. The teacher's expectation and acceptance that the children will both communicate with each other and be in charge of organising and extending their own work also makes this happen. In addition to this, she gives them scope to devise and refine their own ways of recording. Finally, the teacher's interventions serve to keep the children's thinking momentum going rather than interfering with it or stifling it. Overall, what we have seen in this Year 6 classroom is a mixture of opportunities to use and apply mathematics in two of the three ways mentioned in the National Curriculum:

- in practical tasks
- within mathematics itself.

The third requirement in the National Curriculum is that children should be given opportunities to work on real-life problems, and setting this up is considered in Section 2.6.

GLOSSARY

Warning: The information provided in the glossaries is background information for teachers. It is not presented in a form that would be helpful to children!

Generalisation: A generalisation in mathematics draws on the evidence of specific cases to suggest a general property. For example, noticing that 3+5 = 8, 1+7 = 8, 7 + 3 = 10 and after testing out lots of combinations of odd numbers a child suggests the generalisation that *'If you add two odd numbers you get an even number.'*

Hypothesis: The generalisation may also be described as an hypothesis: it is a guess based on the evidence. An hypothesis may be shown to be true or shown to be false. Tammy (Figure 1.2) disproves the hypothesis: *'The longer your legs the faster you can run'* with a single counter-example. The statement is not true in *all* cases although there may be a general correlation.

Proof: A proof in mathematics is a series of logical statements to convince you that an hypothesis is always true, that it *must* be true. Children can be encouraged to move towards proof and logical reasoning by questions such as: 'Are you sure? Why do you think that? Can you explain? But what if...?'

The mathematical ideas above can be found in the National Curriculum 'Using and Applying' programme of study:

- *At Key Stage 1:*
    (a) recognise simple patterns and relationships and make related predictions about them;
    (b) ask questions including 'What would happen if?' and 'Why?'
    (c) understand general statements, e.g. 'all even numbers divide by 2', and investigate whether particular cases match them.

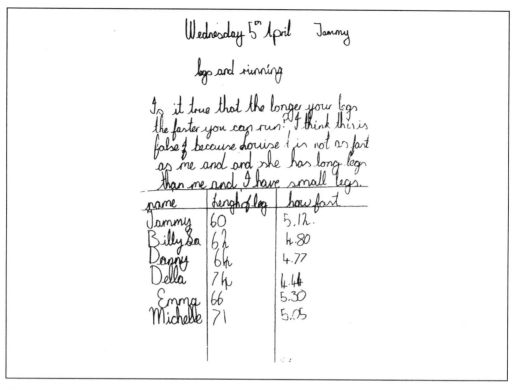

Figure 1.2 True or false?

- *At Key Stage 2:*
    (a) understand and investigate general statements;
    (b) search for patterns in their results;
    (c) make general statements of their own, based on evidence they have produced;
    (d) explain their reasoning.

Section 2: Number

2.1 INTRODUCTION – THE TEACHING OF NUMBER

Having identified the themes of mathematical decision-making, communicating and reasoning as applying across all areas of mathematics teaching, we turn now to the content area of number. The primary number curriculum can be seen as a cycle of learning about the number system whilst using and applying that knowledge. In the early years children are learning to count and beginning to use and apply their counting with simple calculations. Counting develops through an understanding of the place value system which enables very large numbers to be named. A further cycle begins when children extend their understanding of numbers to include negative numbers and fractions of numbers.

Since Victorian times criticisms by inspectors of the teaching of mathematics in schools have focused on children being given too much practice of skills without understanding, without meaningful contexts and without attention to mathematical patterns and relationships. What teaching approaches will enable children to become confident and expert in applying their knowledge of number to familiar and unfamiliar situations? The emphasis in the National Curriculum for 'Number' is on flexibility and the use of a variety of resources and methods, including *mental methods* and a variety of *methods of recording*. Here are some examples:

> Pupils should be given opportunities to:
> (KS1) develop flexible methods of working with number, orally and mentally; record in a variety of ways, including ways that relate to their mental work;
> (KS2) develop flexible and effective methods of computation and recording, and use them with understanding;
> use calculators, computers and a range of other resources as tools for exploring number structure and to enable work with realistic data;

This fits with the emphasis in 'Using and Applying Mathematics' on children being taught to:

> (KS2) select and use the appropriate mathematics and materials; develop their own mathematical strategies and look for ways to overcome difficulties;

If teachers are to realise these objectives successfully, they need:

- to understand the structure of the number system and the calculations on which the children are working;
- to be aware of common misconceptions;
- to encourage children to explain their methods – and to build on the children's answers in their teaching;
- to find the appropriate balance in the use of schemes, practical apparatus, mental mathematics, calculators and computers.

Currently, the two most contentious issues in the teaching of mathematics are the excessive use of schemes and the appropriate use of calculators.

With reference to schemes the OFSTED Report on Science and Mathematics in schools (1994) comments:

> As in all developments, the key issue is one of balance. A framework was needed and the National Curriculum has provided an essential and successful definition. However, most teaching continues to rely on published schemes which provide sequencing in excessive detail and can damage teachers' confidence in their ability to make their own decisions. These schemes tend to overemphasise standard written methods at the expense of mental techniques and common-sense calculations.

Since *mental mathematics* underpins and drives all other methods, teachers can greatly increase children's confidence by explicitly working on and developing skills at working with numbers 'in the head'. There are differing views on the balance between written algorithms and the use of calculators and these are explored in Section 2.3.

The section on Number is arranged in chronological order to give a sense of progression. Some recurring themes are reasoning, encouraging mental strategies for calculations and creating a number environment in the classroom through language and display. The strands of the National Curriculum can be found, as follows:

- Developing an understanding of place value   2.2 and 2.3
  and extending the number system   2.4
- Understanding relationships between numbers 2.2 and 2.5
and developing methods of computation   2.3
- Solving numerical problems   2.3
  and Measures   3.4

2.2 NUMBER IN THE EARLY YEARS

Learning to count

A range of different kinds of knowledge and skills have to be acquired in order for children to learn to count. Schaeffer *et al.* (1974) for instance, suggest that children go through the following stages:

- *Recognising small numbers* like one, two or three without counting but just by looking (sometimes called *subitising*: we do this when we recognise numbers on a dice).
- *Being able to compare more and less* when two sets are paired up.
- *Being able to say the number names in order:*
  - One to twelve. These numbers must be learnt by rote, there is no pattern to help.
  - Thirteen to nineteen. Here the numbers from three to nine are repeated, though not exactly; 'thir' is not quite 'three'. Each number is followed by 'teen' for ten, though the children will need to learn that thirteen is written 13

with the 1 representing the ten before the 3.

- – Twenty to ninety-nine. Quite a lot of pattern spotting has gone on for children to count past twenty: they have to combine two patterns, the one to nine pattern and the twenty, thirty, forty ... pattern. You can see children grappling with these two patterns by watching when they get stuck, which is usually at a nine (e.g. 29) or a tens number (e.g. 40). By reciting the sequence of number names past thirty children are beginning to learn about the decimal structure of our number system.

- ● *Being able to say one number for each object.* To accomplish this task successfully, children need to synchronise touching an object and saying the next number word in the sequence. In the learning stages children can be observed to say two numbers for one object, skip an object or lose track of which things they have counted. It seems to help if they count things arranged in a line and actually *move* the things as they count them, as on an abacus, rather than counting static things like pictures.

- ● *Knowing the last number you say is the number of the whole collection.* This is the *cardinal* aspect of numbers.

  If you ask children how many things there are after they have counted, say, five objects, they may say, 'eight' or 'three'! A child who understands cardinality is likely to be able to fetch you five pencils when asked, rather than bringing back a whole handful.

- ● *Being able to compare and estimate numbers.* Knowing which numbers are bigger than which, for all the numbers up to ten seems to be the last aspect of counting that children grasp.

Some aspects of learning about number are now receiving less emphasis than previously. For instance, Piaget (1952) emphasised the idea of conservation. In Piaget's experiment, this was tested by pairing two sets of objects of the same number, then spreading one set out and asking if there was still the same number in both sets (Figure 2.1).

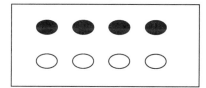 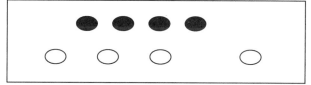

Figure 2.1 Piaget's experiment

Piaget found that generally children under six or seven could not say *that the number must the same because none had been added or taken away.* This was a startling discovery at the time, which revealed that children may not be attaching the same meaning to numbers as adults do. However, so many researchers have found that altering the context and wording of the test allows younger children to succeed at this, and that even those who do not succeed can count and solve a range of number problems, consequently such great importance is no longer attached to conservation. Similarly, the importance for teaching of other ideas emphasised by Piaget, such as sorting, ordering and one-to-one matching (or one-to-one correspondence) is being questioned: although interesting in terms of children's number understanding, they may not be prerequisites for this, and should not be treated as a teaching scheme. The work of Vygotsky (1978), a Russian psychologist, has proved influential in focusing attention on what children can achieve with assistance.

Other aspects of young children's understanding of numbers are now receiving more attention. Close observation of what children do know about numbers has made it clear that some young children have a range of informal and individual strategies for solving problems. Some very young children can count verbally to high numbers and write numerals, perhaps because someone does this with them at home. Hughes (1986) found that most young children can write a label for a box containing a small number of objects, by drawing tallies (Figure 2.2).

Figure 2.2 How many objects are in the box?

He also found that 3 year olds could add and subtract mentally with very small numbers, in the context of a game with bricks being added to or taken away from some in a box. Close observation of young children reveals that their number knowledge is developing on several fronts at once: they may be able to count verbally to quite high numbers while still learning the cardinal value of small numbers. At the same time they may be moving from tallying to understanding the meaning of numerals. They can also compare, estimate, add, subtract and share small numbers of objects. What is interesting to observe is how children solve these kinds of problems: do they use fingers, visualise or count aloud?

It is clear that what we do not need to do is protect young children from big numbers: they seem to be naturally interested in them. Some will just want to talk about big numbers but a small proportion of 3- and 4-year olds will know quite a lot about them. How many children are competent with the reception class mathematics curriculum *before* they enter school? We need to be sure that we allow children to show us what they know, and not to put a ceiling on our expectations. Through observing individual children in everyday activities we should be able comfortably to challenge all of them at an appropriate level, and provide unpressured but stimulating experiences to develop their skills and understanding.

What children may need help with is seeing what the point of counting is: they need to see *purposes* for counting, like comparing amounts or laying the table, and they need to be encouraged to put their counting skills to use. Similarly, since the many examples of numerals which children meet in everyday life – for instance on buses, telephones or birthday cards – often do not clearly represent a number of things, but are used more as a code or label, children also need help in recognising the meaning of written numbers.

What activities help children to count and learn about numbers and numerals?

Research in New Zealand (Young Loveridge, 1987) found that 5-year-old children's expertise in number was associated with a family focus on number which included counting while preparing food, attention to money, lots of game playing including card games and bingo, and especially discussions related to time. Using the calendar to count down to birthdays and other events and pointing out times on the clock seemed to be particularly significant. Discussing numerals wherever they occurred was also important, for instance when playing with calculators, watching 'Sesame Street', reading distances on signposts or the speedometer in the car. It is interesting that in the past we would have considered some of these experiences too difficult for very young children: it seems that some 3 and 4 year olds can cope with telling the time, interpreting speedometers and even doing the same sums as their older siblings. Children in this study who had not had these kinds of experiences, and who did not see their parents using numbers to solve problems in everyday life, were less competent with numbers. It therefore seems important that in school we replicate and build on these kinds of experiences, but we may need to organise more regular group activities so that we are sure that all children benefit and so we can monitor this systematically.

Activities for counting

● Discussing ages, birthdays, cards, badges and candles; counting down to birthdays and other events; using a calendar; discussing times of the day, 'how many minutes to', relating to different clocks.

- Counting when preparing food or equipment 'How many do we need?'
- Making lists that include numbers.
- Counting children for dinners and registers and recording these.
- Playing games which involve counting objects, or moving yourself as you count (e.g. skittles or skipping).
- Encouraging children to record scores of games in their own way on easels or clipboards.
- Putting out number apparatus and charts for children to refer to as they need to, with numbers up to 100 or beyond!
- Reading and making number books.
- Discussing numbers in books and magazines, including page numbers, prices in catalogues and brochures.
- Labelling things with numbers, so you know how many there should be when tidying up.
- Using computers and calculators.
- Providing objects with numerals on and demonstrating their use: scales, height charts and rulers, tape recorders, video and washing machines, thermometers, timers.
- Having numerals conspicuous in role play areas, on clocks, telephones, calculators, appointment books, tills and price labels, tickets, dials on cars, trains, planes.

Number rhymes and action songs

Rhymes help children to become familiar with the number names. Spoken and written numbers can be linked by having children hold up large numerals to accompany games and action rhymes. Rhymes can be adapted to provide extra challenge, for example by counting back two or three at a time. Here is a number rhyme that emphasises doubling. The finger actions are given in italics:

- One and one make two. *Two thumbs are held up to show 'two'.*
- Saying 'how do you do?' *The thumbs bow to each other.*
- Two and two are four. *Thumb and first finger on each hand are held up to show 'four'.*
- Looking at the door. *Thumbs and first fingers made into 'binoculars' through which children look at the door.*
- Three and three make six. *Three fingers open out from binoculars*
- Six and six and six. *And moved in front of the eyes for emphasis.*
- Four and four make eight. *The four fingers of each hand are held up then placed horizontally with fingertips touching to make a gate.*
- Open up the gate. *Hands moved from the wrist to open and shut the gate.*
- Five and five are ten. *Five fingers of each hand are held up.*
- Little flapping wren. *Join thumbs to make a bird. flap wings to fly. Show shadow with torch or OHP.*

Case study: A nursery shopping game

I was visiting the nursery school, and wanted to take an activity which would engage the children and allow them to show me what they knew about numbers. I decided on a miniature shop, with a dice to decide how much money you had to spend. Although this introduced a turn-taking element involving waiting, in my experience this is more bearable with miniature shop games because children can spend time inspecting their purchases, counting their money and deciding what to buy next, as well as checking that others are playing correctly. It would also allow me to focus on one child at a time, while working with a group.

I hoped this activity would show me:

- how the children counted, and whether they understood cardinality;
- whether they could compare numbers:
  - add or subtract in a practical way;
  - recognise numbers of dots without counting, or numerals;
  - represent numbers by tallying or writing numerals.

I set up shop with five teddy bears (one large shopkeeper and four small shoppers, each with a miniature shopping basket) and miniature grocery boxes from the local toy shop, which I arranged in a tray with sections labelled with prices from 1p to 4p. I also had a container of real one penny coins, a box for a till and a numeral and spots dice, numbered 1 to 6. In reserve I had another dice numbered 5 to 10 and, for those who had trouble counting the little spots on the dice, six beans coloured blue on one side, which could be thrown instead of a dice and the blue sides counted. I also had other coins, felt-tips, blank labels and Post-its. I was all set to assess the children's number knowledge, or so I thought.

I started off with Sanyu and the two coloured beans. However, since she did not pay any attention to whether the beans came up blue or white, but insisted on counting all six beans each time, despite my reminders, and matched six pennies to six beans, I changed to the numeral and dots dice.

Sanyu threw two, asked where the two pence coins were and was perplexed as to what to do, until I suggested getting two pennies. Next time she threw five and immediately got five pennies, recognising the numeral on the dice and counting the pennies. She then looked for something costing five pennies and seemed unhappy about buying things for less, which suggested that she was not confident either about shopping or about the relative values. When I encouraged her to buy something from the section of items priced at three pence, she wanted to take three of them, as did the other children who had joined the game. I then felt totally confused as to what this showed about the children's understanding: presumably they did not see the price label as an indicator of cost or value, but as a label directing them as to which items they should buy. Presumably for some children of this age the idea of exchanging money for goods is complex enough, without the added complication that some things cost more than others. I have noticed that when children as old as five or six play shops, they tend to just hand over any number of coins in exchange for items bought, without paying attention to actual prices or relative values, so this may be a much more sophisticated idea.

However, just when I was thinking it was too difficult for her, Sanyu got the hang of the rules and started instructing the other children, getting boxes back out of the pockets of over-eager shoppers. After a few goes, as she was shouting at the children as to what to do, and to 'up' the pace of the game, I made her shopkeeper instead of the large teddy and she managed this with apparent satisfaction.

When some children could not read the numerals on the price labels, I drew some circles to stand for the number of pennies on them: one child commented, 'Ohs', presumably seeing the circles as letters. Wishing I had put sticky coins under the numerals to illustrate their value, I decided to put the labels away and have everything costing one penny, as the many for one relationship still seemed to create a problem for several children and put too many steps between throwing the dice and getting your purchases in your basket. This worked fine, and the game still gave plenty of opportunities to count and recognise numbers.

The children had enjoyed the role play between the teddies ('Good morning, what would you like?' 'Thank you!') and the children carefully put pennies into the paw of the shopkeeper. Some were engaged by making their teddy do the shopping, and tried to get it to hold the basket, which was too big; others found fitting the teddy into the baskets more satisfying, or making it fall on the floor, and then comforting it. Most children held the teddies, some commented on the shopping and decisions about what they would buy (sweets for the kids' tea), and opened and closed the boxes while waiting for turns. It was interesting how much more some children were engaged by the role playing and story element than others. This made the turns and waiting longer, and yet could obviously be beneficially developed further. This is a tension I have often felt with maths and shop role play: insisting on the counting and prices often seems to interrupt equally valuable imaginative play. I wondered whether it would be better to separate the two and make the game more tightly focused on dice and money for goods exchange without any story line of the teddies. But then were the teddies not attracting some children and giving the maths and money a softer and more comforting image? Or on the other hand, was it me and the staff, rather than the children, who needed to make the counting cuddly? Perhaps the children just needed to have their attention drawn to each others' turns a little more.

Most children could read the numerals or count the dots on the dice. The group with me just before 'fruit time' could all read numerals to six confidently. At fruit time they counted round the group of 16 children. The teacher and some of the children counted up to 27 pieces of fruit, so I decided to see if they could use a five to ten dot and numeral dice. Most children needed help with this, but several in the group could recognise the numerals, or count the dots, and all seemed happy to be helped to count the dots, or be told, and then count out the money, sometimes with help. This seemed a comfortable level of challenge, which surprised their teacher.

I showed the children who were less expert how to count by arranging the coins in a line and moving them as they (or the teddy) counted them. Fadilah would check the number of coins, usually being one out with numbers up to five, but adjusting this completely by herself. Tom could not count nine pennies accurately without encouragement to check, but then would do this, arranging his pennies in a line by himself and moving them to count. Several other children spontaneously attempted to do this after I had shown them. I was interested that Tom, and most of the others, although they estimated a handful for numbers over six, were often only two pennies out. Tom was interested in the number he had left, e.g. when he had nine pennies and spent six, he counted the three left. Did this show an awareness of subtraction? I would need to ask him some hypothetical questions about spending, preferably with small numbers, to get a better idea of his understanding. With the higher number dice, the children accumulated several coins which gave opportunities to count higher numbers, as did the large baskets of groceries.

There were interesting variations in the children's awareness of having to pay for groceries. Sean was identified by his teacher as interested in numbers. He took the wooden numerals and went off and laid them in a line on the floor grouping identical numbers together, and pointed this out to me insistently and with satisfaction. He started off by identifying six as nine, and maintained this, despite my inviting him to look at, and then count, the dots. He could recognise ten on the dice. Does his teacher mean he is interested in numerals rather than counting or numbers in general?

When Sean became the shopkeeper, the rule of one penny per object, which Sanyu had enforced, became varied. Some children would fill up their basket at one go, or have one or a few things, and Sean requested apparently arbitrary amounts from one to seven pennies, unrelated to the amount of shopping, and more to how much money individual children had. However once when I asked if he was sure, when he had asked for five pennies (all that the child had) for one box, he reasoned that there might be problems when we ran out of groceries. (However the children suggested putting everything back and starting again, 'or doing something else...'.) Sean certainly seemed to understand that one item could cost several coins, but did not seem to have an idea that there might be a reason for this in terms of varying value.

Early on, I got out more boxes, when we ran out, and invited the children to write price labels on Post-its. Sanyu wrote 4 confidently, and Tom's 4 was less conventional. Sanyu wrote 2 and a reversed 2, which she distinguished confidently, and stuck both on as 'price labels', but we did not use them to pay for things. Perhaps because I had already introduced numerals on labels, this was what the children did. Dawn said she could not write 3 so I got out the wooden numerals and she and Tom copied this. (Tom wanted to draw round it, but I asked him to copy it, which he attempted.) He repeatedly held up 2 back to front and said it looked like 5. Denny did 7 and said, 'Denny is going to be this' (a sibling with approaching birthday?). Tom said, 'I am going to do 10, no 20' (jokingly, as though aware this was a ridiculously high price) and finally said it was nine. This seemed to show quite a lot of knowledge of and interest in numbers and numerals amongst the children.

The activity seemed generally successful, with some children staying 5 minutes and some, like Tom, an hour. They seemed interested in the dice and the boxes and money, so I judged I would miss out the teddies the next time, but would definitely play the game again with this age group. Some of the 3 year olds were more interested in throwing the dice and filling their baskets with as many boxes as they could, rather than attending to numbers or counting pennies and goods, but they were enjoying playing at playing the game. They were all careful with the money, and were more interested in pocketing the boxes if anything!

I had found out quite a lot about the children's counting and number recognition, although as I did not know the children, I found it hard to remember who had done what unless I managed to note their names and jot something down. Some of this had surprised the teacher and raised her expectations for this age group: for instance, that Tom could count to nine and several 4 year olds enjoyed working out the numbers five to ten on a numeral and dots dice. I could try cards like this on a future occasion. Obviously I would need to see what they did another time in a different context to make any hard and fast assessments, but I had some clues. With hindsight I realised that I tended to assume quite quickly that the children did not understand or that something was too hard for them, when *given time* they grasped the situation and adjusted their behaviour; or if shown how, learned how to do things quite quickly, like counting objects by moving them one at a time. Again, I would need to see what they did on another occasion to say they had really learned something. What I was not sure about was the children's understanding about shopping and transactions with coins. What do they think is going on? What do they understand about the different coins and why we have them? I would have to ask them.

Revised version:

- Start with everything costing one penny.
- Use dot and numeral dice to 6, keeping 5 to 10 in reserve.
- Have extra boxes in reserve, to stimulate rearrangement of rules.
- Have a till to pay into, and possibly smaller baskets for the teddies.

Extensions:

- Everything costs three pence?
- Ask the children to price the things, using objects more obviously differing in value, and then read the labels when shopping.
- Introduce labels with different prices and sticky money illustrations.

STARTING TO CALCULATE

A Year 2 class were doing some mental arithmetic in the few minutes before dinner time. Nobody could do '20 take away 6' and the teacher suggested they count back 6 on their fingers. This was tricky, as you had to keep track of how many you had counted back as well as actually counting backwards. It is also quite a slow method. The children could have counted out 20 blocks of course, but this still leaves the problem of how children get from counting blocks to being able to calculate mentally, which is what we want them to do for small numbers like this. There will be some children who are still not calculating mentally by

Year 5 or 6, and have to get out the blocks, or do complicated things with their fingers, to do sums like '42 subtract 17'.

So how do children move from practical to mental addition and subtraction? It is easy to train classes of very young children to do sums on paper: they read the numbers, count the bricks, add or subtract them, then count again and write the answer. They may have got the idea of putting two lots together for add, and taking some away for minus, but they are not yet able to calculate.

Martin Hughes (1986) asked some 3 year olds to work out how many bricks there would be in a box containing, say, three bricks if two were taken away. He did other addition and subtraction problems with small numbers in the context of a game where children could see the number of bricks in the box to start with, and how many bricks were being added or taken away, but not the resulting number. He found that many 3 year olds could solve these problems, either mentally or by using their fingers. Some children just knew the answer and others seemed to be visualising the bricks. What is important here is that very young children are already capable of mental calculation with very small numbers, if they have something to think with. Hughes found that this did not mean that the activity always had to be practical: if he asked the children hypothetical problems involving, say, imagining sweets, they could also answer. If, however, he asked them problems using just abstract numbers, like 'three take away two', they usually could not answer. Some could, however, using their fingers. Fingers seem to be potentially very important in helping children generalise from one context to another: if they realise that they can represent two bricks or two sweets or two anything with two fingers, they are well on the way to abstracting relationships between numbers. It seems therefore that we can build on this capacity for mental arithmetic with young children by providing problems in meaningful contexts, such as games, and by encouraging them to visualise and to use their fingers to solve the problems.

There is often a progression in the way that children solve problems with bigger numbers. When adding two numbers, children begin by counting all their bricks or fingers: for instance, for 3 + 8 they get three, then five, then count all eight from the beginning. Later children will just count on from the three to get eight. Later still, they will reverse the numbers to count on from the larger one, so they count from five, three more to get eight. This, the commutative principle, seems to be discovered spontaneously by children. Finally children will just know the answer without having to think about it, or they will have instant recall.

Counting on and back have been seen as important strategies to bridge the gap between having to count all and having recall of number facts, and this has led to an emphasis on number lines in helping children to visualise this process.

Another strategy which some children use spontaneously is recomposing numbers. For instance, a child may add 3 and 4 by thinking of a related fact, like 3 and 3 making 6, and therefore adding one more to get 7. The child is using a derived fact, by adapting one which is well known. (The doubles, e.g 3 + 3 = 6, 4 + 4 = 8, seem to be easily learned and this seems well worth encouraging.) Another child may use their fingers to think of numbers like 8 as made up of 5 and 3. This helps when adding numbers like 6 and 8, which can be thought of as

'5 and 1' and '5 and 3', so the two 5s are added to make 10 and the 1 and 3 added to make 4, giving 14 altogether. Although this sounds long-winded, the visualising may be done in a flash. This child is using the ability to recompose numbers using 5, which fits in well with using fingers to represent numbers from an early stage. When children are very familiar with number bonds for 10, they can use this to look for ten complements when adding: with 6 and 8, they can quickly see they need to take 2 from the 6 to make 8 into 10, leaving 4 more to make 14. Both strategies are also useful when subtracting: if 7 from 15 is seen as taking 5 from 15, then 2 more from 10, the answer should be instantly recognised as 8. These strategies have an advantage over counting on and back, in that they are quicker, and less susceptible to errors due to losing track. They are also genera lisable to bigger numbers, where counting on and back becomes even more problematic.

When the children are waiting for their dinner they can be encouraged to recall the number bonds to 10, and to look for ways of recomposing numbers like 20 as 10 and 10. Of course a lot of experience is required in splitting up numbers in different ways, with a variety of apparatus, as well as using fingers, before children can calculate mentally in fast and effective ways. Interestingly Japanese and Korean schools, whose children do very well in number in international tests, put a lot of emphasis on finding patterns in number bonds for small numbers, and on recomposing numbers with 5 and 10, encouraging the use of fingers at this stage. It is the encouragement to visualise, to look for patterns, and to look for ways of recomposing numbers which seem to be the important elements in developing mental calculations.

A summary of ways to encourage mental calculation

- Use meaningful contexts, e.g. from situations in the classroom, stories, money problems.
- Encourage and emphasise:
  - representation of problems with fingers
  - adding or subtracting one or two to start with
  - learning the doubles facts
  - recomposing numbers to 5 and something, and 10 and something
  - spotting complements to 10 when adding or subtracting
  - number facts for all the numbers up to 10
  - and up to 20
  - looking for patterns
  - looking for ways of turning unfriendly numbers into friendly numbers.

Children's number stories

Making up number stories is an activity which can provide a variety of learning opportunities. A group of children can be asked to draw pictures illustrating number bonds to 10 (Figure 2.3) or to make up a story involving numbers. As well as being able to calculate, children need to be able to decide what kind of operation

$8+2=10$

Figure 2.3 A picture for 8 + 2 =10

is required to solve a particular problem. They need to be able to relate abstract sums on paper or on the calculator to a problem set in a context. Asking children to make up stories to match sums is another way of helping children to relate abstract symbols to meaningful contexts. In the following example the children were asked to make up a number story, and this shows the children developing a flexible feel for the composition of numbers, and playing around with addition and subtraction. They might then go on to replicate their story on a calculator. The story is quite complicated (Figure 2.4) and requires careful reading!

SOME ACTIVITIES:

How many ways? To gain familiarity with number bonds

Provide children with lots of apparatus so they can show all the ways of making:

- multilink models with five
- unifix towers of 10 using two colours
- plates of six biscuits using two kinds
- cakes with seven candles using two colours
- trains of cuisenaire worth nine using different rods
- dominoes with eight spots altogether
- baskets of five eggs using two colours
- 10p using different coins

Example (ii) Ismail (5 years 11 months)
              Sean (5 years 11 months)

Once upon a time there was 6 men on motor bikes. They went out and 1 disappeared and then there were 5. They went to see their Mum and Dad because they are grown up. There are 7 people. They went home. 1 fell off the bike and there are 4. 1 went to sea and he got lost and then there are 3. 1 went to the pictures and then there were 2. The next went to the supermarket, he got some food and the other got lost and then there was 1.

Figure 2.4 A number story

• different sets of 10 beans sprayed blue on one side

Then they can record using pictures and numbers, spot patterns in the number bonds, e.g. 1 & 9, 2 & 8, 3 & 7... and investigate the number of combinations for each total: (Figures 2.5 – 2.8).

Yoghurt pots: To learn faster recall of number bonds

Take a set number of counters and put them under an upturned pot. Take some out and challenge the children to tell you (by holding up their fingers) how many are still under the pot. It is interesting to see how the children work this out. Do they:

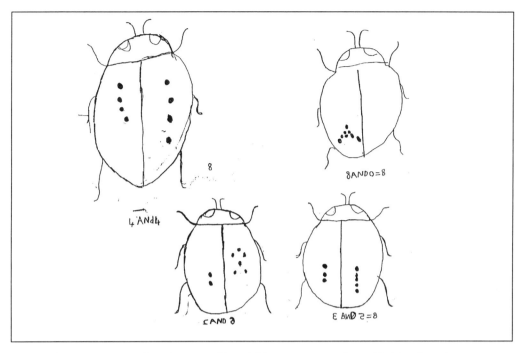

Figure 2.5 Ladybirds with eight spots. The child was given cardboard ladybirds and counters and asked to give each ladybird 8 spots

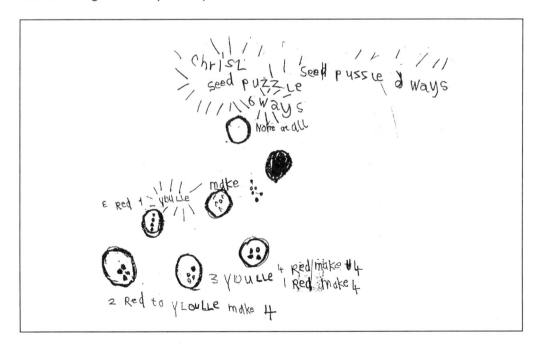

Figure 2.6 Seed puzzle. The child was given red and yellow counters and some pots. The task was to put 4 counters in each pot in as many different ways as possible. Here the child finds all five combinations (e.g., 3 red and 1 yellow, 4 red, etc.) but intriguingly includes 'none at all'

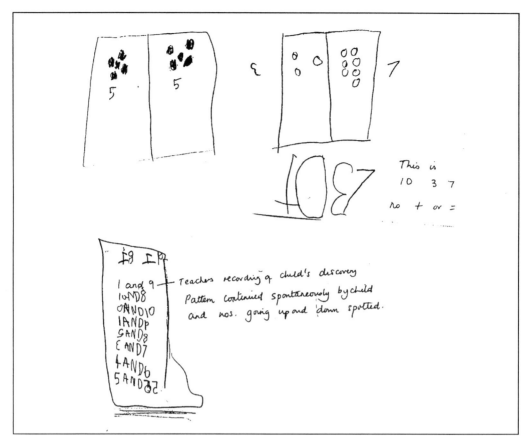

Figure 2.7 Ten counters on a divided baseboard. Child's work annotated by teacher

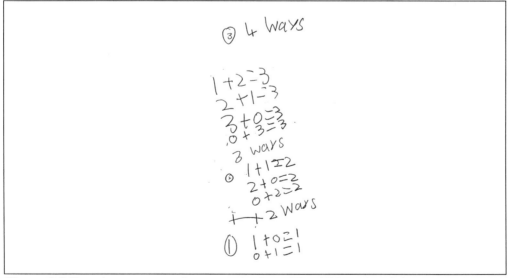

Figure 2.8 How many ways are there to make three. The child continued the patterns systematically to find how many ways to make two and then one

- Visualise, or count the hidden counters?
- Use their fingers in some way?
- Consult number lines on the wall nearby?
- Just know?

Children can play this in pairs, putting some counters on top of the pot and leaving some hidden underneath. It is interesting to see how they record the possibilities in their own way. Figure 2.9 shows a child's recording for six counters.

Figure 2.9 Six counters and a pot

Board games

Board games can be adapted, so that two dice are used, and the scores added, subtracted or doubled. This is more challenging if dice numbered 1 to 9 are used.

2.3 DEVELOPING A FEEL FOR NUMBER

A skilful early years teacher draws on skills similar to those used by child psychologists in trying to analyse what is involved in activities such as learning to count. Gradually an activity which seemed straightforward is seen as involving a whole range of skills and understandings. The need for insight into what is involved in an activity continues in working with older children and the teacher will also need deeper understanding of the mathematical ideas. Whatever activity the children are involved in, the teacher will need a grasp of the ideas on which the activity depends together with a sense of direction, a sense of what comes next. It is this sense of direction which enables a teacher to intervene successfully to encourage learning.

Understanding place value

The system of numerals which we use, called Hindu-Arabic, has important features and regularities which, once mastered, enable us to write larger and larger numbers. Built into this way of naming and writing numbers is the idea of grouping and counting in tens and using the position of a numeral to indicate its value. In this system a two-digit number like 44 is interpreted by saying that the four on the left is worth four tens and the four on the right four units. Adults learning the names for numbers in another language such as French can gain some insight into the difficulty of memorising the numbers with non-standard names (e.g. onze, douze, treize, quatorze, quinze...) and the pleasure of realising that vingt et un, vingt-deux, vingt-trois... have easy standard names. In some classes there will be a range of languages spoken and children can learn from each other. Children can repeat the numbers in a language they know and listen for patterns in languages spoken by other children. Once they have grasped the patterns in the place value system children can carry on saying larger and larger numbers. Writing the numbers down, however, presents some difficulties. Common errors for children learning to write numbers in the 'teens' are to reverse the digits, perhaps to match the order of pronunciation, as in writing 31 for 13. Larger numbers, such as 24, are written as they sound, 20 followed by 4 giving 204 rather than 24. In the following section ways of working on the links between spoken and written numbers are considered.

The classroom may provide an environment which helps children to appreciate the structure of the number system. A large number square with the numbers from 1 to 100 set out in rows of 10 can act almost like a dictionary helping the child who wants to write '19' independently without asking the teacher for help. A large clear number line always visible on the classroom wall can help to develop a strong image of the progression of the numbers. Number lines marked in tens and blank number lines for the children to work on provide familiar images to which the children and their teacher can turn when working on problems. Caleb Gattegno emphasised the value of a chart (Figure 2.10).

1	2	3	4	5	6	7	8	9
10	20	30	40	50	60	70	80	90
100	200	300	400	500	600	700	800	900

Figure 2.10 Gattegno whole number chart

As the teacher points to the number the child says the number. Initially this helps to connect the words with the numbers, for example, four hundred and the symbols 400. Later the teacher can point to 400 and 30 and 5 and teach the condensed way of writing this. Place value means that the place occupied by a number indicates how much the number is worth:

- Without place value we would have to write 4 hundreds and 3 tens and 5.
- With place value we can write 435.

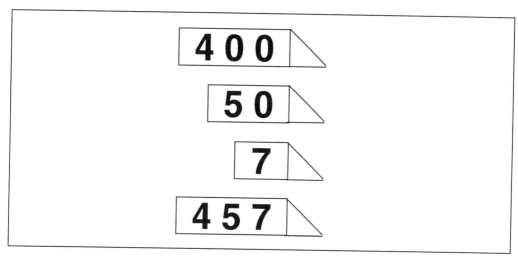

Figure 2.11 Stacking number cards for place value

Sets of number cards showing hundreds, tens and ones, which can be placed on top of each other to show the condensed way of writing numbers, provide a useful image of the information 'hidden' in a number (Sugarman, 1985). The number system condenses a great deal of information: this makes it powerful but also explains some of the difficulties children experience later with algorithms for subtraction and multiplication. Lots of varied experience with counting and writing and problems with numbers will provide a sound basis for later learning. Hundred squares in different scripts will give children opportunities to see patterns of tens and ones in a variety of systems from different cultures.

Activities

- Using the calculator to 'count' by using the constant function can help a child who has spotted the tens and ones pattern in verbal counting to relate this to the way numbers are written. On most calculators using the constant function to count in ones is done by pressing + 1 =, then pressing = repeatedly.
  A computer program called Counter enables many variations on this theme using a large display and associating sounds with the digits. It is available from the Association of Teachers of Mathematics.
- Filling in blank number lines, starting at 100 and going up in tens, starting at 800 and going up in hundreds or starting from zero and going up in tenths.
- Making jigsaws of the 100 square and fitting these together helps children use the patterns of tens and ones (Figure 2.12).
- Dienes apparatus can be used for activities and games which require children to think of numbers in terms of numbers of tens and ones.

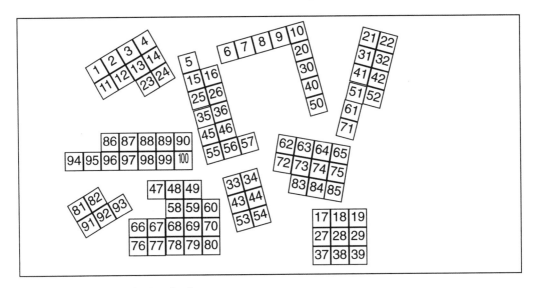

Figure 2.12 Jigsaw of a hundred square

Dienes apparatus provides a physical model of the number system. It consists of single cubes, sets of 10 cubes joined in a line to make a 'long', sets of 10 longs joined to make a 'flat' representing 100 and sets of 10 flats joined to make a cube representing 1000.

- Guessing How Many Things Are In The Jar can be a daily event, with the counting done by grouping in tens. The number of objects can be varied to help children gain a feeling for estimating large numbers.
- Investigating the system of metric measures gives a practical context for work on place value. Finding how many 10 cm rods make a metre, how many 100 gm weights make a kilo, or how many 100 ml measures make a litre, and calibrating a scale on a bottle, together with practice in reading measures, can help children in visualising relationships between numbers.

Mental mathematics

Mathematics happens inside people's heads; paper or computer screens are used to record the reasoning and to help the memory. The separation of the thinking and reasoning which goes on in the head from the written recording can be helpful in realising the importance of encouraging mental mathematics. The term 'mental arithmetic' is a narrower one associated with ten questions to be answered quickly in a test situation. 'Mental mathematics' is used to emphasise the importance of what goes on inside the head in all aspects of mathematics. Ways of developing mental strategies for addition and subtraction were considered in Section 2.2. Mental mathematics focusing on number can involve children in:

- carrying out a calculation and describing how they did it;
- a calculator game designed so that lots of possibilities have to be tried out in the head before a move is made;

- saying number rhymes or counting backwards in threes;
- mathematical discussion led by the teacher with a group or the whole class;
- becoming skilled with operations on simple numbers 'in the head'.

The last item, particularly the learning of tables, is often emphasised in public discussion of children's number skills. For the teacher, tables or multiplication facts are just one part of confident mental calculation which involves many other aspects of number, including addition facts and the important realisation that subtraction is the opposite of addition whilst division is the opposite of multiplication. Communication with parents and enlisting their help in developing children's mathematics is, however, very important so the informal term 'tables' is used here.

Tables

Learning tables is important: it gives children confidence to tackle numerical problems if they can easily recall the answer to 7×8, for example. It is probably a myth that at some point children stopped learning their tables: what did happen is that teachers, becoming more aware of how often children felt humiliated by the process of public testing, found other ways to motivate the learning of tables and assess the children's learning. It is important to realise that the inverse operation of finding factors is even more useful than the multiplication facts (for example, the understanding that if 6×7 is 42 then 7 divides into 42 six times). Questions such as, *'Is 49 a square number?'* or *'Can you find a number that is a factor of 64 and also of 40?'* will seem impossible to children who have to chant their tables to work out the answers. Children need to do more than learn their tables; they need to learn 'to be friendly with' all the numbers from 1 to 100.

If that seems very demanding then a comparison with spelling may help. Children learn to spell hundreds of words, many of them non-standard ones, but there are only 100 basic multiplication facts. A junior-school child who feels bogged down by tables can be encouraged to take a multiplication square and to cross off all the ones that seem easy (twos, threes, fives and tens perhaps).There is a way of doing the nine times table on the fingers which takes care of the nines (see Circle Game on page 35) – leaving just a core of obstinate facts to be learnt.

Learning tables, or knowing multiplication facts and being able to apply them, begins in the early years with children learning to count *pairs* of things. This is quite a leap, in terms of being able to think of numbers of numbers, rather than numbers of individual items. Learning the totals of double numbers, like two and two and three and three, will similarly begin at an early age. Children need to practise counting groups of things, and to build a familiarity with the number sequences of counting in twos, threes, fives and tens. This can be done in practical ways, with objects and pictures, for instance by counting:

- pairs of eyes, shoes, gloves, wheels on bikes, 2p coins;
- threes in multilink or cuisenaire rods, tricycle wheels or segments of fingers;
- fours with legs on animals or tables, sides of squares or rectangles;

- fives with hands, 5p coins, petals on flowers, groups of children in PE;
- sixes with hexagons, egg boxes, legs on minibeasts, chairs round tables;
- sevens with heptagons, spots on ladybirds
- eights with spider legs and octopi, octagons.

If children build up a staircase pattern physically with shapes, rods or other apparatus, they can record this with numbers and relate to the pattern made by circling these on a number line or number square (Figure 2.13).

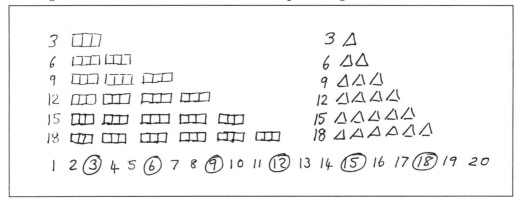

Figure 2.13 A 'staircase' pattern of threes made with multilink or triangles made out of sticks. The pattern is circled on a number line

Children may need help in verbally counting in twos and threes. It is useful to practise counting in which the multiples of 3 are said loudly whilst the in-between numbers are whispered, later the children can just 'think' the in-between numbers:

$$1, 2, \mathbf{3}, 4, 5, \mathbf{6}, 7, 8, \mathbf{9} \ldots$$

While building up these patterns children can relate the multiplication facts to division, and begin to look at the factors of numbers in a practical way. For instance they can take, say, 24 blocks and see if they can count them in twos, threes, fours, fives and tens, recording which ways work with none left over. Describing the different rectangles which can be made with 24 squares is another way of investigating the factors of numbers in a practical form which helps to build useful visual images.

These sorts of activities help children to think of recomposing numbers in different ways, and to develop a flexible feel for numbers, while appreciating the interrelationships between numbers and operations. As well as learning the number facts from practical activities and investigations, children need activities which help develop speed of recall and situations and stories which require their application.

Mathematical language

Many different words are used to describe the same operation in different contexts. Just a few of the possibilities are:

+   add, sum, total, more than, plus
−   take away, subtraction, minus
×   times, multiply, use repeated addition
÷   share, divide, use repeated subtraction
=   equals, is equivalent to, makes

When working on mental mathematics the teacher may vary the language used and listen to the children's language. Skills in carrying out operations are of little use if children cannot identify the appropriate operation to use when a problem is encountered.

Common misconceptions

> Learning is more effective when common misconceptions are addressed, exposed and discussed in teaching.
>
> (Askew and William, 1995)

Studies with large numbers of children have revealed some very common misunderstandings. By introducing these difficult ideas and discussing children's views, teachers can help children to clarify their ideas.

Misconception 1: To multiply by ten you add a nought

This misconception arises from over-generalising a pattern that is true for whole numbers.

$$20 \times 10 = 200$$

$$400 \times 10 = 4000$$

But 0.2 × 10 is *Not* 0.20

Teachers can help to avoid the misconception by talking about shifting numbers along rather than adding a nought, e.g. for 20 × 10, the 2 shifts from 2 tens to 2 hundreds. Asking children what they expect 0.2 × 10 to be and then trying it out on a calculator will get a discussion started.

Misconception 2: 0.25 is bigger than 0.3

Again early experience leads to the correct conclusion that *for whole numbers* a longer number is always larger than a shorter number, for example 273 is larger than 99.

This mistake is more likely to arise if the numbers are read as nought point twenty five and nought point three. With that way of reading, twenty five *sounds* larger than three. The correct way to read the numbers is 'nought point two five' and 'nought point three'. This way of reading, together with work on number lines and scales, can help to make clear that the numbers to the right of the decimal point represent smaller and smaller divisions. This is also important when reading calculator displays: 1.333 needs to be interpreted as between 1.3 and 1.4 (Figure 2.14).

Calculator work is very useful for emphasising that a long number is not necessarily a large number.

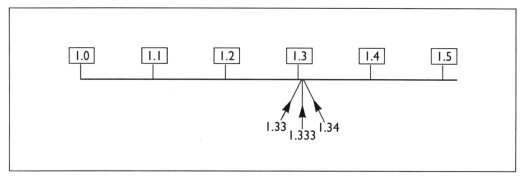

Figure 2.14 Finding 1.333 on a number line

A complication is that in working with money we do read £4.25 as four pounds twenty five. Measurement is a useful bridge with children encouraged to verbalise and notice the difference between:

4 m 25 cm which is read as four metres twenty-five centimetres;

and 4.25 m which is read as four point two five metres.

Misconception 3: If you can't take a large number from a smaller one then taking the small one from the large one will do

$$\begin{array}{r} 34 \\ -17 \\ \hline 23 \end{array}$$

Putting the calculation in a context in which the answer has to make sense can help to make clear why this doesn't work. For example, 34 children in the class, 17 children go singing this would seem to leave 23 children in the classroom. But 17 children singing and 23 in the classroom is 40 children altogether – something has gone wrong. The teacher may also choose to present another similar problem in which the mistake is more obvious because of the size of the numbers. For example, 34 —7 = 33 uses the smaller from larger misconception to give an answer which clearly cannot be true. It needs skilful teaching, first to identify the systematic error and then to help the child to realise that the method doesn't work whilst boosting the child's confidence that with a little help the problem can be identified and a correct method identified. Computer programmers never expect programs to work first time; they expect to perform many trials and to 'de-bug' the program. The idea of finding the 'bugs' in a piece of mathematics can be used rather as the idea of editing is used to work on and polish a piece of writing.

Case Study: Circle Game

The work was carried out with a Year 6 class in a mixed-ability group. The introductory activity was a circle game, a simplified version of an activity developed by Adrian Pinel. Its purpose was to practise and to develop confidence in recalling number facts and in mental calculation.

On this occasion the children sat on the carpet and I sat with them. The activity works just as well with the children sitting at their tables or desks. They each had a card on which there was an answer at the top of the card and a question written below the answer.

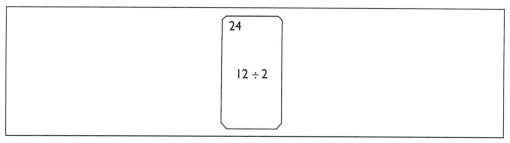

Figure 2.15 The first Card

I started off the game by asking the question written on my card (Figure 2.15).

I knew someone was holding a card with the answer 6: it was Jane. She called out 6. I then instructed Jane to read out the question on her card. *'Six nines?'* she asked. There was a bit of a pause. I suggested: *'Just have a look at the cards of the people near you. Give the person who has the answer a gentle nudge if they haven't noticed it's their turn.'* There were smiles all round at this. By making it clear that it was all right to help each other my intention was to remove any anxieties about making a mistake in public and at the same time I wanted to make it clear that everyone was expected to keep on task, even if their turn had gone. (Everyone had at least one card but several children had two.) Robert had the card with 54 at the top and so the game continued until the last question: *'Double 12'* instructed Gemma. The answer, 24, was on my card – the first card of the game. We had completed the circle.

The children loved it and asked to play again. Some children wanted to keep their cards, others wanted to 'swop'. Negotiations were completed quickly and we played one more time. I jotted down those calculations at which there was some hesitation for my future reference. This introductory activity contained fairly straightforward table facts and my intention was to make sure those facts which caused some difficulty were highlighted and reintroduced in other activities.

I wanted to make sure the children knew the value of such an activity. When asked, they offered:

'You have to listen all the time'
'You do lots of calculations in your head'
'You have to work out every answer'
'It's tables practice'
'It's fun'

I suggested the children really practised ways of recalling number facts and quick ways of calculating numbers which worked well for them. This led to a discussion about the children's preferred strategies for recalling their table facts. They acknowledged that there really wasn't time to *'count on in ones'* when playing a game. You needed to either know the answer or have a quick method of finding it out.

'Six times nine' was one question we discussed. The children offered these favourite strategies for finding the answer:

> *'I know 6 tens, so then it's easy to find 6 nines.'*
> *'I find the nine times table easy because of the pattern the nines make. Look it's 9, 18, 27, 36, 45, 54.'*
> *'I always work out times 5 and add on from there, so if I need 6 nines, I do 5 times 9 (which is the same as 9 times 5) and add on another 9.'*
> *'I know my square numbers, so I know that 6 X 6 is 36 and I need another 3 sixes which is 18 and I do it that way.'*

Pete had a finger method taught to him by his uncle which he demonstrated to the rest of the group. They helped to teach each other (Figure 2.16).

The group was intrigued to find their friends worked things out in so many different ways. It reminded me once again of the importance of listening to the children's explanations of how they think and also of the futility of insisting that one algorithm has merit over all others. These particular children had not only experienced a rich variety of number activities, they had clearly been encouraged to see possible links between them, e.g developing square numbers. Visualising them and learning them had given one child easy access to the table facts he found difficult to learn.

Following the introductory activity, I moved to the main activity which was to make a circular card game. The purpose of the activity was to develop logical thinking and to encourage an awareness of the links between number operations. I told the children they were going to make their own version of the game to play in a small group, on their own or at home. They worked in groups of four or five. Tim, a child with Down's syndrome, worked in a pair with his assistant but participated with the whole group for the introductory activity and for the feedback session.

Each group played a mini-version of the circle game. They then set to work to produce a game themselves. Where children found it difficult to get going, I intervened by first playing the practice game with the children and then setting out the cards which made the completed circle on the table (Figure 2.17). I then removed one card, inviting them to suggest possible questions which could complete the circle if the card had been lost. They soon got the idea and began to offer a range of possible answers to fill the gap, showing not only that they understand how to proceed with making the game but that they had a growing awareness that the same answer could be obtained by a variety of methods. Some children went on to:

Figure 2.16 (a) and **(b)** 9 x 7 = 63. Paul is demonstrating 9 x 7 = 63 by folding down the seventh finger. This leaves six fingers standing up on the left and three fingers standing up on the right, so the answer can be read off as 9 x 7 is 63. In the same way 5 x 9 can be read off by folding down the fifth finger, etc.

- 'Patent' their own set of cards by putting a logo on the back to identify their games.
- Realise they needed to mark those cards which belonged together in a set with a symbol or letter.
- Mix the operations, use decimals, fractions and measurement.

Tim had been working on change from 10p. His assistant worked with him to produce sets of cards in this context. When the class reassembled on the carpet to

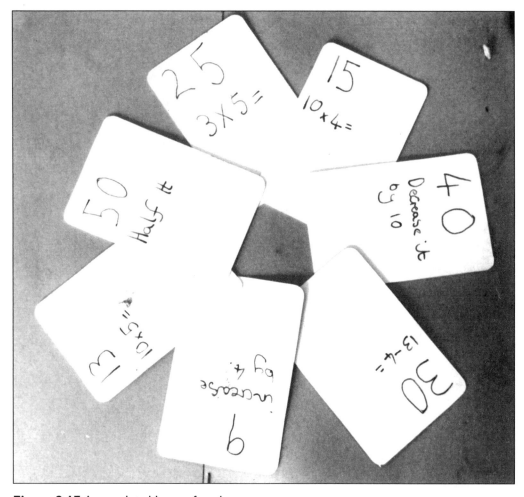

Figure 2.17 A completed Loop of cards

discuss their version of the game, Tim's version was of considerable interest. Nobody else had thought of doing a money game and Tim was clearly pleased at the positive response he received.

A RANGE OF METHODS FOR CALCULATING

Calculators

The main arguments used for and against calculator use are as follows:

- For:
  - There is evidence that children using calculators learn more rapidly about large numbers, decimals and estimation.
  - They are widely used in adult life.
  - They enable more complex problems to be tackled, using 'real' data.
  - The skills involved in using calculators effectively need to be learnt.

- Against:
  - Children are observed using calculators for very simple calculations.
  - Facility with pencil and paper algorithms for multiplication and division may be reduced.

As is often the case with polarised arguments, these positions often become self-fulfilling prophecies. That is, where a teacher values the use of calculators they are used effectively and appropriately; where a teacher feels strongly that calculators make children lazy, the children accept this view and prefer pencil and paper methods. A balanced view is most likely where there is a carefully thought out school policy which emphasises calculator activities that make children think. The essential element in an effective calculator policy is the corresponding emphasis on *mental mathematics*.

If calculators are to be used effectively then teachers and children need to be clear about the purposes of calculator use. It can be helpful to distinguish two quite different ways of using them in the classroom:

- calculators as a learning device;
- calculators as a tool.

(1) Calculators as a learning device

The teacher decides that some aspect of the children's understanding can be developed through the use of a calculator activity. The calculator may be used to provide rapid feedback or to generate lots of examples from which the children can deduce a pattern.

Activity 1

- *Teacher's decision* – The teacher identified a group of children as needing to work on place value. This task was chosen to assist their learning.
- *Reason for using the calculator* – To provide rapid and accurate feedback about the number system.
- *Children's role* – Thinking and learning about the value of each digit in a number.

Children work in pairs. Each child puts a three-digit number less than 500 into the calculator without showing the other child. They then ask each other for one of the numbers from 1 to 9, thus:

First child: *'Do you have any threes?'*

The second child has 238 on her calculator and so must say *'Yes you can have 30'*.

The first then adds 30 to her total and the second child takes 30 away from 238. The game continues until one child's total is reduced to zero or when an agreed target – say 700 – is reached. (*Note:* The game works better if the target is not too large as throughout the game the sum of the children's numbers remains the same, if the target is too large the game only ends when one child reaches zero.)

The main learning point of the activity is in seeing that taking 30 away from 238 wipes out the 'tens' leaving 208; similarly subtracting 200 would wipe out the hundreds.

Activity 2

- *Teacher's decision* – An open-ended activity is required which enables children to demonstrate their understanding of number.
- *Reason for using the calculator* – To encourage the children to experiment and explore number relationships.
- *Children's role* – To be imaginative in their exploration, to reason and to make sense of the number operations.

One of the findings of the Calculator Aware Number Project (PRIME, 1991), a major project on the use of calculators, was that a small number of open-ended activities could be used repeatedly to explore the number system. A useful activity involves drawing three blobs joined with arrows (Figure 2.18). A number is put in the first blob and an operation on the first arrow.

Figure 2.18 Blobs and arrows

This gives the number in the second blob and an operation can be chosen to give the number in the third blob. So far the calculator has been doing all the work BUT now the child must find an operation to bring them back to the number in the first blob – this is where the thinking occurs (Figure 2.19). In practice children rapidly learn to look ahead and choose their early numbers and operations to make it possible to complete the circle. Their choices give information to the teacher on the level of their mathematical understanding. Once the activity is familiar, children can return to it to try out increasingly complicated ideas.

(2) Calculators as a tool

When faced with a problem involving calculations, such as working out how much money the class should have brought in for the school trip, the child needs to:

Step 1 – Consider the problem and decide which type of calculation is needed.

Step 2 – Choose whether to use head, calculator or pencil and paper.

Step 3 – Calculate.

Step 4 – Check reasonableness of the answer.

Step 5 – Loop back to Step 1 if working on a substantial or open problem.

Studies by the Assessment of Performance Unit have indicated that an overemphasis on Step 3, involving the practice of standard algorithms, resulted in children who lacked skills in the essential Step 1, deciding which type of calculation to perform. If a calculator is used to work on a practical problem then Step 1 is essential because of the need to decide which button to press.

For Step 2, deciding which method to use, children need to be encouraged to take some degree of personal responsibility in deciding what sums they can more sensibly do in their head.

Step 4, checking the reasonableness of the answer, is the essential skill required if children are to make effective practical use of their mathematical calculations. It is possible only when children have developed skills in mental mathematics and are able to see when their answers make no sense.

Informal written methods and standard algorithms

Algorithms are step-by-step procedures such as those used to multiply large numbers. The National Curriculum requires children to:

> (KS1) develop a variety of methods for adding and subtracting
> (KS2) extend mental methods to develop a range of non-calculator methods of computation

The National Curriculum indicates what children are expected to achieve but leaves to schools and to teachers decisions as to how these targets are to be reached. There are some important decisions for schools to make about approaches and timing.

Here are two very different possible approaches:

- Analysing into small steps:
  - practise simple algorithms;
  - introduce problems leading to simple algorithms;
  - practise harder algorithms;
  - practise word problems leading to harder algorithms.

- Analysing into substantial elements:
  - develop children's mental maths skills;
  - introduce problems and encourage children to discuss the problems and develop their own methods;
  - work on estimation and a 'feel' for the size of the answer;
  - introduce standard methods and/or ensure that children have a robust, effective non-standard method;
  - practise problems leading to harder algorithms.

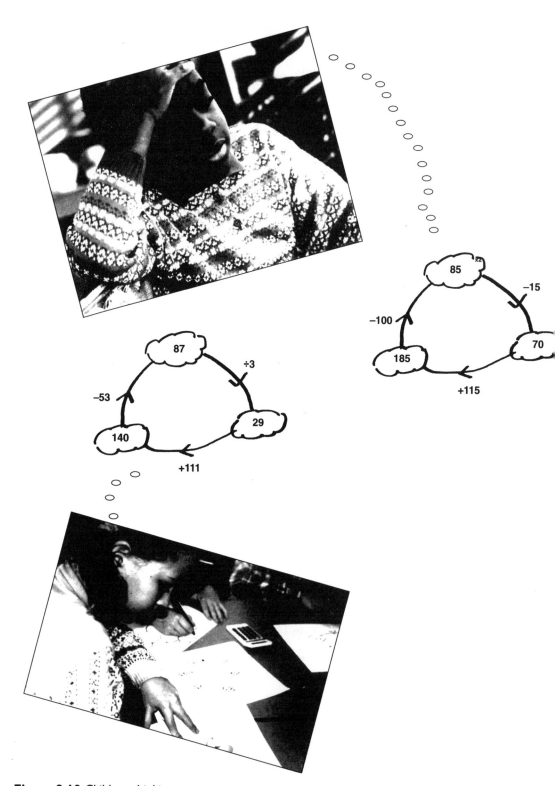

Figure 2.19 Children thinking

54

÷14   ×7

756   378

×2

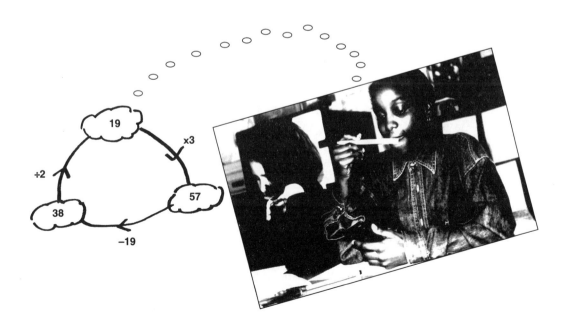

19

÷2   ×3

38   57

−19

The first method based on individual written work typifies a scheme-dominated style, practice dominates and the teacher's role is to correct mistakes. The second method uses the scheme as a resource: the teacher anticipates the children's learning needs and emphasises mental and oral work. A valuable reference is: OFSTED (1993):

> Good standards were more evident in those classes where the teacher used a range of methods to teach knowledge, skills and understanding. In such classes the pupils received direct teaching and thus benefited from the teacher's appropriate explanations and questioning, and from discussion which challenged pupils to think in greater depth about number concepts and relationships.
>
> Where standards were less than satisfactory the teaching failed to address the range of ability in the class. Much of the work was poorly planned and executed, or was superficial. Too many pupils worked largely alone on inappropriate and undemanding time-filling exercises while the teaching time was taken up with organising the work, instead of direct tuition.

Some people argue that children who learn simple vertical algorithms first, tend to generalise inappropriate methods – for instance by subtracting the smaller unit from the larger no matter where its position, because this has always been the case in the easy examples.

$$\begin{array}{r} 89 \\ -53 \\ \hline 36 \end{array} \qquad \begin{array}{r} 83 \\ -59 \\ \hline 36 \end{array}$$

When children meet the harder subtraction, they continue to take the smaller number away from the larger, because this is what they have been doing in all the previous examples.

It could be argued that using the written algorithm for easy two-digit subtractions, like 89 – 53 is like using a sledge-hammer to crack a nut, since these can easily be done in the head, as indeed we should be expecting children to do. It would make more sense to introduce a written method only when there is a need for it, i.e. when the calculation becomes difficult to do mentally. Mental calculation, it is argued, is more likely to require the child to understand what they are doing. Children can complete written algorithms by memorising 'tricks' without understanding, or make mistakes by not remembering the procedures correctly, having no sensible means of reconstructing the procedure. In either case, of course, it is important that children are encouraged to check by another method, so they have a fallback strategy available.

Introducing vertical algorithms for addition and subtraction

It seems logical that children should not be introduced to the sophisticated, standard vertical written methods of computation until they have some basic mental skills, number knowledge and understanding. If you check to ensure children have these, there should be no danger of them completing two-digit calculations by having to count cubes or secretly drawing lots of tallies as some children do.

Before they are introduced to:

$$\begin{array}{r} 34 \\ + 28 \\ \hline 62 \end{array}$$

Children should, for instance:

- know 9 and 8 is 17;
- know 29 is 20 and 9;
- be able to add 34 and 22 without counting in ones,
    (by adding tens and units separately and
    by counting on in tens from 34, then adding the 2).

They could then be asked to do some detective work to see what is going on. In this way, they are being asked to make sense of the algorithm and explain how it works, rather than being taught to memorise a procedure with fragile understanding.

Similarly, children should be asked to spot what is going on with:

$$\begin{array}{r} 53 \\ -29 \\ \hline 24 \end{array}$$

and they should already have some mental strategies to check the answer.
They need to:

- know bonds to ten
- be able to count on in tens from 29
- and then add on the units to get to 53.

They should also be encouraged to look for ways of making 'unfriendly numbers' friendlier and to look for quick ways. For instance in working out 53 – 29, they might notice that 29 is one less than 30 and, by adding one on to both 53 and 29, make the easier calculation of 54 – 30.

When they understand the method of computation, children can try harder numbers where they cannot work out the answer easily in their heads. Then they will need to be encouraged to check using strategies like looking at the final digits and approximating the size of the answer.

Children also need to be encouraged to explain methods and share them, and to develop a flexibility in expressing numbers in different ways, by splitting them up or recomposing them and thinking of relationships with other numbers. For instance when adding 8 + 9 children might:

- Think of complements to ten – make the 9 up to ten by taking 1 from 8 giving 7 + 10 or 17.
- Use the nearest double – 8 add 8 is 16 and 1 more is 17.

If they are encouraged to make and look for patterns, they will know that 18 + 9 and 28 + 39 will also end with 7.

Informal and formal methods for multiplication

Evidence that very few adults used the formal methods which they had been taught at school has led to an interest in methods which, whilst they include some paper recording, were developed by the children themselves. Teachers can explore these strategies by asking children to explain how they have worked out a calculation. In this example the child is trying to work out 16 x 15. She has noticed that 15 is five times three. After her first attempt she said, 'I see what I need to do I must multiply the top line not add it' (Figure 2.20). This same child was also able to do the calculation in a number of other ways including the more conventional (Figure 2.21).

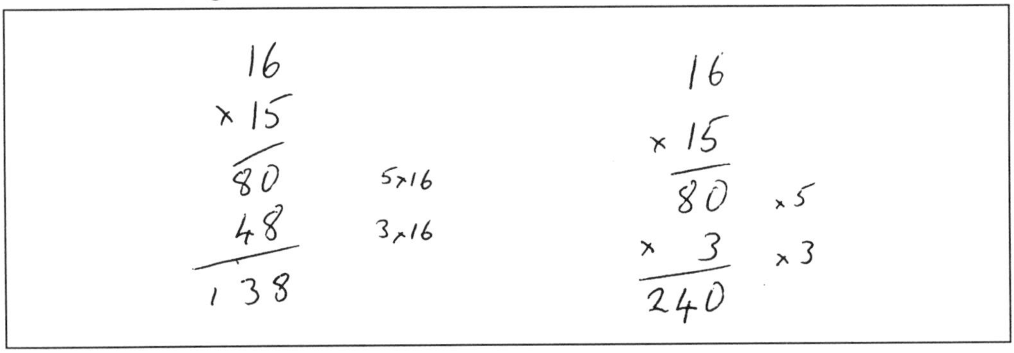

Figure 2.20 First and second attempts – can you follow the child's reasoning?

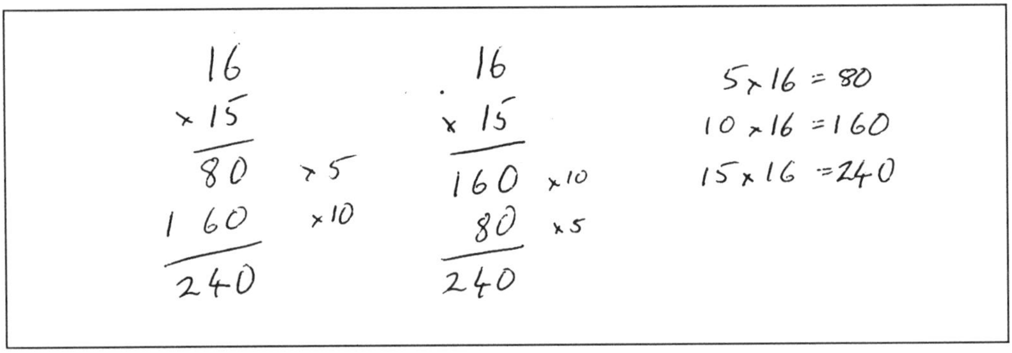

Figure 2.21 More than one way to multiply

Problems requiring several similar calculations give children a chance to hone their methods:

The problem. Using 6, 8 and 5 work out 68 x 5

Then try other multiplications using the same digits.

Which way gives the largest answer?

Figure 2.22 shows a child's response to this question which demonstrates a robust, effective non-standard method for two-digit by one-digit multiplication. Figure 2.23 gives a child's method showing all the understanding needed to move to a more compact form of recording.

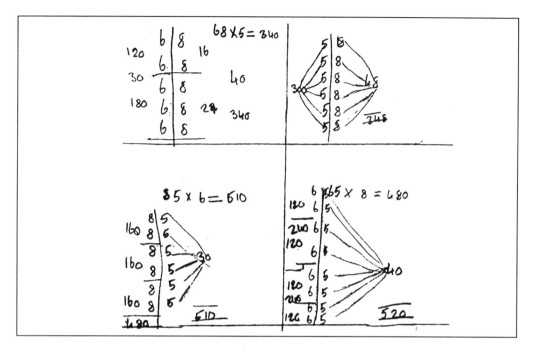

Figure 2.22 68 x 5 by a robust, non-standard method

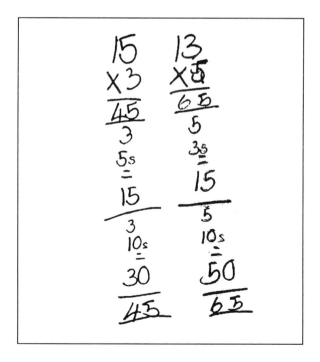

Figure 2.23 A near formal method

Children's experiences of division

(1) Children will encounter division in a variety of forms and be expected to make a variety of responses

- *Sharing* – Children need to learn that sharing in a mathematical context means equal shares. Sharing in a family context is a much more complicated idea: consider sharing out the potatoes for lunch; sharing your teddy with your baby brother.
  Here are 12 sweets, let's share them between these four teddies. One response is a physical dealing out: one for me, one for you, etc. Then you count up to see how many sweets each teddy has. Alternative responses might be to sweep the sweets into four piles or for larger numbers to count them out two at a time.
  (In a sharing problem you know how many groups to form and are trying to find out how many will be in each group.)
- *Grouping* – There are 28 children here today, can you get into groups of three. The expected response is to join hands in threes and then look round to see how many groups of three have been formed.
  (In a grouping problem you know how many in each group and are trying to find out how many groups can be formed.)
  Take a handful of cubes and see how many groups of three you can make. The expected response is to take groups of three until there are no cubes left, then count the number of *groups*.
- *Fractions, decimals and percentages* – Find a third of nine counters. The expected response is to partition into three equal sets. (to find one third you divide by three) (Figure 2.24).
  0.1 as one divided by 10.
  1% as one-hundredth part of a whole.
- *Division as the inverse of multiplication:*
$$4 \text{ multiplied by } 3 = 12$$
$$\text{means } 12 \text{ divided by } 4 = 3$$
$$\text{and } 12 \text{ divided by } \quad 3 = 4$$
- *Division button on a calculator* – Planning events offers real-life problems. This six-pack of Cola costs £2.60 – is it a good buy? How much is that for one can? The child needs first to interpret the problem as division, then to enter in the correct order 2.60 divided by six and finally to interpret the result, 0.4333333.

(2) Children will also be exposed to a variety of language styles

- *Formal written language in the scheme* – How many sets of 2 make 8? Share 6 sweets equally between 2.
- *Spoken language of parents and older brothers and sisters* – How many twos in eight? Twos into six.
- *Spoken language in the classroom* which is likely to contain elements of both formal and informal phrases: share equally, share between, share by, into.

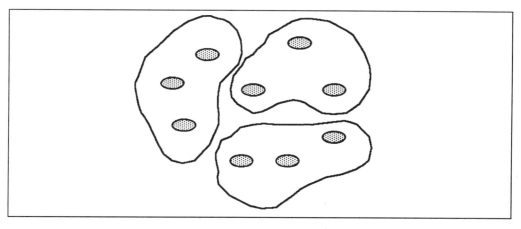

Figure 2.24 Find a third of nine counters

(3) Several recording methods are likely to be encountered

An added complication with division is that, where there is no real-life context for the problem, it is never clear what to do with remainders.

- *Child's informal recording.* Take a handful of cubes, count to see how many you've got. Can you group them in threes and write something down to show me how you worked it out?
  e.g. counting the cubes, 37 cubes.
  Splitting up in some way, such as

  > 10 lots of 3 are 30
  > 2 lots of 3 are 6
  > and 1 left over

- *Formal recording.* Children working from a scheme are likely to be required to use two or three distinct methods of formal recording designed to clarify the very compact 'standard' written methods for larger numbers.

  44 divided by 3

  44
  30 take away 10 lots of 3 ⎫
  ――   ⎬ that makes 14 lots of 3
  14   ⎪
  12 take away 4 lots of 3 ⎭
  ――
  2 left over

(4) Images offered to help understanding of division

These include:

- Objects such as counters, in piles.
- Drawings of rectangular arrays:

  . . . .
  . . . .
  . . . .

- Structured apparatus of unit cubes, strips of 10 cubes and blocks of 100.
- All the mental images built up in earlier number work (See sections 2.2 and 2.3).
- Counting in 2s, 3s, etc.
- Multiplication square used to find factors.
- Gattegno chart to emphasise multiplying and dividing by 10.

To chart a course though all these variations the teacher will need a clear sense of direction. The easy route out may seem to be handing over the problem to a scheme, but when a child working from a scheme approaches the teacher saying *'I don't understand'*, a teacher will typically pause for only 1 or 2 seconds before replying. In that 2 seconds she will need to have decided:

- What's the purpose of this exercise?
- What do I know about this child's previous experience and understanding?
- What language or image shall I use in my response?

One interpretation of initial teacher education and continuing professional development is that the years of education are all needed so that you know what to say after 2 seconds! With increased levels of school planning there are opportunities to discuss in detail the approach used in any scheme the school has adopted, to accept it fully or to modify the approach. This marks the difference between the scheme-as-resource and the scheme-driven approach. Some suggested principles are:

- crucial ideas underpinning division are: the knowledge of multiplication and division facts, particularly multiplying by 10; the ability to split up and recombine numbers in a variety of ways;
- estimation makes more sense when the problem is in some context (see sections on measure and data-handling), a context is also needed for making sense of remainders.

In practice this may well mean establishing some activities which can become part of the classroom ritual to be worked on several times a week for short periods. These familiar activities, the images shared by teacher and children, can be referred to when the children get 'stuck' on individual written work.

Activity 1 – Towers

This provides a useful image for sharing problems. You will need multilink cubes and a variety of cardboard shapes, equilateral triangles, squares, regular pentagons and hexagons.

The child takes a handful of multilink cubes, counts them and selects a shape. The task is to build a tower at each corner of the shape. The towers must be of the same height, any left-over cubes are placed in the middle. So if 16 cubes are taken and towers built on the triangular mat, there will be five cubes in each tower and one left over. The children can be encouraged to predict the remainder, to try to find a mat where there is no remainder. See the *Count Me In* games (page 193) for a version using scoring.

Activity 2

A collection of calculator activities selecting numbers which will multiply to reach a target number (see Section 2.4).

Activity 3 – 'Spotting division'

Newspaper articles expressing concern about falling standards always include a problem including division. It would be very satisfying if we could educate a generation of children who could solve these problems! The first hurdle seems to be in identifying that the problem is a division one in a problem without clear verbal clues:

- The exchange rate is 7.5 francs to the pound. *(General information.)*
- A menu costs 30 francs. *(Specific information.)*
- How much is that in pounds? *(Question that doesn't specify division.)*

Helpful tactic 1 – Estimation. If the problem is changed to an exchange rate of 10 francs to the pound, the success rate shoots up. Many children will answer £3 immediately and can then see that what they did was work out 30 divided by 10. They can then tackle the harder problem of working out 30 divided by 7.5; they can at least get started.

Helpful tactic 2 – Familiarity at *identifying* the operation.

A local map is placed on the classroom wall with the scale clearly marked. A route for a walk is measured using a piece of string:

- Scale is 4 cm to 1 kilometre. *(General information.)*
- The walk is 17 cm on the map. *(Specific information.)*
- How far is that? *(Question that doesn't specify division.)*

The activity can be repeated changing the walk, the map, or both, linked perhaps to the work on geography or history, until identifying the operation becomes familiar. Similar activities involving conversion from one currency to another can be based around a Euro-corner in which information on the culture of another country includes numerical information to be interpreted. Such classroom displays provide a parallel for older children to the home corner full of numerals which supports mathematics in the early years.

Activity 4

Real-life problems such as planning an event will provide further contexts in which a variety of operations are needed (see Section 2.6). Activities checking for 'value for money' are particularly useful for division. A collection of varying sizes of packages for tea, coffee, cereal, etc. marked with prices is a useful resource.

Estimation

Whatever method of calculation is chosen, when the calculation is complete the child must take notice of the answer. 'Is this answer daft?' is the essential question that needs to be internalised. How can a child learn to answer that question? A crucial factor in estimating is to have something to compare with. To decide whether a bookcase will go through a door, you need to see both the bookcase and the door. To decide if 27 is a reasonable answer to 13 times 14, you need to be able to compare with a familiar benchmark such as 10 times 10 is a hundred – so 27 is *far* too small. A collection of familiar benchmarks can be used to make judgements, as follows:

- For calculations:
                    10 x 10 = 100, 20 x 20 = 400
                    a thousand times a thousand is a million.
- For ratios: Three-quarters is 75%, which is 0.75, which is a half plus a quarter.
- For heights: my height is 1 metre 20 cm, my sister is 1 metre 40 cm.
- For measures: a bag of sugar weighs a kilo, which is about 2.2 pounds.
- For numbers: the number of children in the class, the school, the number of people in the city, town or village in which the children live.

Children can be encouraged to develop their own set of bench-marks or to make a display of significant bench-marks.

Rounding

More formal methods of estimating use rounding. Using a calculator to find out how many 43p cans of soup can be bought for £4.00 gives an answer of 9.30232. This must be rounded down to give 9 cans and some change.

Using a calculator to find out how many coaches are needed to take 400 children on a trip when each coach takes 43 children gives the same answer of 9.30232, which this time must be rounded up to give 10 coaches if some children are not to be left behind.

The decision to round up or down is taken by considering the sense of the question.

There are two formal systems of rounding: by decimal places and by significant figures.

e.g.   To one decimal place   3.92   is 3.9
                                               4.090 is 4.1
                    To one significant figure 3.92   is 4
                                               357   is 400

With both these formal systems the convention is to round up if the digit is 5 or above but the overriding consideration is to give an answer that makes sense in the context of the question.

2.4 EXTENDING THE NUMBER SYSTEM

The process of learning to count, which begins with the counting numbers 1,2,3... and proceeds with an ever more confident grasp of how to count on and on, is the beginning of an exploration of number. With increased acceptance of calculator use children are beginning to use larger numbers, negative numbers and decimals at an earlier age.

Really large numbers

There seems to be a certain pleasure in using numbers larger than you have ever used before. The moment of counting on beyond 20 for the first time, or beyond 100, can be very satisfying. Children need to continue to develop their counting skills just as they continue to develop their reading skills. Calculators can be used to explore large numbers and children encouraged to read out the numbers, e.g. four thousand nine hundred and ninety-nine, and then to predict what number will be obtained by adding 2. The computer program 'Counter' (Association of Teachers of Mathematics) displays large clear numbers and can be used to count up or down in ones or twos or any other step forming a useful focus for group or class discussion. Children can be encouraged to invent their own problems using numbers as large as they please. A million is sometimes used to mean 'an amazingly large number', a number so big it is hard to imagine. So why not try to imagine it: suppose you did have a million of your favourite chocolate bar – what would that look like? Would it fill a suitcase? Or the classroom? Or the school? (A word of warning: one class decided to collect 1 000 000 empty drink cans and found they had taken on far more than they bargained for!!)

A really large number called the **googol** was invented by a physicist George Cranow for his daughter; it has become accepted and appears in reference books. A googol is 1 followed by 100 noughts:

10 000 000 000 000 000 000 000 000 000 000 000 000 000 000 000 000 000 000 000 000 000 000 000 000 000 000 000 000 000

Activities using large numbers

- Have you been alive for 1000 000 seconds?
- What is the distance round the equator? Make a poster that helps to make sense of this distance by comparing it with more familiar distances, for example the distance between two familiar cities or the distance run in a marathon.
- What is the largest number you can find in the newspaper?
- Developing and extending the number line. One way of thinking about the progression in children's understanding of number is to think of gradually developing a more and more complicated idea of the number line:

    (a) An early number line of large numbers on the floor or in the playground which children can walk along or jump along two steps at a time.
    (b) Number lines with the numbers 10, 20, 30 ... emphasising the pattern of counting in tens.
    (c) Number lines with space to put in $2^1/_2$ and $4^1/_4$ (Figure 2.25).

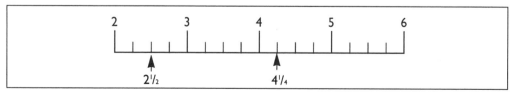

Figure 2.25 Fractions on a number line

(d) Number lines going up in really large steps to a million (Figure 2.26).

and then there is the negative number line....

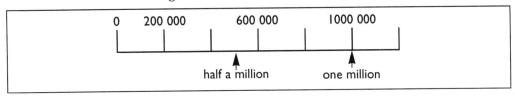

Figure 2.26 Really large numbers

INTRODUCING NEGATIVE NUMBERS

Negative numbers are very strange.

You could have three cats, you could have 253 cats but who ever saw a minus cat? Mathematics is considered such a sensible, serious subject that children are sometimes expected to swallow it whole without protest or logical argument.
Negative numbers are an invention. They were invented because it was convenient. They fit in well with some existing ideas (such as adding and subtracting numbers) but they are not *counting* numbers. You can't count negative three cats!

Negative numbers are useful when there is some zero or base point from which measurements are made. You have three pounds in the bank, you deposit five pounds – and then withdraw 10. You owe the bank two pounds. It seems sensible to label it with the number two and a sign to show that you owe two pounds: –2.

You describe a hill as 100 metres above sea level, so how would you describe a cave 10 metres under the sea? –10 m.

You put 5 into your calculator and take away 7. The calculator reads 2 – oh, no it doesn't, there's a small sign in front of the number: –2.
You have some marbles in a bag, you are not sure how many:

– You put in three marbles and take out five.
– You have two less marbles in the bag than you started with –2.
– You add three marbles. How many now? One more than you started with: +1.

This last activity works well as a whole-class activity. The children can follow up the ideas by creating their own marble problems. When asked to invent problems, children always seem to use much harder numbers than those found in exercises. If the teacher seems a little concerned about the difficulty, the children will happily produce even harder problems. This playful self-confidence can help the children to become enthusiastic about their mathematics.

Once you are using negative numbers it can seem appropriate to put a plus sign in front of the counting numbers to emphasise the difference. The positive numbers, zero and the negative numbers together are called the **Integers**.

Glossary

This provides background information for the teacher

Whole numbers: These are the counting numbers 1, 2, 3, 4 ....etc. (0 is sometimes included).

Integers: All the negative numbers, zero and the positive numbers
$$. . . -4, -3, -2, -1, 0, +1, +2, +3, +4 . . .$$

Ratio: A ratio is the comparison of two numbers. It can be written as 3:4 or as a fraction 3/4. If one person pays 80p towards a lottery ticket and another 20p, then it is only fair that their winnings should be divided in the ratio 80:20 or 4:1

Rational numbers: The word rational has the same root as ratio. Rational numbers can be written as the ratio of one integer to another. So all the fractions are rational numbers, for example 3/4, 5/3, −4/5. Whole numbers are described as rational because they can all be written as the ratio of two integers. For example 2 can be written as 2/1. Decimal numbers of finite length e.g 0.725, are all rational because they can be written as fractions 725/1000. Surprisingly, some infinite decimals (the ones with repeating sequences of digits) can also be written as fractions. For example 0.333333333... even though it goes on for ever can be written as 1/3, 0.0909090909... can be written as 1/11.

Irrational numbers: It would be reasonable to assume that the rational numbers filled up the number line *but* it turns out that there are some numbers which can't be written as one integer divided by another. The first irrational numbers usually encountered are $\sqrt{2}$ and π. We always use approximations for these numbers as the decimal expansions are infinite and never repeat. This isn't a case of waiting for a bigger and better computer; it has been proved that these numbers will never end and never settle down to a repeating sequence!

Fractions, decimals and percentages

It is disheartening when children who have in their books correct exercises completed several weeks ago can appear to have forgotten large chunks of what they learnt – but what experiences do we offer that are memorable? Many of the activities advocated include physical movement, large wall charts, discussion/arguments about misconceptions or extended projects with interactive wall displays. These are intended to provide mathematical signposts, significant events which children can recall and build pon. It is skilled teaching of a high order to provide interesting memories of fractions, decimals and percentages!

So what do we want children to remember? The National Curriculum emphasis is on *understanding* fractions, decimals and percentages and *using them in context*:

(KS1) recognise and use in context simple fractions, including halves and quarters, decimal notation in recording money and negative numbers

(KS2) understand and use, in context, fractions and percentages to estimate, describe and compare proportions of a whole.

Fractions

Understanding the meaning of fractions is the first crucial stage. Studies of common errors and misconceptions have provided useful information about how difficulties might arise from the language and images used for fractions. Consider this scenario of a father having lunch with his children. There are three fish fingers left:

Child: Can I have some more?
Father: OK then, you can have half.

Everyday use of language can be vague. In this situation would you expect the child to get half of a fish finger, or 'one and a half fish fingers' that is 'half of the three fish fingers that are left.'? Many of the mistakes that children make occur because they are not sure what they are finding a fraction *of*.

Children whose main experience of fractions is shading in shapes which have already been divided up for them may develop a strong sense of 3/4 as one 'whole' divided into four parts with three parts shaded (Figure 2.27). If they don't have to divide up the shapes themselves, they may never pay attention to the fact that all the component parts have to be the same size. Again everyday language in which it is not uncommon to hear 'I'll have the big half' is unhelpful and needs to be challenged. Children need to explore a variety of images to give them a robust understanding of fractions (Figures 2.28 and 2.29).

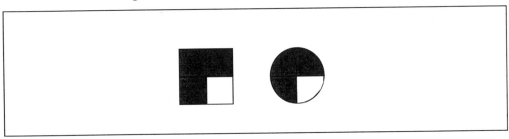

Figure 2.27 Three-quarters of square and circle: a familiar (perhaps over-familiar) image?

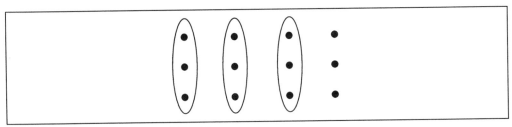

Figure 2.28 Three-quarters of 12 objects

Figure 2.30 shows an image for three divided by four, or three things shared between four people. This is just one way of dividing up the shapes, children can be encouraged to explore a variety of possible ways.

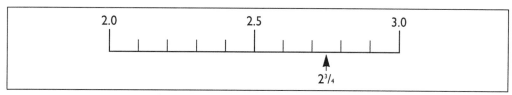

Figure 2.29 An image of two and three-quarters on a number line

Just as children at Key Stage 1 work to explore whole numbers, at Key Stage 2 children need to explore and become very familiar with a few basic fractions. Fractions greater than one, such as two and a quarter, need to be familiar as well as fractions less than one.

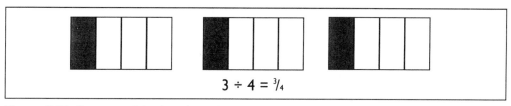

$$3 \div 4 = \sqrt[3]{4}$$

Figure 2.30 One way of dividing three things between four people

Activities involving fractions

- Measuring with paper strips one metre long, which the children fold themselves and mark as a quarter of a metre, half a metre and three quarters of a metre, can be helpful.
- Favourite dice games can be adapted using dice marked $\frac{1}{4}$, $\frac{1}{2}$, $\frac{3}{4}$, 1, $1\frac{1}{4}$, $1\frac{1}{2}$.

Activities in which the children divide up and label shapes can give a feel for the relative sizes of simple fractions and prepare the ground for the addition of simple fractions (Figure 2.31).

What is a half? Providing children with a set of objects to halve can be challenging. A piece of string, a packet of sweets, a bag of marbles, a litre bottle of water, a piece of Plasticine, a paper triangle, a paper circle. (*Note:* This means finding both a fraction of one whole, such as a whole piece of paper, and a fraction of a (whole) set of objects, such as a bag of marbles. The set of objects needs to include both odd and even numbers to halve.)

Using paper strips folded in half and then again and again is a useful way of comparing fractions and discovering those which are equivalent. Children taking turns to shade fractions of the strip can soon make up a game by throwing a dice to determine what fraction to shade in and chasing each other to the end of the strip.

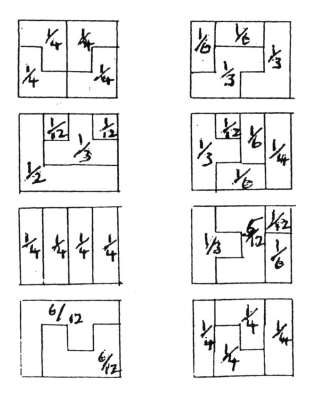

Figure 2.31 Fraction activity

Cuisenaire rods or colour factor can be used to explore fractions. The rod representing 10 units may be chosen to represent 'one whole' or the children may choose the rod which represents 8 units to be 'the whole'. Halves, quarters, eighths can be measured against each other, fractions can be added and subtracted and the results recorded, children can produce an impressive array of statements which they have generated by comparing the rods.

Decimals

Decimals are a special type of fraction in which the whole is divided into ten parts. Because our number system is based on ten, there is a simple way of writing decimals:

for one tenth we write 0.1

for one hundredth we write 0.01

Decimals can be seen as a natural extension of the place value system. In the section earlier on 'Developing a feel for number' a variety of representations were discussed, and these can be revisited and extended to explore decimals. The Gattegno chart can be used by pointing to a starting number such as 500 and asking the children to divide by 10 to get 50, then again to get 5, and then again to get 0.5

0.1	0. 2	0.3	0.4	0.5	0.6	0.7	0.8	0.9
1	2	3	4	5	6	7	8	9
10	20	30	40	50	60	70	80	90
100	200	300	400	500	600	700	800	900

Number lines can be reintroduced and divided into tenths and hundredths. Calculators can be used to explore what happens when numbers like 2 000 are divided by 10 again and again. The principle of using physical movement to emphasise and make memorable the patterns in the numbers can be applied by using children to represent the digits in a calculation. For example, three chairs can be set out to represent hundreds, tens and ones with three children holding large cards with the digits 2 and 4 and 0 to make the number 240. The instruction from the teacher is 'divide by 10'. After some discussion amongst the children with the numbers, the child with the 0 moves away, the child with the 4 moves up and the child with the 2 moves up to show 24. To divide by 10 again will need some form of marker for the decimal point and another chair to represent the 'tenths'. This simple activity, requiring only a set of large cards marked with the digits 0 to 9, can be elaborated by the teacher and used to draw out any misconceptions. It emphasises that it is the *digits* which move to *positions* of different value. It then provides a useful 'shared memory' when the children are working with pencil and paper or calculator: 'Do you remember when we were dividing by 100 on the chairs......?'

Misconceptions about decimals

In the section on mental mathematics misconceptions about the size of decimals were discussed (e.g. the longer the number, the bigger it is). A further misconception, which does not become obvious until children are involved in multiplying decimals – perhaps using a calculator to solve a practical problem, is the assumption that 'Multiplication makes bigger'. This is true when multiplying by numbers larger than 1 *but*:

$9 \times 0.1 = 0.9$, which is smaller than 9.
a half times a half is a quarter

Confronting the paradox is again effective in helping children to think through their ideas. The teacher may discuss with the children sequences involving multiplying by smaller and smaller numbers to get the children thinking and then provide activities in which the children have to use their understanding that multiplying doesn't always make bigger, such as the calculator activity described below.

Discussion activity

12×4	$= 48$	9×9	$= 81$
12×2	$= 24$	9×3	$= 27$
12×1	$= 12$	9×1	$= 9$
$12 \times 1/2 =$	6	$9 \times 1/3 =$	3
$12 \times 1/4 =$	3	$9 \times 1/9 =$	1

Children will usually agree that 12 lots of a half is 6, and be able to work out that 12 lots of 1/4 is 3. The teacher's role is to emphasise that multiplying by 1/2 has given the *answer* of 6 which is smaller than 12.

Calculator activity

This activity involves choosing numbers which multiply to a given target. To emphasise that multiplication can result in an answer which is larger or smaller than the starting number, a mix of whole and decimal numbers is used.
Starting numbers are displayed for all the children to see:

| 5 | 8 | 0.2 | 0.5 | 10 | 2 |

A target number is chosen from a set of cards prepared by the teacher to include products of the starting numbers:

| 5 | 16 | 1.6 | 50 | 40 | 0.4 | etc.

From the list of starting numbers the first player must choose two numbers which will multiply to hit the target.

The second player uses a calculator to see if the target has been hit. It is natural to discuss whether the numbers are too big or too small and this gives the teacher an opportunity to ask if there are any numbers the players can multiply by to make the answer *smaller* than the starting number. The vehemence with which some children will claim this to be impossible gives some indication of the power of this misconception.

Percentages

Yet another way of expressing parts of a whole is to use percentages, that is to divide the whole up into hundredths. The essential idea of percentages can be gained by working with frequently occurring examples such as 10% or 50%. An understanding that 10% is ten pence in the pound provides the basis for a robust method of working out percentages when money is used. Ways of working out 20%, 50% or 15% can be derived from this.

When expressing part of something, it is often possible to choose whether to use fractions, decimals or percentages. It is helpful to emphasise the connections between the different forms from an early stage.

A large number line on the wall marked in decimals, a set of cards and some string can form the basis for many activities linking fractions, decimals and percentages (Figure 2.32).

Activities involving percentages

10% off

10% is a very useful 'bench-mark' for estimating and understanding percentages. This activity enables children to get a sense of what 10% means. There is a story of a disgruntled worker on a building site who cut 10 cm off all the metre rods used for measuring. The house was duly built using these false measures and the m the problems emerged: you would hit your head on the door and have to stoop to use the sink. Imagine there was ten per cent off everything in your classroom. What would the effects be? How long would your pencil be?

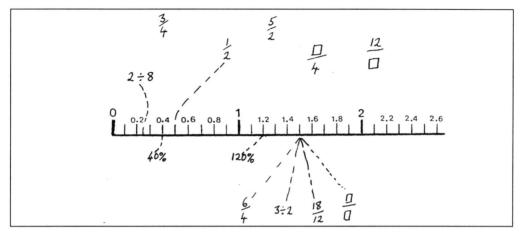

Figure 2.32 The links between fractions, decimals and percentages on a number line

Newspaper headlines

Percentages are sprinkled liberally around in newspaper articles and on the television news. They are often used to support arguments. Arguably, one of the most important reasons for understanding percentages is to support children's growth as citizens in understanding the world around them. Headlines such as '25% of water lost in leaky pipes' and 'School class size to rise by 5%' invite value judgements, but what do these figures mean and how can children be helped to understand and interpret them?

When children are making a newspaper using word-processing facilities as part of their activities in some other curriculum area, the following requirement can be included. The newspaper should contain at least three statements including percentages. In one of these statements the percentage given by the writer should be deliberately far too high, in one far too low and in the third statement the percentage should be quite reasonable. When the newspapers are displayed the children can discuss and identify the misleading percentages in the newspapers produced by other groups.

A simpler version of this activity is for the teacher to produce some headlines, real or invented, for the class to discuss.

Properties of numbers

Odd, even, multiple, factor, square, prime, cube, square root

Part of becoming familiar with the numbers from 1 to 100 involves learning addition and multiplication facts and being able to invert the facts to subtract and divide. There are also numbers with special properties to be encountered and named. It is useful to have several activities for each property so that the children meeting the numbers in different contexts become familiar with them. 'Oh, it's square numbers again' – is the sort of response to be hoped for. This familiarity can be aided by the use of display. The class can also build up a database of numbers on a computer recording for each number all the properties they can think of. The entry for 7 might read:

A prime number.

A factor of 42 and 49.

Number of days in a week.

The fourth odd number.

A guessing game can be developed with one group entering the properties and another group guessing the numbers.

Activity 1: Odd and even numbers

As children become used to working in an open way, they will respond confidently to very general questions, e.g. What can you find out about adding odd and even numbers? The apparently vague question is actually carefully designed by the teacher to give the children room for interpretation. A more precisely phrased question would mean the teacher doing the work rather than the child (see questions in Section 1). The techniques used to encourage creative writing involving different responses from different children can be adapted to encourage creative mathematics. Figure 2.33 shows the work of a child who interpreted the question by adding not just two numbers but several!

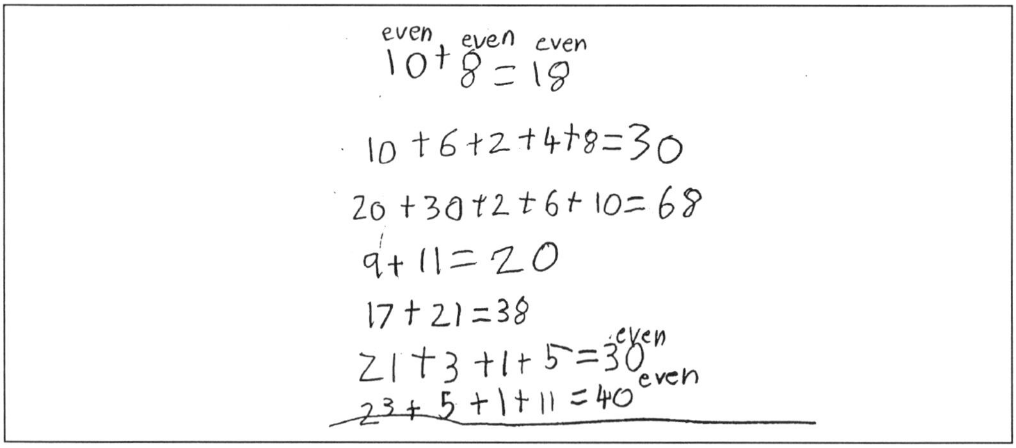

Figure 2.33 What can you find out about adding odd and even numbers

Activity 2: Factor trees

This is a useful large group activity for bringing together lots of work on the properties of numbers. The children will need a good grasp of multiplication facts.

● Draw a tree trunk and write the number 24 in the middle of the trunk (Figure 2.34).

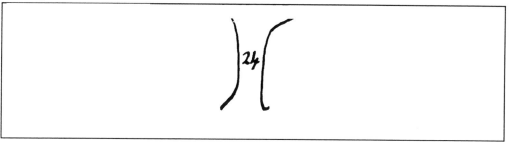

Figure 2.34 Starting a 24 tree

● Draw in two branches and ask for two numbers that multiply to give 24.
● There are several possible answers, 3 x 8 or 2 x 12 or 4 x 6 – any of these will do.
● Write the numbers on the branches.
● Now move to one of the branches, draw in two more branches and ask for numbers that multiply to give 8.
● Stop when you get to a number like 2 or 5 which can't be broken down (Figure 2.35).

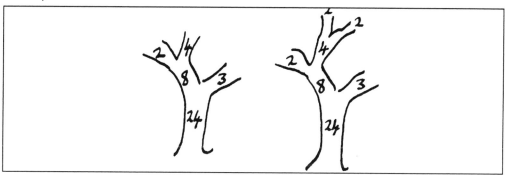

Figure 2.35 One way of continuing the tree

It is very easy to slip into adding, so the children can be warned to watch out for addition sums creeping in and to make sure that they have a 'multiplying tree'. With children choosing different starting numbers the group will soon have a forest of trees which can be sorted into different kinds (Figure 2.36):

● Trees where all the branches end in 2, e.g. 32 and 64 and 8. These are the multiples of 2.
● Tree-stumps with no branches at all, e.g. 7 and 13 and 29. These are the prime numbers.
● Trees with only two branches, both the same, e.g. 9 and 25 and 49. These are the squares of prime numbers.

When the idea of factor trees is well established a good activity for spare moments is to ask for a special tree, e.g. *'I'd like a tree where all the branches end in 3'*. The child then has to try various starting numbers to try and make such a tree. *'I'd like a tree with lots and lots of branches'*, is a challenging request.

Figure 2.36 Looking for similar trees

Making these trees requires careful work. A useful check for the teacher and for the children is to multiply together all the numbers at the tips of the branches. This should give the starting number.

Glossary

Factor: 3 is a factor of 12 which means that 3 divides into 12 exactly

Multiple: 12 is a multiple of 3 which means that 12 is in the multiplication table for 3.

So the **factors** of 12 are 1,2,3,4,6 and 12 and only these.
The **multiples** of 12 go on for ever: 12, 24, 36, 48, 60, ...1 200....

Prime numbers have only two factors, themselves and 1. So 2, 3, 5, 7 and 11 are Prime BUT 1, 9 and 15 are not. (Note that 1 is not prime as it only has one factor.) The list of primes goes on and on. Indeed it has been shown that there is an infinite number of primes.

Square numbers are 1,4,9,16.... They can be written as a number multiplied by itself, e.g. 1 x 1, 2 x 2, 3 x 3, 4 x 4...or represented by a square of dots (Figure 2.37).

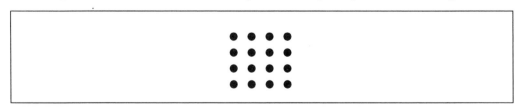

Figure 2.37 16 is a square number

Cube numbers are 1, 8, 27, 64.... They can be written as $1 \times 1 \times 1, 2 \times 2 \times 2$...etc. and could be represented by fitting together multilink cubes to form larger cubes.

Square root: Pressing 10 and the square root button on the calculator gives 3.142... this is approximately the number which multiplied by itself will give 10. The name 'square root' is appropriate, since if a square has area 10 then the square root of 10 gives the length of the side of the square. Examples:

> Square root of 25 is 5.
> Square root of 100 is 10.

2.5 FROM PATTERN TO ALGEBRA

Early generalisations: the search for pattern

Pattern is a very important element in mathematics because recognising a pattern or relationship leads to the possibility of predicting or generalising. Seeing a pattern means focusing on what is the *same* in a situation and what is *changing*. By asking children to describe what they see as clearly as they can, early work on pattern becomes a natural part of encouraging children to be observant and to develop their language skills.

Pattern can lead to work in Shape and Space as well as to number patterns. Looking at patterns in wallpaper, wrapping paper and materials can provide ideas for potato or lino printing patterns. To provide instructions for printing the paper requires careful analysis.

Looking at number squares can reveal patterns in the numbers. Large number squares, or number lines which can be unrolled on the floor for children to stand on, provide an opportunity for children to 'feel' patterns in their body. Counting in twos on a number square sends you jumping along the first line of the square, then back to the beginning of the second line. Counting on in nines moves you diagonally across the square. Making a pattern with multilink cubes red, red, blue, red, red, blue...can be developed as a mathematical activity by asking questions such as: *'What colour will the 12th one be?* How do you know?'

The following case study describes some work with Year 6 children which gave them opportunities to work with patterns in shapes and in numbers and to make generalisations. The practical activity of making the shapes and checking the number of cubes needed is the basis for the insight into the general rule.

Case Study: Growing shapes

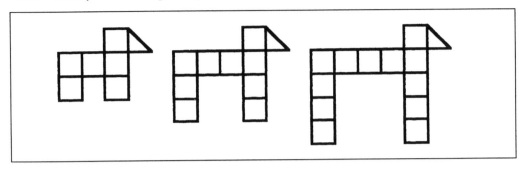

Figure 2.38 Family of dogs – in graded sizes

A group of year 6 children were shown a family of animals of carefully graded sizes as shown in Figure 2.38. These were made from multilink cubes and, although hardly life-like, were accepted by the children as 'dogs'. I set the dogs up in line in the centre of the table and asked: *'Can you tell me what the next dog in the family would look like?'* One child started to count the cubes in the largest dog, another moved the dogs closer together to compare the sizes. *'How many cubes would it need?'* I prompted. I had expected partial answers, perhaps an observation on how many cubes there would be in the legs but one pair of children who had been talking together said more or less simultaneously *'Fifteen' 'Fifteen? How do you know that?'*, I asked in an admiring tone, *'One more on the legs and one more there'* was the response – pointing to the body of the animal.

I asked for instructions on how to build the next animal in the family. I wanted to build it myself rather than ask the children to build it so that they would have to consider and verbalise the number of cubes used at each stage. Another pair of children were chosen to give the instructions. *'Four for the legs'* came quickly. Finding the number for the 'body' needed more conferring, with different views as to whether four or six cubes would be needed. When I had made the animal, I placed it in line. Again one child rearranged the dogs side by side to judge 'by eye' whether the shapes were right. Small folded pieces of card were now distributed so that the children could make a label to stand by each animal giving the number of cubes.

It was easy for the children to spot the 'going up in threes' pattern. (This was what the first child had spotted when she said *'one more on the legs and one more on the body'*. This 'going up in threes' pattern made it easy for the children to see that the next dog would need 15 cubes and the one after 18 cubes *but* the challenge I gave them now was to describe how to make the tenth animal. By jumping to the tenth animal and asking not for the total number of cubes but for instructions on how to build the legs and the body, I was shifting attention away from the 'going up in threes' pattern to the pattern that the third animal had three cubes in each leg and the fourth animal had four cubes in each leg so that the tenth animal would have 10 cubes in each leg.

Figure 2.39 Making labels for the dogs to emphasise position and number of cubes

After much counting and thinking, the children came up with two rival descriptions. One pair claimed it was: *'10 cubes for the legs, 12 across and the head making 33'*. Another pair were convinced that it was *'11 cubes for the legs and 10 across'* (Figure 2.40).

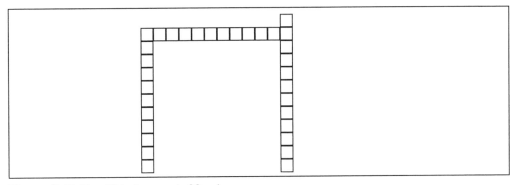

Figure 2.40 The 10th dog needs 33 cubes

After some argument/discussion it was agreed that both methods gave 33 cubes and that both methods were right. The animal (which was not very stable and didn't look much like a dog!) was made and labelled.

The children, in pairs, then made their own animal families (Figures 2.41 and 2.42). The gorillas (Figure 2.42) were far more convincing as animals than the dogs. The children designing them lined them up and seemed to judge by eye rather than counting cubes. All the animal families the children made gave clear number patterns. Amazingly, as long as it is quite clear how to make the next one in the family, there will always be a number pattern.

Seeing the link with algebra

The tenth animal needed two lots of 10 cubes for the legs, 10 + 2 cubes for the body and one for the head:

Figure 2.41 A family of giraffes

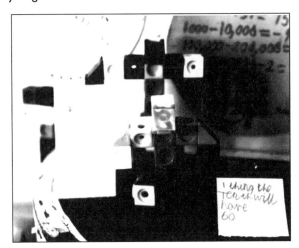

Figure 2.42 A family of gorillas

$$2\,(10) + (10+2) + 1 = 33$$

So the *n*th animal would need two lots of *n* cubes for the legs, *n* + 2 cubes for the body and one for the head, making:

$$2n + \quad (n+2) + 1 = 3n + 3$$
LEGS   BODY   HEAD

With this particular group of children introducing the formal algebra did not seem appropriate; *but* having a sense of progression, knowing where the activity could lead, encouraged emphasis *not* on the 'going up in threes' pattern but on making the jump to predict how many cubes for the tenth or for the hundredth shape. Some children would find that this would enable them to leap to abstract generalisation and their own first algebraic statements.

Further activities where patterns in numbers can be expressed as simple relationships in words or symbols can be found in Section 2.6.

2.6 USING AND APPLYING NUMBER

A very effective way of developing children's understanding of number is to select problems which encourage them to use and apply their knowledge. In this way children can be simultaneously working on a problem, using their creativity, developing logical and organisational skills and practising their number skills. The *Using and Applying* section of the National Curriculum is not a separate element of work but a description of approaches to the teaching of mathematics which is intended to permeate all the mathematics learning. Early monitoring of how the mathematics National Curriculum is being implemented has indicated that schools are tending to emphasise some aspects of Using and Applying but seldom all the aspects. The *Using and Applying* programme of study says:

> Pupils should be given opportunities to use and apply mathematics in practical tasks, in real-life problems and within mathematics itself.

Practical tasks

Practical tasks and real-life problems are given as separate categories so it is necessary to untangle the meaning behind the general phrases. The two following sections give examples of *Real-life problems* which can be thought of more formally as applied mathematics and *Problems within mathematics itself* or pure mathematics. Practical tasks need to be found in both applied and pure mathematics. Practical in the context of applied mathematics tends to mean realistic, such as everyday tasks involving measuring and constructing, weighing or using money. Practical in a pure mathematics context means using apparatus such as cubes, geo-strips and geo-boards so that the children are working in a practical (in the sense of using their hands) rather than a theoretical way. Practical activities, in both senses, have been suggested throughout the book as a means of deepening children's involvement with their mathematics.

Real-life problems

Real-life problems should have some 'real' outcome, although they can vary in scale. Many classroom contexts involve the solving of mathematical problems such as displaying work in books or on walls. Children can be encouraged to estimate the amount of paper required to frame work, to measure (sometimes using a paper trimmer) borders for work and to cut card to size for book making or game card making.

Classroom statistics such as absences, numbers for dinners and so on are real contexts for the application of numerical skills. Involving children in collecting and accounting for money transactions can provide other opportunities. In one class a teacher handed over (under a watchful eye!) the collection and recording of small amounts of money brought daily to school by children for tuck shop at the after school play centre. This Year 1 and Year 2 mixed class learned about different combinations for amounts such as 20p, how to list names and record amounts in chart form and how to count money out at the end of the day. They were also encouraged to help children plan how to spend their money: 'Kerry has 25p today. What could she buy?' At first the younger children were generally reliant on the teacher and their older peers to convince them that one coin (20p) was worth the same as the two coins they had parted with in the morning, but they gradually came to understand some key ideas about cost and to develop skill in addition in this real-life context.

At the other end of the scale are more elaborate real-life problems such as organising a class or school event such as a party or sports day. Reorganising the classroom or involvement in ordering stock from catalogues can all provide insights, opportunities and practice in problem solving. The teacher needs to think carefully about the potential for mathematics, decide on how far the problem can be 'real' (will there be a putting into practice of the children's solutions?) and still allow for children to come up with suggestions and approaches in dealing with the problem. A spin-off from this kind of work is in the opportunity for assessing how children apply what they have learned in context. Do they use strategies encountered in other contexts such as purer maths problems? Do they approach calculations as we would expect from our teaching? Are they independent in developing approaches to the problem?

To take planning a party as an example (other related contexts could be a picnic or a disco), a whole class will need to be organised to break the problem down and so some kind of initial brainstorm of what will need to be done will help. The amount of autonomy given to the children will depend on their age and experience but groupings will allow you to look at aspects such as co-operation as well as mathematical understanding. There will be many possibilities for mathematical thinking. Surveys might be involved in planning food – what would most people like to drink? This would lead into work on value for money and capacity. How many bottles will we need? Is it cheaper to buy larger bottles? Are we likely to have fine weather to have the party out of doors? The teacher will be able to think of many more questions and can have ideas in mind to prompt if children are less forthcoming. If the context is one with which children are familiar and there will be a party at the end, motivation will probably be high. Often, too, these contexts reveal surprising insights into the understanding of individual children, which are not always apparent in more usual classroom mathematical tasks.

Problems 'within mathematics itself'

This slightly strange phrase is a reminder that children find interest and involvement not only in practical, realistic problems but also in puzzles and problems presented as a challenge or in an imaginary, playful context. Two activities are described here which can be adapted to challenge and involve children from the age of five to eleven. The activities can profitably be used many times by the same children in a variety of increasingly demanding forms. Both activities give the children the opportunity to demonstrate many aspects of their numerical knowledge. They are therefore very useful when working with a group of children for the first time to give one a sense of the children's potential.

Activity 1: Function machines

The basic idea of a Function machine is that numbers are fed into a machine, as illustrated in Figure 2.43, the machine performs the same action on each number (e.g. adds 4 or divides by 2), and a number is then fed out of the machine. This simple idea can be the basis of a wide range of activities with all ages of children.

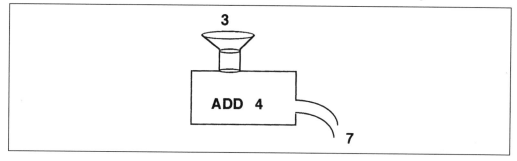

Figure 2.43 An 'ADD 4' Function machine

At Key Stage 1, the activity can be set up with a cardboard box large enough for a child to sit inside. One child is chosen to sit inside the box and given secret instructions as to what the 'machine' must do. The first secret instruction could be 'add 2 cubes'. A train of multilink cubes is handed in, the child adds two cubes and passes out the train of cubes. An easel placed beside the box can be used to record with drawings or numbers the cubes going in and the cubes coming out. After a few goes the children outside the box are encouraged to predict what will happen to the cubes. When everyone in the group knows what the machine is doing a new 'secret instruction' can be used.

At Key Stage 2, a similar activity can be set up with a smaller box, using slips of paper to feed into the machine. The child acting as the machine each time performs the same operation, e.g. multiplying each input number by 7 (Figure 2.44).

(a)   (b)

Figure 2.44 Children represent a linked Function machine. (a) (5 + 3) x 2 =16   (b) (6 x 2) ÷5 = ?

Function machines can be drawn on paper with children working in pairs to create machines and to guess what the machine does. Whatever the form in which the activity is set up, the children should be encouraged to implement their own ideas.

A little more background information will help to make clear the potential of this apparently simple activity and indicate how the teacher can use it to help the children progress in their understanding of number.

In working with Function Machines, children are:

- noticing number patterns
- guessing and predicting
- practising number skills.

The Function machine can be used to emphasise the **Operation**

5 – 3 = 8 is a common mistake

It has been suggested that even though children correctly copy out the subtraction sign and the equals sign, they don't *attend* to them and are using the well-practised skill 'see two numbers and add them.' A child cannot just operate as a '3 machine' with no other instruction but needs to know whether she or he is, for example, an 'ADD 3' machine or a 'TAKE AWAY 3' machine.

The Function machine can be used to emphasise **Prediction**

If the operation is unknown, each new number fed in and fed out gives a clue as to what is happening inside the machine. Predicting what will happen to the next number fed in provides an opportunity to test the prediction.

The Function machine can be used to emphasise the **Inverse operation**

Using Function machines 'backwards' is particularly important.The Function machine helps to make concrete the idea that even though the number fed in is unknown, if you know what happens to the number and what comes out at the end then you can work out the 'unknown number', thus:

? + 3 = 9

The activity can be extended by having linked Function machines. For example, I put in a number, the first machine doubles the number, the next machine adds 5 and the answer is 13. What was the number? The idea of an 'unknown number' can then lead to algebraic ideas and the solution of equations such as

$$2x + 5 = 13$$

As children learn to count, they are provided with a range of practical experiences to help them make sense of the formal notation and signs, such as

3 + 5 = 8

Using a Function machine backwards is a practical experience which provides a useful basis for later algebraic work.

Once the children are used to working with the function machine, the teacher can encourage mathematical developments by use of the powerful question:

What would happen if....?

- What would happen if...we put in complicated numbers like $2^1/_2$?
- What would happen if...we knew the numbers coming out of an 'ADD 5' machine, but not the numbers going in?
- What would happen if...two machines were linked together?

Extension

A spreadsheet can be set up to act as a Function machine. For children who have not yet used a spreadsheet, this is a good introductory activity which uses just two cells (Figure 2.45).

	A	B	C
1		**3**	
2			
3			
4			**16**

Figure 2.45 A spreadsheet set up as a Function machine

First set up the spreadsheet with a large cell size and clear numbers. The activity can then be introduced to a large group with the children later following up the work at the computer in pairs:

- *Step* 1 – Move cursor to cell B1 and input the number 3.
- *Step* 2 – Move cursor to cell C4, hide the screen from the children whilst you input the secret formula = B1*5 + 1 This means 'take the number in cell B1 multiply it by 5 and add 1'. When you press return the number 16 will be entered in cell C4.
- *Step* 3 – Before you let the children see the screen, move the cursor back to B1, this will hide the formula.

To enter numbers into this 'Function machine' a number is entered to cell B1, cell C4 will immediately alter to give the output number. The children's task is to guess the formula. Numbers such as 10, 20 or 100 are very useful as they seem to make it easier to spot the formula. Some children will also realise that entering 0 can be helpful. Perhaps surprisingly entering 1, 2, 3, 4... systematically is often not helpful as it tends to focus attention on the gaps between the output numbers 6, 11, 16, 21, 26.... The patterns are interesting but don't help to spot the formula.

When the children think that they have guessed the formula, move the cursor to any empty cell and enter the children's formula. Then move back to cell B1. If the children have guessed right, their formula will give the right answer whatever number is placed in cell B1 – usually to celebratory cheers!

Later the children work in pairs with one child entering a formula for the other child to guess.

Activity 2: How many ways?

Rather than giving children a list of sums and asking for the answers, the activity may be turned on its head by giving the children the answer and asking them to invent the sums. 'How many different ways can you find...?' is a key question. It encourages children to search for lots of different possibilities. In this next activity there is no limit to the answers the children can find.

I was working with half a Year 6 class in the carpeted area whilst the rest of the class worked on another number activity. I had an easel with a large sheet of paper, some coloured pens and a pack of cards labelled from 1 to 100. Circular sheets of paper, a large number line and some pieces of string were available.

I asked one of the children to choose a number from the pack and she chose 48. I wrote a large 48 in the centre of the sheet of paper and asked: 'Can you tell me a sum with the answer 48?' Hands went up and the first response was '24 + 24'. 'Is that right?' was the next question. There were murmurs of agreement and no protests, so I drew a line from the 48, and wrote 24 + 24. Several children now suggested sums: '40 + 8, 6 x 8, 38 + 10.....' and these were recorded. '7 x 7' was also suggested, but greeted with 'No, it's not': so I asked how we could change it to make the answer 48, and '7 x 7 – 1' was agreed and written up. After a while I pointed out that all the suggestions so far involved adding and multiplying so I asked, 'What else could we have?'

Gradually the children's suggestions became increasingly varied. When the large sheet of paper was satisfyingly full, each child was asked to choose a personal target number and to record many different ways of making their target on a circle of paper (Figure 2.46). The next day, a number line was fixed to a wall and the circles were attached by strings, like balloons, to the appropriate position on the number line (Figure 2.47).

Assessment

This activity gives a lot of evidence of the level at which children spontaneously work with numbers and the level they can reach with encouragement from the teacher. In this class, a few children could confidently use fractions. Further work indicated that they could add fractions involving quarters, eighths and three-quarters in their heads.

Children who stick to addition can be encouraged to generate strange looking sums such as the long string of 1 + 1 + 1 + 1....... The proud owner of this sum went on enthusiastically to search for more ideas.

Glossary

Function: In everyday language, a four- function calculator is one that will add, subtract, multiply and divide. More complex calculators have more 'function

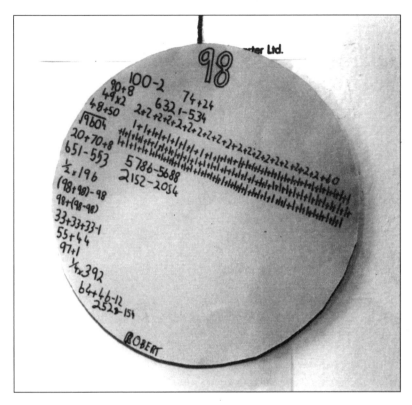

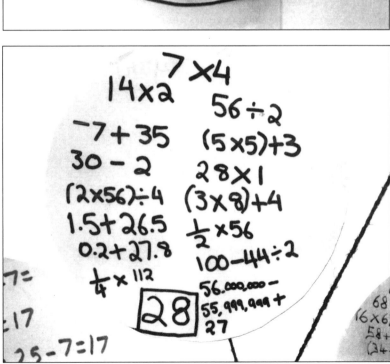

Figure 2.46 A simple question allows children to show their potential

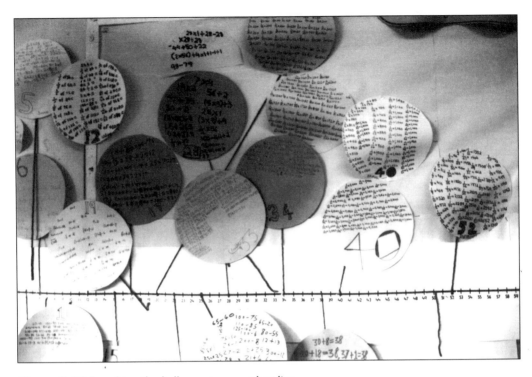

Figure 2.47 Attaching the balloons to a number line

keys' such as square root, cube, sin and cos. The function is an operation, an action which is applied to numbers.

So examples of functions are: ADD.3   DIVIDE BY 4.

Inverse: In everyday language, the inverse is the opposite. The inverse of 'walking 3 paces North' is 'walking 3 paces South'. The inverse of 'putting on your coat' is 'taking off your coat'. The idea of an inverse is one of the powerful ideas which keep cropping up in mathematics. It is well worth looking out for opportunities to do an action and then the opposite action, using the term 'inverse' in your conversation with the children:

The inverse of 'add 3' is 'subtract 3'
the inverse of 'multiply by 4' is 'divide by 4'.

Section 3: Shape, Space and Measures

3.1 SHAPE AND SPACE: INTRODUCTION

There is currently a strong tendency to overemphasise arithmetic as if this were the only mathematics children need to learn. Of course working with numbers is important, but a full mathematics curriculum will also develop children's spatial and problem-solving skills. In 20 years time, when these children are adults, computer technology – a very visual medium – will be all-pervasive. Thinking visually is an important and often neglected dimension of intellectual activity. Some children instinctively form images to help them solve problems: they see how to find a solution. Far more children can be helped to develop the skills of thinking about a problem by forming and manipulating an image in their heads or *visualising*. The ability to visualise has received new emphasis recently, including in the National Curriculum. As the spatial aspect of *mental mathematics*, it is increasingly being seen as of central importance to children's learning. Valuing the space and shape curriculum is an important start to developing children's spatial mathematical ability.

There is a reasonable degree of agreement about the Number, Algebra and Handling Data content of the National Curriculum. The Shape and Space section is more vague because historically there has been much less agreement among mathematics educators about what is important in this area. The National Curriculum identifies two strands of Shape and Space to be studied:

- Understanding and using properties of shape
- Understanding and using properties of position and movement

Work on Shape and Space can sometimes lack a sense of purpose and progression, degenerating into just the learning of names of shapes and transformations. (Of course, there are technical terms to be learned, and there are definitions in the Glossary at the end of this section for reference.) Coherence can be given to shape and space work, by considering the essential nature of mathematical activity as given in Section 1. If children are *making and monitoring decisions* to solve spatial problems, developing the ability to *communicate mathematically* verbally and visually, and above all *reasoning* and generalising about spatial properties in increasingly sophisticated ways, they are engaged in the mathematics of shape and space. The activities in this section are therefore of an exploratory or problem solving nature and emphasise:

- reasoning
- communicating and
- visualising.

Since the reasoning, communicating and visualising in these activities is about the properties of shapes and transformations, children will necessarily also develop their understanding of how shapes are classified and their technical vocabulary.

It is important to present children with a variety of examples for a technical word, otherwise they may get a limited idea of what the word refers to (Figure 3.1). Many children think that a 'tilted' square is not a square, because they have only learned to match one image to the word rather than being encouraged to identify the key properties and to confront tricky examples. Similarly some children think that only equilateral triangles can be triangles, refusing to recognise irregular triangles or even 'upside down' ones, because they have only learned to attach the name to one kind, and that always with a 'horizontal' base. Other children may include, in a set of triangles, shapes which are nearly triangles, but with four sides, because they are 'triangular looking'.

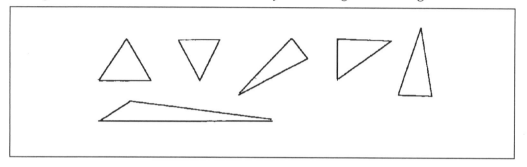

Figure 3.1 A range of triangles

In *Recent Research in Mathematics Education 5–16* (OFSTED, 1995) it is stated that:

> Careful choice of examples improves children's concept formation. The ideal examples to use in teaching are those that are 'only just' examples, and the ideal non-examples are those which are very nearly examples.

It can be useful for children to make a Shape and Space dictionary in which they illustrate terms with diagrams and explanations. Children's dictionaries could include two or three examples of a concept as well as an example which does not fit the concept. For example, Figure 3.2.

Teaching points

One important principle here is that children are given the opportunity to discuss the *properties* of shapes as well as to learn the names, in order to understand the definitions. The term 'properties' usually refers to features or attributes of shapes, such as straight or curved sides, flat or curved faces, numbers of angles and sides, equality of angles and sides, parallelness and symmetry. Another important principle is that this discussion is associated with *actively* manipulating, constructing and distorting shapes, either practically or mentally. Children may investigate what happens when alterations are made, looking at what changes and what stays the same. If children discuss *trying* to make circles with string and chalk, with their bodies, or by programming with robots or LOGO, they will have a clearer idea of what is and what is not a circle and develop an internalised understanding of the definition. They will then be doing more thinking than if they are just asked to say the word 'circle' in response to a few images of the shape.

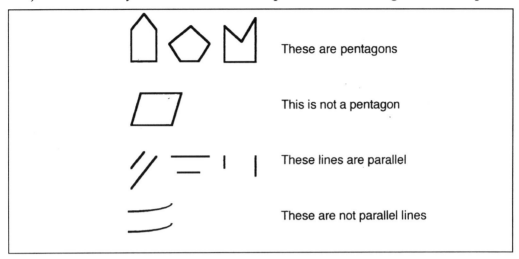

Figure 3.2 Shape dictionary

Case study: Visualising: an initial assessment activity

Asking children to visualise can be quite revealing as an assessment activity (Figure 3.3). At the beginning of a topic on shape, I asked some Year 4 children to close their eyes and:

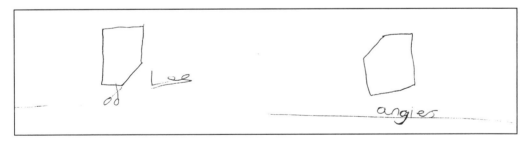

Figure 3.3 Lee's shape

Imagine a square. Cut off one corner, take the corner away.
Can you describe what you have left? What does the shape look like now?
Angie: *It has three corners.*
Me: *Count the corners.*
Angie: *It has five corners. It has four sides.*

Angie initially focuses on just three corners, perhaps the right-angled ones. The question prompts her to include all five corners. Her response of four sides is puzzling – perhaps Angie thinks that the cut side in some way 'doesn't count' as a side.

I asked the children to draw their image secretly to help them 'fix' it and then to look at it.

Natalie: *It's like a square. It has five corners. Three sides are the same, one is different. Three have L-shaped corners.*

Natalie counts the corners, but, like Angie, seems to count only 4 sides. She recognises right angles but does not use the term.

Bilal: *There are two bits sticking out. One facing left, one facing down. The corners don't join up. The top two bits have two corners and there is a corner at the bottom left.*

I am not quite sure what Bilal is describing! He seems confident about corners, but his description, presumably of sides as 'bits facing left and down' would benefit from some more standard vocabulary to make his meaning clearer.

These responses are beginning to make me think we will need to do a lot of work, exploring not only the effects of chopping off corners, but indeed exploring shapes in general, using paper and scissors, and also geoboards and elastic bands, and making shapes out of dough, Plasticine, geostrips and straws.

Next, I asked the children to describe their shape to me, so that I could draw it:

Bilal: *Draw two corners just at the top. Join the corners together. You know the left corner, if you just go down and draw another corner. From the bottom left corner, draw a line across. From the right top corner, draw a line down to nothing, not too far, to make a square* (Figure 3.4).

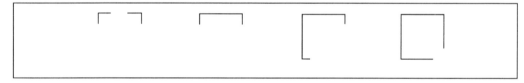

Figure 3.4 Trying to follow Bilal's instructions

This exercise is clearly making Bilal try to give clear instructions and to imagine himself in the place of his listener. It is very good for communication skills – I will try this with the class working in pairs to describe shapes to each other when we have talked about the terminology more. Bilal's skilful description would be much easier to understand if he used standard vocabulary, for instance 'right angle', 'vertical' and 'horizontal'. I had great difficulty in understanding what to draw, much to the children's amusement, until I realised that Bilal's shape was an outline – so his corner cut off would create a space, not more corners! This was the surprise element of the activity – but perhaps not so surprising really: there is usually someone in the group who visualises in a way that has never occurred to you before.

Visualising activities

An interesting aspect of visualising activities is that the children are put in the powerful position of knowing what *their* shape looks like. The teacher or partner can listen and ask for clearer instructions, but the child who is doing the describing is the authority on the shape. Examples of activities are:

- Imagine that you pick up four straws and arrange them, touching, on the table. What do your four straws look like?
- Imagine that you are inside a cube. You touch a corner of the cube, and then another corner – how many corners can you touch?
- You are sitting in the corner of a square – what can you see?
  The square starts to grow bigger and bigger and bigger – what can you see now?

Once the children are used to the idea of visualising in this way, it can become part of regular discussion activities. A few minutes spent visualising can be used by the teacher to remind the children of shapes and vocabulary that they have recently met and to assess the children's understanding of the properties of shapes.

3.2 SHAPE AND SPACE ACTIVITIES

Activities in this section have been selected because they represent some key approaches to the shape and space curriculum, and require children to be actively engaged in thinking. They also use various kinds of apparatus and give the children opportunities to, as the National Curriculum states, *'gain a wide range of practical experience using a variety of materials'*.

Any approach can usually be used at a variety of levels: for instance you can engage 3 year olds or adults in predicting what shape a folded and cut piece of paper will reveal when it is unfolded (see Activity 2, page 85). The mental challenge rapidly increases with more folds or changes of angle, but the requirement to justify the prediction turns a simple game into a logical problem, demanding mathematical communication skills as well as reasoning. Simple questions like *'Why?'* and *'How do you know that?'* can intensify the intellectual demands of a simple practical activity like folding and cutting.

Through these activities, various aspects of properties of shapes and properties of position and movement are addressed. For instance, properties of shape are the main concern of the classifying activities, while the concept of angle can be introduced through Body Maths and IT activities. Some activities deal with several aspects at once: LOGO, for instance, will involve children in ideas of movement and position, especially angle, as well as properties of shapes. Table 3.1 gives the main coverage of the different aspects of the National Curriculum strands at Key Stage 1 and 2 in the activities.

Table 3.1

Activity	National Curriculum requirement
1. Hide and describe	2a visualising and describing shapes and movements
2. Folding and cutting	3a describing positions
3. Making boxes	2b making 3D shapes with increasing accuracy recognising their geometrical features and properties
4. How many different	2c recognising and using properties to classify shapes and solve problems; understanding the congruence of simple shapes; recognising the reflective symmetries of 2D and 3D shapes, and rotational symmetries of 2D shapes
5. Making patterns	3a recognising movements and transforming 2D shapes, by translation, reflection and rotation; copying, continuing, making and describing patterns
6. Using IT	2b making 2D shapes 3a transforming 2D shapes by translation, reflection and rotation, visualising movements and simple transformations to create and describe patterns 3c as below
7. Body maths	3c understanding angle as a measure of turn, recognising and using right angles, quarter and half turns,and later, degrees to measure rotation, using the associated language

Activity 1: Hide and describe

Visualising and describing shapes, positions and movements

This activity can be used to develop children's language in precisely describing properties of shape. It also involves more general communication skills such as putting yourself in the place of someone who cannot see what you are describing, or listening with attention to detail:

- With a partner, each take five multilink cubes (all the same colour) sit back to back and fix the cubes together so that your partner cannot see what you are doing.
- Then, still keeping your model hidden, describe it so that your partner can make it with his or her five multilink.

This will involve the children in using positional language like: on top of, underneath, next to, left, right, middle.

Variations

An easier version uses cubes of different colours. It might seem obvious, but individualising the cubes in this way makes instructions less challenging to follow since each cube can be identified separately by colour.

Drawing *different viewpoints* on squared paper involves children in relating 2D representations to 3D models. Combining several views requires skill in visualising from the partner who tries to build the model from the drawing (Figure 3.5).

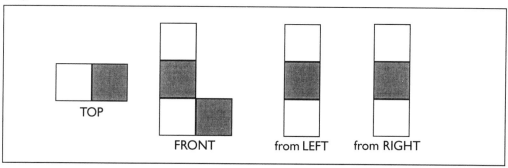

Figure 3.5 Different viewpoints

Drawing models on isometric paper is a more challenging task for older children (Figure 3.6).

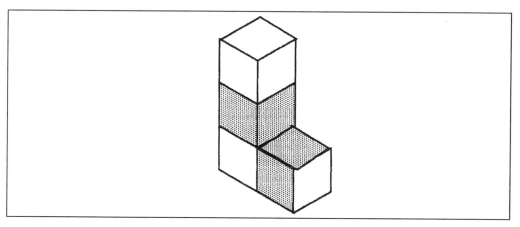

Figure 3.6 Drawing the 3D shape on isometric paper

Describing a **geometrical drawing** for a friend to draw can involve shapes and properties of varying degrees of difficulty. Language may relate to:

- fractions – *half way up, a third of the way along,*
- angles – *right angle, very pointy,*
- other properties – *diagonal, parallel.*

Or children can describe a simple pattern to each other, in which case they can use language of position and movement, such as *reflection* and *rotation* (see activity 5) (Figure 3.7).

This activity is more fun if the describer does not look at what their partner is drawing until they have finished. It is sometimes best to organise this as a whole class activity, so that no one is disturbed in trying to do quiet work while it is going

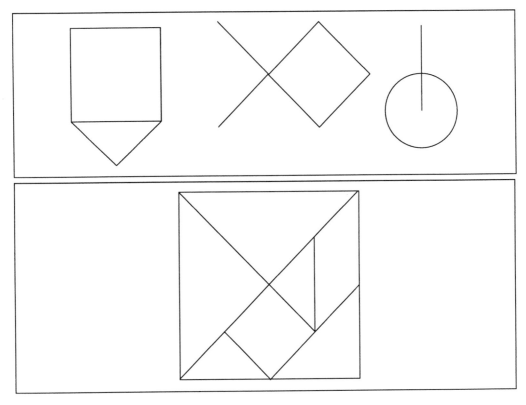

Figure 3.7 Shapes to describe

on. Identifying children as A and B in pairs, each with a different 'secret' sheet, as well as sheets with boxes for them to draw in, will help children who are not used to this kind of activity. Young children can offer positive criticism to partners, and can be heard saying things like, '*Well that's* **quite** *good, you've nearly got it right, but the triangle should be in between the squares*', whereas older children enjoy deliberately exploiting lack of preciseness by drawing the unexpected, and the describers can then be more self-critical: '*Oh, I should have said the lines were straight!*'

The teacher can playfully demonstrate alternative interpretations by drawing on the board according to the children's instructions (for instance by drawing curved lines if straight ones are not specified, or obtuse angles when a child says 'corner' but means 'right angle'). However, beware rising frustration levels!

Feely bag activities usually involve a bag or box with objects. One person puts their hand in, and selects one object to describe without looking at it. If you provide a set of objects identical with those in the bag, the listening group can try to pick out the one matching the description. To focus children's attention on particular properties, provide items which are similar except in one respect: for instance, a collection of quadrilaterals of different shapes and sizes will encourage children to talk about angles and relative length of sides. Instead of providing a matching set of objects, children can be invited to draw the object from the description and then compare results.

Activity 2: Cutting and folding

Visualising and describing shapes, positions and movements

This activity involves prediction and visualising, and can easily be adapted to provide varying degrees of challenge.

Fold a piece of paper in half, then in half again. Can you make one cut so that you get a square when you unfold it?

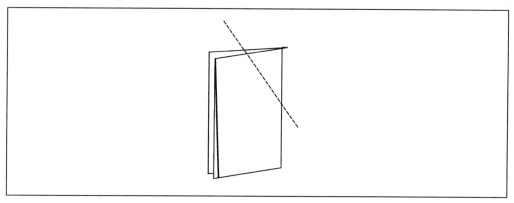

Figure 3.8 Will this cut give a square?

Can you explain how you know where to make the cut so that you are sure of getting a square?

Children usually judge by eye, but asking them to instruct someone else in where to make the cut will often produce some idea that the cut has to be made between two points which are equidistant from the central corner or that the angles at the new corners must be the same. Can you explain why this works (Figure 3.9)?

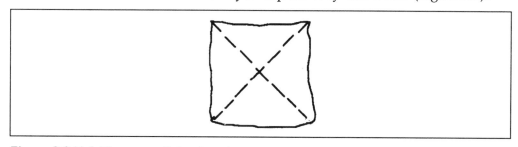

Figure 3.9 Unfolding to see if the shape is a square

This question challenges more experienced children to reason that the angles of the corners they are cutting must be half a right angle in order to form the corners of the square. Alternatively, the edges of the triangle they cut out form the bisected diagonals of the square and so must be the same length. This requires children to articulate their visualising and to think logically about the relationships between properties. You are unlikely to get answers in quite these sophisticated terms, but the underlying reasoning can be expressed by children in their own language.

Variations

Can you make an octagon with one cut? Can you make your shape regular (all angles and sides the same) (Figure 3.10)?

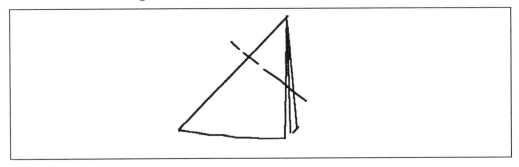

Figure 3.10 How do you cut to get an octagon?

This involves children in thinking how many equal triangles make up an octagon. A hexagon can be made by folding a piece of paper in half, then folding into thirds from a central point and cutting to get six triangles folded on top of each other. (This requires a bit of adjusting to get the thirds equal, matching the sections overlaying each other, before creasing the folds definitely.)
For younger children, fold a square cloth or large sheet of paper in half and half again.

Can you cut a folded piece of paper to make a person, a tree or a dog?
Cutting from a folded piece of paper to produce symmetrical shapes encourages children to think in terms of half a shape. Depending on scissor skills, more complicated designs can be made with people holding hands, doilies or snowflakes (using hexagons as a basis). In many cases these activities are creative. However, to make them explicitly mathematical, children need to be required to think about the changes and shapes used. Children can investigate the relationship between the number of folds and the resulting number of shapes. Setting children specific challenges, giving instructions to partners and asking them to predict before unfolding, all help to encourage reflection on properties and relationships between them.

Activity 3: Making boxes

Making 3D shapes, recognising their geometrical properties
Using and understanding measures

Can you make a box for something tricky?

Provide children with a collection of irregularly shaped items, such as toys, dolls, tea pots or watering cans, a ball, a pyramid, ...and some interlocking plastic shapes such as Polydron or Clixi.

This will involve the children estimating or measuring the dimensions of their chosen object, and thinking about the plane shapes needed to make the net of the 3D shape they select for the box. As a design activity, children will benefit from having a go and then thinking about improvements in terms of the elegance of the design and the practicalities of making a snug fit.

Can you make the net for your box out of card?

To make the net children will need to think about the arrangement of the shapes and their dimensions in 2D, and then transform this to 3D mentally and practically. Again, children will benefit from having several attempts, and refining rough drafts in sugar paper before a final version in card.

Other constraints can be introduced, such as: What is the best design which uses the least amount of paper (Figure 3.11)?

Figure 3.11 Folding a box from an A4 sheet of squared paper

Children need to consider how to measure the area of different nets: squared paper will help here. Relationships between surface area and volume can be systematically explored as a follow-up.

An investigation with surprising results is **maxbox**: take an A4 sheet of centimetre squared paper, and make an open tray by cutting out a square at each corner and folding up the sides, fixing with Sellotape. Now try making different open boxes by cutting out larger squares at the corners, making the sides higher.

Which box holds the most?

This is particularly useful for assessing children's understanding of finding the volume and their strategies for multiplication.

Can you make a miniature version of your box which is half the size? How many little boxes will fit into your big one (Figure 3.12)?

Children usually halve all the dimensions of their box, which they expect will produce a box with half the volume. They are surprised when, for instance, a cube with all three dimensions half of another cube, fits more than twice into the larger one. Explaining why this happens is the challenge to reason mathematically in this activity. A variety of commercial packaging can be a useful stimulus. Chocolates are often packed in interesting ways, with different arrangements for fitting smaller versions inside larger ones, for instance with chocolate triangular prisms inside boxes shaped as trapezoid or hexagonal prisms.

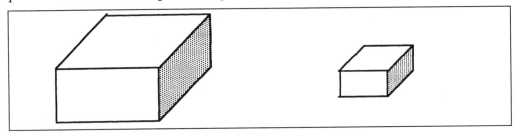

Figure 3.12 Halving all the lengths makes a surprisingly small box

Can you go into mass production and make several nets which tessellate from one piece of card?

Environmentally and economically, this is encouraging children to consider cost of materials and wastage but also to visualise and investigate different arrangements (see also Activity 5, Patterns, page 93).

Can you make designs on the faces of your net so that they are the right way up when it is assembled?

Essentially this is a creative activity, which involves relating the 2D image to the 3D by visualising where the faces will be in relation to each other when the net is made up (Figure 3.13).

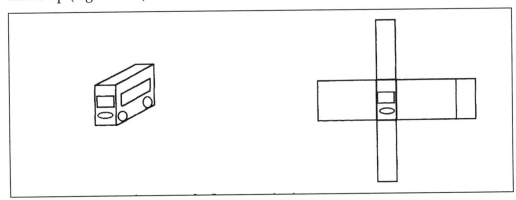

Figure 3.13 Designs on a net

Activity 4: How many different...?

Recognising and using properties to classify shapes and solve problems, understanding congruence and recognising symmetries

This activity can be structured to focus attention on different properties of shapes, according to the resources used. Here the focus is on properties of symmetry and parallelism. If the children work as a group, with the requirement that they must reach agreement through discussion, then they can clarify meanings and give reasons for arguments. This provides the teacher with valuable insights into their understanding.

Take four geostrips and make sure you have different lengths among them – (It does not matter how many of each length you have, so long as you have four strips altogether: you can have two of each length, or three the same and one different or all different.)

How many different four-sided shapes can you make?

Everybody make one shape.

Compare yours with other peoples' shapes. Are any the same? The advantage of geostrips is that you can easily change the angles, while keeping the same arrangement of side lengths. Two children with the same geostrips can make different shapes, turning a rectangle into a parallelogram, for instance. (In some cases this is trickier: can you change a kite into something else, for instance?) (Figure 3.14.)

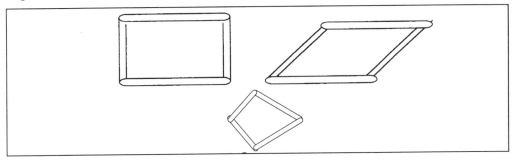

Figure 3.14 Geostrip shapes – how can they be changed?

You should now get some discussion about what the same means. Children may debate whether different size versions of the same shape are allowed, or whether the same shape in different orientations is really the same or not. This involves them in ideas of *similarity* and *congruence*. Congruent shapes are exactly the same shape and size. Similar shapes have the same angles and their sides are in the same proportions.

Keep one example of each shape and then make some different ones – You will probably have discussions about some non-examples: open shapes with four sides, for example. Definitions and rules about allowing or not allowing variations will have to be agreed.

Do cross quadrilaterals of the bow-tie variety count as quadrilaterals? The justifications put forward in this kind of discussion are very valuable and may be quite sophisticated, involving issues of what a *side* or a *shape* means (Figure 3.15).

In the case of the kite (Figure 3.16), is an arrowhead a *different* shape, or just a special kind of kite? Does a kite have to be something you can fly, or is the

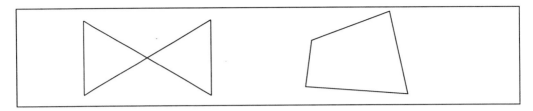

Figure 3.15 These shapes are made from 4 geostrips? Are they quadrilaterals?

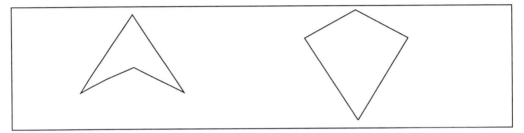

Figure 3.16 A kite is a quadrilateral with two adjacent pairs of sides equal in length

mathematical meaning different? The important issue for the children's learning is the reasoning about the relationship between properties and the appreciation of the need for a consistent definition. With the arrowhead, the discussion will focus on acute and obtuse angles and whether having obtuse angles stops a shape from being a kite. Kites are usually considered to be shapes with two pairs of adjacent equal sides giving one axis of symmetry, so an arrowhead can be considered a special kind of kite.

Check these are different. Now are there any more possibilities? This requires children to *imagine* examples and calls on skills of visualising and logical thinking about what might be possible.

Can you find a way of checking that you have them all? Developing a system for checking requires more logical thinking: children may vary the angles within one shape at a time. This means keeping one property fixed (the relationship between the length of the sides) and systematically varying another (the angles). This is an important way of thinking mathematically.

Decide on a way of making groups of shapes that go together, and label your collection – Depending on their experience, children may classify shapes according to a range of properties – shapes which:

- remind you of shapes in the environment, e.g. house shapes
- have one or more axes of symmetry
- have right angles
- have angles larger or smaller than right angles *obtuse* or *acute* angles
- have pairs of parallel sides
- have pairs of equal sides.

With older children you can ask them to make some rules for other groups to identify as **true** or **false**, along the lines of:

- All quadrilaterals with an axis of symmetry...
- You cannot make a shape with parallel sides with...

If you challenge children to explain *why* statements are true then you are encouraging them to reason mathematically and to provide arguments which may verge on proof. This kind of investigation can result in the children discovering some important geometrical relationships. In working with shapes made out of geostrips children can observe what changes and what stays the same. For example, *'However I change the angles of my parallelogram, opposite angles remain the same'; 'However I change the angles of my kite, the long diagonal cuts the short diagonal in half.'*

To ensure that children focus on relationships involving one particular property, you might structure the activity more tightly: *How many different four-sided shapes with at least one axis of symmetry can you make?*

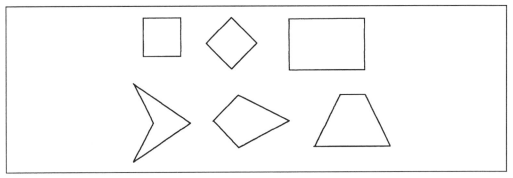

Figure 3.17 Shapes with at least one axis of symmetry

Invite the children to classify the shapes by providing large sheets of paper and some labels for *one axis of symmetry, two axes of symmetry, no axes of symmetry* (Figure 3.18).

Or the children may record their shapes by drawing, cutting them out of paper, or making them with straws.

Children can make squares, rhombuses, rectangles, kites, arrowheads, and trapezia, discovering which ones can be made from each other by changing the angles. Does changing the angles of a shape affect the number of lines of symmetry? It is intriguing that, no matter how hard you try, it is impossible to turn the kite into an asymmetrical shape by altering the angles, whereas a rectangle surprisingly turns into a parallelogram without any axis of symmetry. Structuring the activity in this way will make it more likely that children will discuss relationships between properties like symmetry and pairs of equal sides. There is likely to be discussion about whether a parallelogram has an axis of symmetry, and it is useful to have some mirrors available. Children might go on to investigate shapes with rotational symmetry.

Other questions are: *How many different quadrilaterals can you make with at least:*

- *One pair of sides parallel?*
- *One pair of equal sides?*

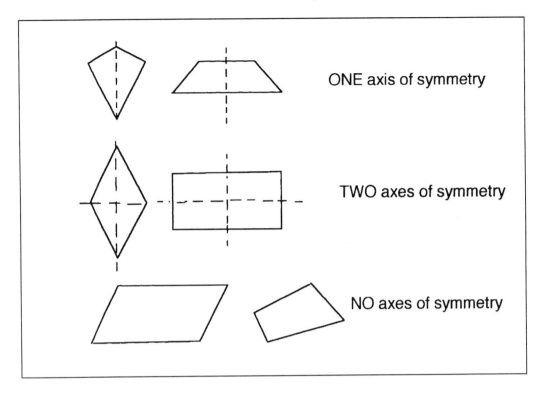

Figure 3.18 Classifying shapes

Other variations

Similar activities can be carried out with other apparatus. In all these examples, the way you start the activity and maintain it will be the same, and similar issues will arise.

Take a three by three nailboard or geoboard. How many different triangles can you make? The same activity could be done by drawing on dotty paper. With triangles you may get:

- ones that are the same but different sizes – similar shapes
- ones that are identical but different ways up – congruent shapes
- shapes which are reflections of each other
- shapes which are rotations of each other.

With pentominoes (five squares joined edge to edge) (Figure 3.19) issues will arise about:

- shapes which are reflections of each other
- shapes which are rotations of each other
- systematic checking by fixing four squares then moving one square.

How many different shapes can you make with two identical shapes? (e.g. two squares, two isosceles triangles). Or you could invite children to make 3D shapes out of:

- five multilink
- six polydron or clixi pieces of various shapes
- a number of straws.

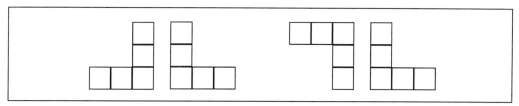

Figure 3.19 Children need to discuss whether they will consider these shapes, made with 5 squares, to be 'the same'

The teacher needs to be aware of the mathematical relationships which children might discover from the activity and also the issues about definitions of shapes: some conventions are more universal than others, and definitions vary. The definition for trapezium can vary on different sides of the Atlantic, according to whether it should have an axis of symmetry. It is generally agreed that a square is a kind of rectangle and both are kinds of parallelogram. The glossary at the end of this section will help.

Guess my rule

When children have had experience of making and classifying 2D or 3D shapes, they can play a guessing game using labels they have written for sets of shapes. For a collection of 3D shapes, such labels might be:

- six faces
- some triangular faces
- one plane of symmetry
- parallel faces
- all right angles
- all acute angles.

One person has a set ring and secretly selects a label for the set. Other people take it in turns to choose a shape, and the first person must say whether it goes in the set or out. Gradually there emerges a group of shapes in the set, and a group outside the set, which children can examine for similarities and use to guide their choice of the next shape to offer. When it is their turn to offer a shape, they can then guess what is on the label for the set. When children have played this game a few times, they may want to write other labels and make up their own rules for the sets. The issue that emerges is the need for precision in doing this. For instance does 'square faces' mean all faces, or more than one face, or at least one face square?

Activity 5: What is my rule? Making patterns

Transforming shapes to create and describe patterns

Patterns can be observed in the natural or built environment, and in the creations of many cultures, so this kind of activity can be linked to many areas of the curriculum. A pattern in mathematical terms is not just an arrangement of shapes and lines, but must have some rule governing it so that it can continue with regularity. If children are asked to analyse patterns, then an absorbing aesthetic and creative activity becomes also a logical and mathematical one, involving articulating mathematical rules and identifying shapes, positions and transformations.

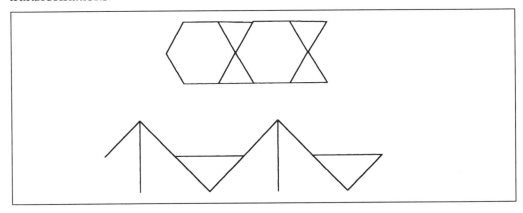

Figure 3.20 Copy and continue these patterns

To copy patterns, and continue them, (as in Figure 3.20) children must analyse the rule that governs the pattern's construction, even if they do this intuitively. The simplest kind of pattern is one that repeats in a linear fashion, by adding on in one direction only. This is sometimes called an AB pattern, with two elements A and B, making up the basic element AB which is repeated (ABABAB......). This can be made more complex by having more elements, as in an ABC or an ABCD pattern, or elements may be repeated within the unit: ABB, ABB, ABB. They become more complex again if the unit is not just repeated, but increased in some way, perhaps by adding on one element each time or doubling:

    AB, ABC, ABCD, ABCDE
    AB, AABB, AAABBB, AAAABBBB
    AB, AABB, AAAABBBB, AAAAAAAABBBBBBBB

Patterns become more complex if they are not just linear, but grow in different directions at once. The simplest way of doing this is to just surround an arrangement, but a variety of rules may be created by children.

Make an arrangement with a few squares. Now grow your pattern, by adding on a few more squares. How did you know where to put them? Can you add some more to make your shape grow, keeping to the same rule for adding on each time? See if you can write your rule down (Figure 3.21).

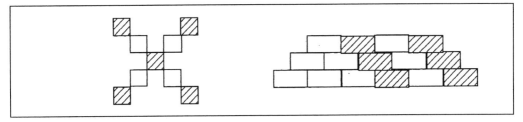

Figure 3.21 Growing patterns according to rules

Can your friend continue your pattern? Can they say what your rule is? They may say something like:

- My rule is that you join onto the outer corners each time, or
- I add one onto each row on the right each time.

Using different colours for each stage is a useful way of identifying these. Children may discover alternative rules for the same pattern. Obviously this can be done with a variety of shapes, and in 3D as well as 2D. Interesting number patterns can be discovered (see Growing Shapes on page 66).

Transformations

One kind of rule that is often used to create a pattern involves moving a figure in a regular way, by reflecting, rotating or translating (sliding). These kinds of movements or transformations, can be found in various combinations in patterns from many cultures. Young children will often intuitively use reflections when arranging shapes, so the resulting patterns have one or more axes of reflective symmetry. Rotations and translations are easily created by printing.

Stick some string onto pieces of card in the shape of some letters. Can you make a pattern for some wrapping paper, so that the pattern could continue indefinitely? (Figure 3.22)

More about transformations can be found at the end of this section.

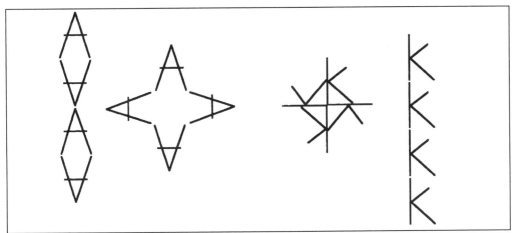

Figure 3.22 Patterns made by reflecting, rotating or translating a simple basic shape

Tessellations

Another way of making patterns is by tessellating or fitting shapes together, so that they will cover a surface indefinitely with the same pattern, as in tiling.

Make some different tessellating patterns with rectangles. Describe the rules for the different patterns (Figure 3.23).

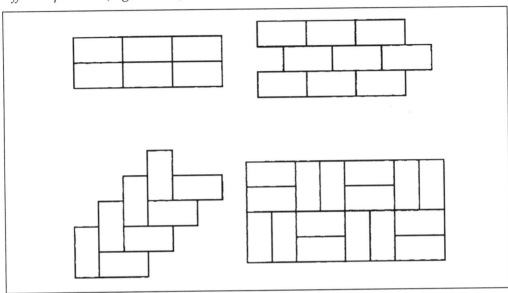

Figure 3.23 Could you describe how to fit the shapes together over the telephone?

Try making other tessellations just using one shape, regular or irregular. Or you can use two shapes (Figure 3.24).

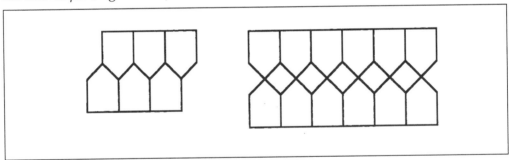

Figure 3.24 Tessellation of irregular pentagons and of irregular pentagons with squares

Again, children can continue each other's patterns. The placing of the shapes should follow a regular pattern so that it is clear that the tessellation could be extended indefinitely.

Older children can investigate what is going on with the angles at the meeting point or vertex of the shapes.

Why do these shapes fit together round a point? Why do some shapes not fit together? (Figure 3.25)

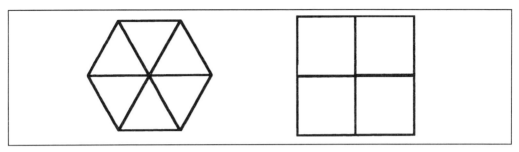

Figure 3.25 Focusing on the point at which shapes meet

This can lead to discussions about angles. If children know that the angles round a point make 360° (or that four 90° angles fit together) they can work out the size of the angles of other shapes, from the number of them meeting round a point. They can also spot corners of shapes which together make straight lines, so the angles add up to 180°. They can also reason that in order for regular shapes to tessellate on their own, their angles must be factors of 360° and they can go on to test this generalisation.

Children can also make patterns using computer programs such as Tiling from SMILE.

Activity 6. Using IT

Making 2D shapes, transforming shapes and visualising movements

LOGO is a computer program based on a cursor in the shape of a turtle, moving around the screen. The children enter instructions to turn the turtle and move the turtle forward drawing a line. There is a natural progression in the precision and complexity of the instructions needed from:

- the children playing at being robots using their own bodies to move around in response to instructions;
- to using robotic toys which move around on the floor or table;
- to working with the computer program.

In all three activities the children need to reason to work out what instructions will give the desired effect and to give sufficiently precise instructions. Working in small groups with IT encourages them to articulate their reasoning to convince each other of what to do.

Playing robots

This activity works well in the hall or playground. One child acts as the robot and a second child gives instructions.

> The robot comes from the factory able to understand simple instructions like 'turn left, turn right, forward 5, back 3 steps'. Can you give instructions to the robot to walk round a skittle to a bench?

The instructions will have to be more precise if the robot is sufficiently trusting to shut their eyes!

Robotic toys

There are several robotic toys available which can be programmed to move around in response to instructions.

One of these is called the Roamer. Children, working in small groups, can program the Roamer to move around obstacles or to trace out shapes on the floor. There is immediate feedback: if the children's estimates of distance and angle are not accurate, the Roamer will not do what they expect.

> *Can you program the Roamer to follow a roadway?*

Children can make roadways or mazes for the Roamer with chalk or masking tape. They can then challenge other groups to program Roamer to follow their route. This is best done if the children decide on the set of instructions for their route, then map out the roadway to follow the actual path of the Roamer. This is because the Roamer will only move in whole units, and the roadway needs to use these too. If the roadway is quite wide this allows some leeway for estimating angles. Inexperienced children will need to put in one or two instructions at a time, then adjust the next accordingly, but later they can be challenged to write all the instructions in one go.

Using LOGO on the computer (Figure 3.26)

The transition to typing instruction to the computer follows naturally from the work with robots:

FD 200 – forward 200 units;
RT 90 turn right through 90 degrees;
FD 200 RT 90 FD 50 RT 90 FD 50...will begin to draw a castle.

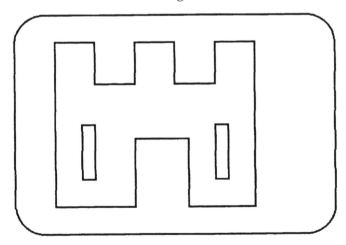

Figure 3.26 Using LOGO

LOGO is very widely available in schools. A great deal of useful mathematical activity can be based on a small set of instructions. As well as direct instructions such as the FD, BK, LT and RT mentioned above, there is a repeat instruction. REPEAT 4 [FD 40 RT 90] will repeat four times the instructions in the brackets, to draw a square.

The children can teach the computer a new word. So if the children would like the computer to draw a castle whenever they type in the word CASTLE, they can do this by entering the full set of instructions for a castle.

If children have decided what to draw for themselves, they will be more committed in trying to solve problems they come across. Once children have created a program for a simple shape, they can draw it in different positions on the screen, or rotate the shape and so create patterns (Figure 3.27).

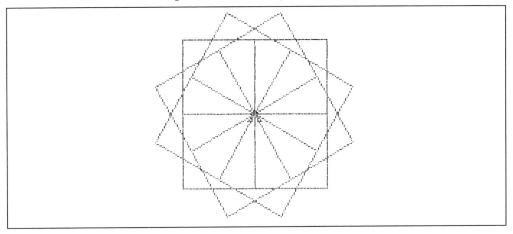

Figure 3.27

Many other programs allow children to create patterns, e.g. Tiling from SMILE.

Children will gain a lot in terms of discussion from working in twos or threes, but the teacher needs to monitor interaction. A chair labelled HOT SEAT and a convention that only the child in this seat can type in instructions can be a useful organisational device.

Activity 7: Body maths

Understanding angle as a measure of turn, and reflection

There is something very powerful and memorable about using your own body to act out a mathematical situation. Possibilities arise when working on many different aspects of mathematics. Some examples are given here but many more activities involving position and movement can be acted out in a similar way. For instance, young children can walk in circles or triangles in different ways, then later relate this to the idea of rotating through 360 degrees in conjunction with work on LOGO, as discussed previously.

Reflection

When the children are working in the hall, a line is marked out on the floor as a mirror. One child stands a pace in front of the 'mirror' and slowly moves an arm or a leg. Another child acts as the mirror image and follows the movement. The teacher can ask the child in front of the mirror:

'Move back one step', or
'Move to the left two steps'
'What must the image do?'

Once the ideas have been explored the children can work in pairs to develop a slow dance type movement.

Rotation

Using a compass the children can find which direction is North in their classroom. With all the children standing up facing North, the teacher can give a series of instructions.

'Turn 90 degrees clockwise. Turn 90 degrees clockwise again: what compass direction are you facing in now?'

If a swivel chair is available, the fundamental idea of angle as an amount of turn can be explored by having a child sitting in the chair with an arm outstretched. The rest of the class can imagine looking down from the ceiling and decide what angle has been moved through from North, or a fixed point. This can help to link the familiar idea of turning with the abstract drawing of two lines which is used to represent angle in books.

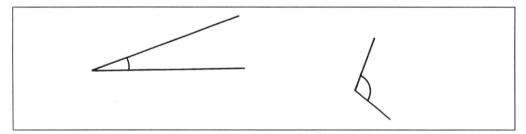

Figure 3.28 Which angle is larger?

In tests of spatial understanding, many children said that the first angle in Figure 3.28 was larger than the second. This misconception seems to be based on paying attention to the length of the lines rather than the amount of the turn. Activities which emphasise the physical turning through an angle, with the lines used to show the starting direction and the final direction, can help to avoid this misconception and will also be helpful at a later stage when children are learning to use a protractor.

Glossary

Warning note: the language of definitions is very formal. These definitions are included so that as a teacher you will be well-informed. The emphasis in working with the children needs to be on the properties of shapes.

A Polygon: Poly (many) gon (angle) is a plane (flat) shape formed by straight lines. Some of these have been given special names, but it is possible to describe them all by the number of their sides: TRIangle, QUADrilateral, PENTagon, HEXagon, HEPTagon, OCTagon, NONagon, DECagon, HENDEcagon, DODECagon ....

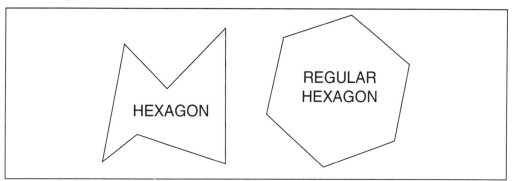

Figure 3.29 Irregular and regular hexagon

Polygons which all have sides *and* all angles equal are called *regular* polygons (Figure 3.29). Polygons which have all sides equal but different angles are not regular, nor are polygons with all angles equal but different length sides. It is important that children do meet irregular shapes.

Triangles may be classified by means of equality of sides:

- Equilateral – all sides equal
- Isosceles – two sides equal
- Scalene – no sides equal

or by the size of the largest angle:

- Right angled – 90 degrees
- Acute angled – less than 90 degrees
- Obtuse angled – more than 90 degrees.

Quadrilaterals are four-sided shapes: they may be classified by means of parallel or equal sides and right angles:

- **Rhombus** – a quadrilateral with four equal sides
- **Trapezium** – a quadrilateral with a pair of parallel sides
- **Parallelogram** – a quadrilateral with two pairs of parallel sides

Notice that the definitions *include* special cases: a square has four equal sides and four equal angles so a square *is* a rhombus; a square has two pairs of opposite sides parallel and so a square *is* a parallelogram.

Congruence is the idea of shapes being identical, despite being in different orientations. They are the same shape and size, so that one will fit exactly on top of the other.

Similarity refers to shapes which have the same angles and whose sides are in the same ratio to each other other, although the shapes may be of different sizes, e.g. a 16 cm by 10 cm rectangle and an 8 cm by 5 cm rectangle are similar (Figure 3.30).

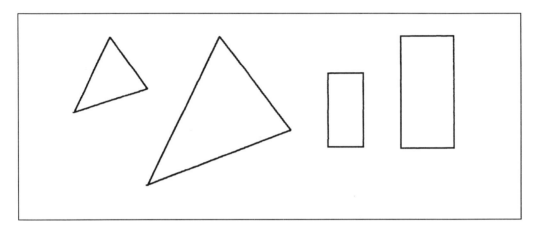

Figure 3.30 Similar shapes have sides in the same ratio

Polyhedron – poly (many) hedron (faces). A polyhedron is a solid with plane (flat) faces, each of which is a polygon. Plural polyhedra.

- *Cuboid* – A polyhedron whose plane faces are all rectangles.
  A **cube** is a special cuboid with square faces.
- *Prism* – A polyhedron whose cross-section parallel to its end faces is the same as both end faces. Toblerone packets are useful examples of triangular prisms. Cuboids and cylinders are also prisms. Prisms are good for making sandwiches because their slices are all the same size.
- *Pyramid* – A polyhedron with triangular side faces meeting at a point. Cross-sections parallel to the base are the same shape as the base but of diminishing size. The base can be any shape.
- *Regular icosahedron* – A polyhedron with 20 equilateral triangles as faces.
- *Regular dodecahedron* – A polyhedron with 12 regular pentagons as faces.

Co-ordinates: Co-ordinates are used to specify locations. A common use is in map references, as in a street finder, where a page is divided into squares which are numbered vertically and given letters horizontally, resulting in references like BQ37. Children can be introduced to these ideas by placing pictures of coloured objects on a two-way grid, so that objects match in rows and colours match in columns. Later children may play games of 'find the treasure' with invented maps of treasure islands. Such work will link strongly with geography, leading to the use of maps such as those produced by the Ordnance Survey, which have numbered scales along two axes, so that numbers refer to lines, not squares. This allows for the intervals between lines to be subdivided into ten, in effect dividing each square into a hundred small squares so that more precise locations can be identified with a six figure reference. There are a variety of computer games which practise the use of co-ordinates, such as Rhino from SMILE. Children can also use co-ordinates to name points which form the corners of 2D shapes. Co-ordinates are used in four quadrants when scales are extended to include negative numbers on both axes. These can then be used to describe the positions of shapes which have been transformed for instance by reflection or rotation. Children can also meet co-ordinates in advanced LOGO work when required to set x and set y to make sprites.

Transformations are different kinds of movement applied to a plane figure:

- *Translation* is movement without turning. Children make translation patterns for themselves when they do potato prints or stencil patterns. They can find these repeating patterns in fabrics, wallpaper or wrapping paper.
- *Reflection* is movement by reflecting as in a mirror. A shape is said to have reflective symmetry if it can be folded along a line of symmetry. When folded one half is seen to fit exactly on the other half. Viewed in the mirror, the reflected half looks exactly the same as the half obscured by the mirror, so the picture looks complete. Some shapes have more than one line of symmetry.
- *Rotation* is turning about a fixed point. All shapes can be rotated through an angle of 360 degrees to fit upon themselves. A shape is said to have rotational symmetry if it fits upon itself when rotated through a smaller angle. A half turn of 180 degrees will fit the letter S upon itself. A square fits on itself four times as it is rotated, so it has rotational symmetry of order 4.

Enlargement: Translations, reflections and rotations all leave the size of the shape unaltered. Enlargement is the term used to describe a change in the size but not in the shape. A photocopier can be used to make enlargements of any picture or shape. An enlargement, scale factor 2, is made by doubling all the lengths of a shape.

3.3 MEASUREMENT: GENERAL PRINCIPLES

Introduction

Measurement is an aspect of the mathematics curriculum which can easily be seen to be 'useful' in everyday life. We buy packaged food labelled by cost per kilogram. We use measurement to work out how much paper and paint we will need to decorate a room, and we organise our working days, journeys and so on around the measurement of time. Sometimes we gauge measurements roughly based on estimation, as in knowing that a cupboard which fits in one space will definitely fit another because it is obvious, by eye, that the second space is bigger. Sometimes it is not quite so clear, and so a piece of string held up against the cupboard and the new space, in turn, will show whether there will be a fit. Where we require a snug fit, it might be necessary to use a standard measuring tool which gives a clear numerical comparison and has small enough subdivisions to make fine distinctions easier. There is a range of approaches to comparison, on which it is helpful to draw in suiting the purpose. All depend on a feeling for measure.

In our society we operate both in metric and Imperial systems of measure, and this is something we have to bear in mind in our teaching. We may feel more comfortable in expressing our body measures (weight, height, etc.) in Imperial measures while we are getting used to buying petrol in litres and shops are required to mark food packaging in metric measures. There will need to be recognition of these two systems in work with children but, generally, the metric system is the main focus for work in the classroom. Imperial measures are discussed where they arise naturally from children's experience, for example in comparing height in the two systems.

Developing in children a 'feel for measure', an understanding of the use of standard measures and experience in interpreting different systems of measure is what this section addresses. The case study offers a view of measures in a problem-solving situation.

National Curriculum

In the current (1995) National Curriculum, measures is included in a section called 'Shape, Space and Measures'. The strand relating to measures is 'Understanding and using measures' in both Key Stages 1 and 2.

At Key Stage 1 the main aspects to be taught are comparison, the use of common non-standard and standard units of length, mass and capacity, beginning to use a wider range of standard units (including time), choosing suitable units and estimating with units. Children should also learn how to 'choose and use simple measuring instruments, reading and interpreting numbers and scales with some accuracy.'

At KS 2 progression is addressed by a greater emphasis on the choice and use of standard units of measure, sensible estimating in 'everyday situations', deeper understanding of relationships between units, conversion of units (metric) and some knowledge of rough equivalent metric/Imperial measures. 'Increasing accuracy' in the choice and use of instruments and in reading scales and in interpreting numbers is clearly identified as progression at this stage. Finally, specific content is identified: perimeter, circumference of circles and introduction to π, areas and volumes by counting and dissection.

Standard and non-standard measures

In the National Curriculum, and in most texts for teachers, a progression of children's learning in measurement is outlined. It is suggested that children develop from *direct comparison* (such as standing back-to-back to see who is taller) to *indirect comparison* using non-standard units (such as finding out how many hand spans tall Child A and B are and comparing through counting the hand spans) and then onto the use of *standard units of measure*, also indirect, but this time heights are compared through metres and centimetres (or feet and inches). It might appear that more formal methods of measure are more advanced and therefore more correct, but sometimes direct comparisons and non-standard units are actually more appropriate. For example, in cooking at home, the size of small cakes is compared by eye, while in a factory an exact weight of cake mixture is measured out.

The key point here is that we use different degrees of formality according to context, and children need to build up confidence in making decisions about the best approach in a given situation. In setting up a task children can be offered a range of materials, including standard measures, and, by observation of how they are used, the teacher can assess what the children know already and what should be taught next.

To help children understand that units need to be equal to make comparison fair, tasks can be set up where children are offered a variety of units (e.g. pencils of different length for measuring length compared with uniform felt-tip pens) and two groups can be asked to measure the same object, both with pencils and with pens. As they record results they should be able to see that the pens give groups the same result but the pencils are less likely to. The teacher will need to structure questions carefully to encourage reasoning:

'Why did you get 15 pencils and 8 pens for the length?'
'Why did this group get 10 pencils and you got 12 pencils?'
'Which is the best thing to measure with and why?'

Through children's responses the teacher will be able to judge understanding and plan appropriate work to build understanding. Do they need more of this kind of experience to build generalised views, or do they seem to understand that the standard unit is more helpful in communication with others?

It would be reasonable to expect that many children at Key Stage 1 will tend to use comparison to tackle measurement tasks. For example, in response to the question *'How can we find out who is the tallest?'*, they are likely to suggest standing next to one another. However, they will also have had the experience of being weighed and will be aware of tools such as tape measures. In allowing them to try to use such standard measures and interpret information from them, the teacher can look out for understanding. With the tape measure, for example, a child might hold it up against the object to be measured but not know about the meaning of the numbers. The intervention here might be to set up tasks involving making rulers with unifix cubes and labelling with numbers to help understanding of the tape or rules as a strip of units stuck together (Figure 3.31).

Calibration

At Key Stage 2 children can develop their understanding of calibration by making calibrated containers to measure capacity. A transparent cup can be marked at each successive addition of an eggcupful of water, for example, and then used to measure the capacity of other containers (Figure 3.32). This can then be compared with a standard measure such as a 500 ml container, and understanding can be helped by discussing how many 1 ml containers would be needed to fill it.

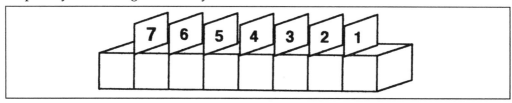

Figure 3.31 Unifix with markers

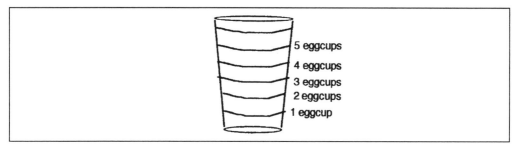

Figure 3.32 Calibrated cup

Relationships between standard units can be explored by such activities as pouring 1 ml containerfuls into a 10 ml container and so on up the scale, getting children to predict how many they think they will use. Similarly, children can place centimetre length strips along a decimetre, and decimetres along a metre, to see that 10 cm =1 dm and 10 dm = 1m. For area, children can compare 1 square centimetre of paper with a 10cm square and a 10 cm square (Figure 3.33) with a metre square. With volume, a metre square (skeletal) can be made with lengths of dowelling, and children can be challenged to work out how many centimetre cubes would fit along one side, across one face and in the whole cube.

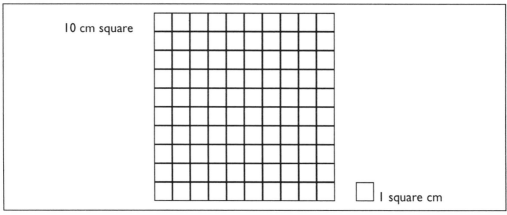

Figure 3.33 Matching smaller units to larger

The names of the units can be analysed for meaning in helping to see the relationships. There is usually a base unit (metre, litre) on which subdivisions and multiples are based. Latin words are used to denote the subdivisions and Greek words the multiples.

So for capacity, litre is the base unit, millilitres (thousandth of a litre) are the usual subdivisions. There are also centilitre (hundredth) and decilitre (tenth).

For measure of distance you will also meet kilometre (a thousand metres).

With grams, there are multiples: hectogram (100 grams) and kilogram (1000 grams). There are also subdivisions: centigram (one hundredth of a gram) and milligram (one thousandth of a gram). The usual prefixes and their values is as follows:

- milli – one thousandth
- centi – one hundredth
- deci – one tenth
- deca – ten
- hecto – one hundred
- kilo – one thousand

Children can be encouraged to make their own posters or dictionaries giving examples and explanations, and these can be used as classroom references. There are also published mathematical dictionaries for the same purpose. The metric system is underpinned by the place value (base 10) system, and it also allows practice at calculations to reinforce number understanding. The history of measures is a rich source of investigation, for example finding out where measures such as feet and inches came from.

Choosing appropriate standard measures

At Key Stage 1, the National Curriculum requires that children 'be taught to both use and estimate with standard units'. In general the base unit such as the metre or litre are given as starting points, and children are asked to find things which measure 'about the same as', 'more' or 'less' than it. Subsequently, the unit is halved (half metre or half litre) and similar exercises are suggested. In both steps children can be encouraged to make collections for a display of objects which can be thus sorted. With weighing, use of the gram presents problems because it is difficult to find simple balances which can accurately differentiate with such small amounts, and so the first standard weight might be a 100 gram weight and, using the appropriate prefix for 100, named a hectogram or hecto. Similarly in other measures it is often suggested that interim measures, not commonly used in 'real life' can be introduced to help children deal with subdivisions (for fractional parts) in steps matching number size more accessible to them. For example, in tackling length, children can move from body measures to the metre, then the half metre (by folding in half) and the quarter metre, and then on to the decimetre (10 in 1 metre), allowing a smaller subdivision but still dealing with numbers accessible to most Key Stage 1 children. Finally, the centimetre can be introduced as a smaller part of the decimetre, followed by the millimetre.

The last two (cm and mm) are usually introduced in Key Stage 2 but there will be overlap where children are able to deal with the numbers involved, have experience of measuring and see the need for them. Children might for example become interested in the relationship between centimetres and millimetres from looking at rulers in the classroom. At each stage, objects in the environment can be compared with the measure so children develop a feel for the measure in relation to familiar objects. As children need to use measure and finer comparisons are required, say in science activities, the subdivisions are seen to be necessary.

Use and interpretation of measuring tools

There is a wide variety of tools for measurement whose use requires understanding and skills. Some examples will illustrate common difficulties which might arise.

For example, a ruler can be used to measure length and children need to understand the nature of what they are measuring (length), how to line up the ruler and how to interpret the number read from the scale. A child might be helped by making her or his own ruler based on units used to measure, for example a ruler based on footprints (Figure 3.34).

Figure 3.34 Foot ruler

Using this to measure in the classroom and discussing the results could then lead into discussion of other rulers and how to measure in centimetres. Centimetre squares could be offered singly to be built up into a strip, if necessary, and then the strip compared with a school ruler.

Another problem with reading linear scales is in reading measures between marked points. This is an area which children will need to discuss in the context of practical tasks, such as reading the scale of a thermometer.

Weighing scales present this difficulty, too. They can also cause difficulty because they show weight (unseen) as a point on a scale. Spring balances, where children can see the object being pulled down and a marker on a scale moving at the same time, can help.

Another measuring tool commonly used in primary schools which needs careful introduction and monitoring is the trundle wheel. To demonstrate that one turn of the wheel measures one metre, paint can be applied (if it is made of suitable material) and a line printed on paper, which can then be compared with a metre stick. Alternatively, string can be cut to the length of the wheel's circumference (a bit fiddly!) and again compared. Then the wheel can be moved and stopped at each click, asking children 'how many metres have we gone now?'

With all these potentially tricky areas, the key is not to avoid or attempt all instruction prior to use of the tools but to set up tasks which require their use and involve the children in making sense of what results they obtain.

Estimating

In measuring we make judgements about *closeness*, according to our purpose. Does this shirt fit? Am I going to be able to get this armchair through the door? Estimation often appears in teacher resource books as a natural part of measurement work and children are routinely asked to estimate, or make a good guess at the result, before actually measuring to check. Children may not be clear about the point of estimation in this situation and are often reluctant to make estimates which are immediately shown to be inaccurate. If we are clear that estimation is about developing a *feel* and sense about measures, similar to a *feel* for number, then the point of estimation will be clearer to children. Estimation, in practice, is likely to relate to rough calculations prior to more careful planning and measuring such as costing a carpet roughly on rounded measures before carpet fitters measure more accurately to cut and fit the carpet. Estimation and a feel for measure also plays a part in rule of thumb conversions between different systems, e.g. a bag of sugar is about 2 kilograms if you want a base for comparison.

To help children develop estimations based on experience, the teacher could ask children to predict whether an object will take more or less (handspans, conkers, cupfuls...) based on a task they have just completed. Then later they can be asked, *'How many more (or less) do you think it will be?'* With standard units, games can be devised to develop estimating skills. A set of objects can be made for weighing (e.g. 50 g up to 100 g). Two players each select an object and estimate the weight. Write estimates down. Weigh the objects and take counters to represent each 10 g you were out by. Count up the counters when all objects are weighed, and the winner is the one with the least counters. Similar games can be set up for other aspects such as length (varying lengths of ribbon are good for this). To extend to larger fixed objects such as 'height of the door', children can have cards illustrating the objects to select but measure the objects *in situ* (Figure 3.35).

Assessing for starting points

To make an assessment of children's understanding of a particular measure on beginning a new topic, there are tasks which can be presented to children with a choice of possible ways to solve them. The methods children use can give the teacher evidence of understanding and allow planning for extension of learning.

The teacher can prepare a set of objects to be compared. For length, these might be objects such as ribbons, sticks, pencils, scissors (curved as well as straight). For weight, a set of parcels could be made, different sizes and weights, some 'tricky', e.g. large but light or small but heavy. For capacity, a set of containers can be collected. Depending on the age and confidence of the children the number of objects could be from three to six.

The teacher asks the children to say which one they think is longest (holds the

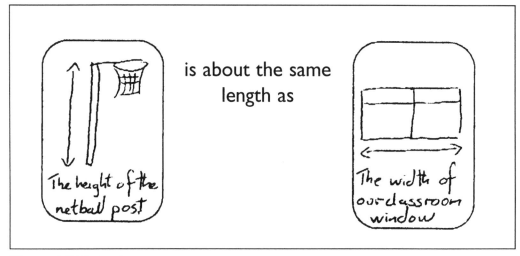

Figure 3.35 Estimation games

most, is heaviest, etc.) and why they think that. They should then be asked how they could check, and offered a variety of material to choose from, including non-standard and standard methods. For example, for length, rulers, tape measures, or string could be offered. Some children might choose to make a direct comparison with pairs of objects and order the objects, from different pairings. If children are stuck the teacher could make suggestions, '*Could you use this to help?*' The approaches used by children can be observed in gathering evidence for assessment to inform planning of the next step. Similarly, for weight and capacity, standard and non-standard units and tools can be available and the teacher can analyse what children select and how they use it.

3.4 ASPECTS OF MEASUREMENT: LENGTH, CAPACITY/VOLUME, PERIMETER, AREA, WEIGHT /MASS, TIME

For each of these aspects of measurement, key concepts and potential misconceptions will be identified together with sample activities for Key Stages 1 and 2.

Length

'*Length is the distance between the ends of an object, along it*' (ILEA Checkpoints. Length Card 1). The concept of length can be difficult if the object is flexible, and children might feel a ribbon is a different length extended than it would be rolled up.

From Piaget's work comes observation of children's perception that the length of an object can be altered by a change in its position (Figure 3.36).

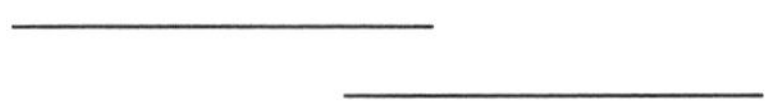

——————————

——————————

Figure 3.36 Are these lines the same length?

It would appear that children look at the ends of the lines rather than at the lines as a whole. Concentrating on the ends of the lines also encourages some children to say that the lines in Figure 3.37 are the same length.

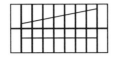

Figure 3.37 (From Dickson, Brown and Gibson, 1984:96)

The idea of the distance (between two points) can also be difficult because instead of an object to compare there is a space to be filled. Children need experience of measuring both lengths of objects, (curved as well as straight) and distances.

At Key Stage 1 children can use body measures such as feet or hands, material such as sticks, straws or interlocking cubes and will need to line up or fill space with repeated units before being encouraged to see that one unit can be used repeatedly by moving it along. Watching how children use units will reveal whether they understand that units must not overlap or have gaps in between. Metre length sticks or paperstrips can be introduced and, again, getting children to place place several end to end can show them clearly how many metres long something is before they develop the idea of repeated use of one unit. Half metres and quarters can be obtained from folding paper strips as children become more concerned about 'the bit left over' (this can also be done with hand and feet measures).

The teacher needs to look out for children using fractional terms, or phrases such as 'and a little bit more', in deciding when it might be helpful to introduce ways to deal with fractions of measures. Decimetre strips (10 cm) can be introduced before centimetres and millimetres as children need to make smaller distinctions in measure.

Use of these last two units is most likely to be developed at Key Stage 2 as children will need to be familiar with larger numbers to be able to read and interpret results. This, however, is not to say that no children at Key Stage 1 can use or understand them but that the teacher needs to assess appropriate intervention for children at both stages.

Problems occur with rulers where children are not sure how to line up with the object being measured. Children often read from 1 rather than from 0 or the end of the ruler beyond the calibration. Matching 1 cm squares to the spaces on the ruler can help because the child can see that one square fills the space between two centimetre marks. To match up with the 1 cm mark, the square must be lined up with 0 at the other end. Children can have a selection of strips of 1 cm squares and be asked to count the squares in each case. Then they can be asked to line them up against the ruler to the number they have counted. Ask them where the end of the strip of squares matches the ruler.

The measuring of length will be needed in many technology activities and in science. For example, if children are testing the distance a toy car will reach after rolling from the end of a ramp, they need to find a way of comparing the distances of each after rolling. They may choose to walk out the distance (*'It's 110 footsteps'*), stretch out lengths of string or use a metre rule. The teacher can observe and discuss the task as they work and make assessments of knowledge and understanding. Older children might be comparing distances of places away from the school. The teacher can discuss with the children how they will approach the task. What will they do if they need to follow curved routes rather than 'as the crow flies'? How will they read the subdivisions on the ruler?

Capacity and volume

Capacity can be thought of as the amount a container holds. It is sometimes refer-red to as 'internal volume'. A practical example to distinguish between volume and capacity is a drink container in a child's lunch box. Its capacity (internal volume) is how much drink it holds, while its volume (external) is how much space it takes up in the lunch box. In some cases, a Thermos flask for example, the container has thick walls and the capacity is much less than the total volume occupied by the flask. Another way of looking at it is that the drink itself has volume (but needs to be contained to be measured) while the container has capacity.

It is difficult for children to know what volume is, especially in the case of liquids. With sand or Plasticine, they can put their hands around it and feel. Looking at the volume of cubes the child has to visualise the building up from smaller cubes and needs also to understand length.

At Key Stage 1, work with capacity (or internal volume) will include practical experience with a variety of containers and a variety of materials to put in the containers, solid and liquid, and also discrete objects such as beans, cubes, conkers. This might be set up in sand or water trays or as story or play contexts, e.g. *How many drinks can you get from this bottle at the teddies' tea party?* Looking at volume (external) can be introduced practically through children's manipulation of material such as Plasticine or playdough. Do they realise that they have the same amount even if they change the shape (if none is removed or added)? These discussions can be included as part of the manipulative experience set up for children.

Children can also be encouraged to look at what happens to water levels when objects are immersed. They can be asked to predict which object will make the water 'go up' more. For experience with sand and water, at times the teacher will provide a set of containers to challenge thinking – flat, wide and tall, thin – and see whether children think they have more or less water as they pour from one to the other. Questions about the level of the water, e.g. *'Why is the water higher now?'*, can lead into looking at children's ideas of what is happening.

Harrison (1987) raised an interesting observation with young children when he saw that they seemed to be focusing on *fullness* rather than capacity. He gave an example of a girl (aged 4) who thought that a cup 'held more' than a teapot. Harrison suggests that she was focusing on the fact that she had just filled the cup. The teacher needs to look out for such phenomena and consider also the language we use. Harrison suggests that since there is not an equivalent to 'longer', when dealing with the comparison of lengths (e.g. 'is capaciouser than') it is helpful to use phrases such as 'larger/smaller than' or 'can hold more than' in the context of capacity. Children can be asked to take a particular measure (a cup, a litre container or a bottle, for example) and pour it into a set of different containers. They can be asked to look at how far up the water comes and discuss why they think that is. Real-life contexts such as the school parties can be used to apply children's estimations and calculations. How many bottles of coke will we need? How can we find out? About how many drinks will each person have?

At Key Stage 2, the range of units should be extended into millilitres and the understanding of the relationship between the units developed through physical experience – find out by pouring how many times you need to empty the centilitre container into the litre to fill it. The most likely contexts for using these measures will be in other curriculum areas such as science.

To measure the volume of solid shapes, a basic unit is required. The most frequently used unit is the cube with sides of 1 centimetre (1 cm^3); larger volumes can be measured in cubic metres (1 m^3). The move towards an understanding of the volume of cuboids can be made through building models with cubes. Calculating the volume can be tackled by various ways of counting the cubes, by addition and multiplication initially (one layer has 4 cubes, there are two layers, and so the volume is 8 cubes). Children could explore the patterns obtained in the numbers of unit cubes used to make different sized cubes. They could be asked to solve a problem of wrapping 12 gift boxes to sent through the post, using the smallest amount of paper.

Area

Area is a difficult concept, but it can be developed early by discussing covering surfaces, for example predicting how many sheets of newspaper will be needed to cover the table. Other contexts relevant here are estimating how much wallpaper or carpet is needed in the Home Corner or in a dolls' house. The language to be developed will involve the amount of material needed for covering and wrapping. Activities could include wrapping parcels, making tablecloths for the Home Corner or covers for the Three Bears beds.

In this section there is a strong emphasis on practical contexts. However, there are many valuable practical activities in the form of puzzles and problems using mathematical apparatus (e.g geo-boards, squared paper, acetate sheets) that are not concerned with practical in the sense of 'everyday'. It is important that children have a strong foundation in number and in geometry, and that they have a secure understanding of mathematical concepts and ideas. It is arguable that area may be rather less important in 'real world' (applied) contexts than it is in a purely mathematical sense.

How accurately do we need to know the area of a garden or a wall? There are problems which can be posed, such as calculating the amount of grass seed required to make a lawn, or the number of pots of paint required to decorate the hall, but these are contrived and hypothetical, rather than realistic and practical.

However, the concept of area is not only important in its own right, but also fundamental to a full understanding of:

(a) Multiplication – the idea of a two-dimensional array is a helpful model of multiplication.
(b) Fractions.
(c) Geometric transformations and operations such as dissection, enlargement, and tessellation.
(d) Higher mathematical ideas such as calculus.
(e) Scientific ideas such as surface tension, pressure, photosynthesis, evaporation, and many, many more.

So area is an important building block in mathematical and scientific development. Whilst accepting that it should be taught meaningfully, it is not always necessary to take a lot of time and trouble concocting practical situations which pretend to contain area. Materials such as transparent grids and geoboards are useful for posing problems involving area. On geoboards ask children to make shapes with a particular area, e.g. 8 squares. Look at the shapes. Will the perimeter remain the same? (Geoboards have nails at the points of a square grid, elastic bands are stretched between the nails to make shapes.)

A common misconception is to over-generalise the correct result that the area of a rectangle is obtained by multiplying the length by the breadth by applying this to all areas regardless of the shape in question. This can be avoided by ensuring that children find the area of many different kinds of shape, including irregular shapes such as leaves, and also insisting that children are precise in their use of mathematical statements, e.g. 'The area *of a rectangle* is length x breadth.'

Perimeter

Perimeter, an aspect of measuring length, is often confused with area. Dickson *et al.* (1984) suggest that this might be due to early formalisation through the introduction of formulae before children have had sufficient experience of exploring the shapes practically. They suggest activities to show that area can be varied while perimeter stays constant, and vice versa. If a shape has all its sides doubled but retains the same angles, its area will be quadrupled. Using squared paper or a geoboard you can ask: How many shapes can you make from 12 squares? What are the perimeters of those shapes? How many shapes can you make with a perimeter of 12. Find the area of each of the shapes. Is it always the same?

The perimeter of a circle is called the *circumference*. When using trundle wheels, children can be asked to measure the diameter of the wheel and compare this with the circumference. Do all trundle wheels have the same diameter? Can you find a cylinder that will roll through 30 cm? What is the diameter for a 30 cm roll? By experiment, children can find that the circumference is roughly three times the diameter. The actual ratio is not a rational number (see Section 2, Glossary). The decimal expansion has been shown to go on and on: 3.141592........

The ratio *circumference of circle/diameter* is called π; when calculating, simple approximations such as 3, 3.1 or 3.14 are used according to the degree of accuracy required.

Weight (and mass)

So far in this section we have referred only to weight and we need to include a comment for the teacher on its relationship to mass. Weight is a force – the gravitational pull exerted on an object – whereas mass is the amount of matter in an object. The weight, or downward force on an object, can change depending on where the measurement is made. The mass of an object, in contrast, remains the same no matter where the measurement is made. With young children there might seem to be little point in differentiating between the two and there may be more familiarity with the term 'weight'. They will also be engaged in the practical activity of 'weighing'. As work in science develops the distinction can be made in the context of weightlessness in outer space.

The difficulty with weight is that it is not visible in the same way that length is. From holding objects, children can feel the pull downwards, and they can see the downward movement of see-saws, bar balances and spring balances. Early ideas about the weight of objects can be influenced by other attributes such as length or shape. In the main, young children will predict that a large box will be heavier than a small one. If children are asked to hold objects they can be encouraged to talk about how they 'feel', but the size of an object can influence how heavy something feels to hold. For example a small, dense object like an iron key might feel heavier than an object which weighs more but spreads more widely over the hand. The pressure on the hand is not evenly spread. This problem can be overcome to some extent by placing objects in bags, held with arms relaxed these can give a clearer sense of the downward pull and make comparing clearer. As previously mentioned, spring balances linked to a linear scale also show this pull. A simpler version of a spring balance can be set up, using a container (e.g. large yogurt pot) with an elasticated loop to hold (Figure 3.38). Objects can be placed

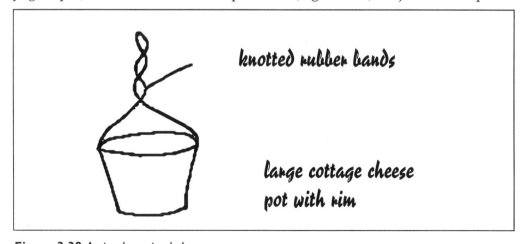

knotted rubber bands

large cottage cheese
pot with rim

Figure 3.38 A simple spring balance

in the container and, if it is held up against paper attached to the wall, starting and end points can be marked and children can see the results of the extending elastic. They can then be encouraged to predict: '*If the scissors made the pot go down to here, where will it go with the stapler inside? Which do you think is heavier?*'

At Key Stage 1, weighing will involve direct comparison. For example, in cooking, recipes can be based on comparisons such as using the amount of flour which balances two eggs. A variety of balances, including bucket sized containers, can be provided together with sand or water, to give experience with a tool for weighing. Stamps can be added to the parcels in a post office according to weight, using standard or non-standard units. For example, if a parcel balances 3 large bricks, it will have a stamp of value 3; but a parcel balancing 5 bricks will 'cost' 5 . Children can make parcels and stamps for their post office. Other 'play' shops can also contain scales as part of the experience provided.

At the early stages of using balancing scales, teachers need to look out for instances where children are having to adjust the amount of material against which they are balancing their object. Often the children will realise an adjustment needs to be made when the scales are not balanced, but they may add more when removing would have been appropriate (or vice versa). These situations are rich in possibilities for discussion and thinking. The teacher will learn more about what it is the child does and doesn't currently understand by engaging in dialogue rather than simply correcting the child, and the subsequent planning then becomes more informed. First, the child can be asked to describe what is happening. Does s/he talk about the link between 'going down' and heavier? Does s/he have an image of what the scales will look like when balance is close? Careful, supportive questioning is important here, e.g. '*Can you tell me...*', *What can you see?*', '*What do you think will happen if... (we put more cubes in/take some cubes out?)*'.

At Key Stage 2, labels collected and read can yield examples of common quantities such as weights of family-sized cans, of cereal packets and of loose-purchased fruit and vegetables. In cooking children can adjust recipes to feed different numbers than those given on the recipe. Questions such as '*Should all ingredients be doubled?*' will lead to discussion of proportions. A context where comparison between metric and Imperial weights arises is in looking at wartime rations and recipes, and children can explore rough equivalences by comparing ounces and pounds and grams with the scales. In using scales they would be expected to develop their understanding of readings between various subdivisions.

Time

The main distinction involved in work on time is that between telling the time and a *concept* of time.

The first involves the reading of a dial which has units like any other measure but is presented in quite a complex display on an analogue clock, where the numerals have different meanings depending on the unit. For example, the 3 can refer to hours (as in 3 o'clock) or a quarter past or 15 mins. With the greater prevalence of digital clocks nowadays, it has been suggested that children are growing up with quite a different model of time, not circular but linear (see BEAM, 1994, Starting from Scratch – Measures). In the classroom it will be necessary to have examples of both analogue and digital clocks and, if the two run side by side, children can see how particular times, significant to them (e.g. 'School starts at...', 'Power Rangers' is on at ...), are shown. It might be the case that, rather than one type replacing the other, the two types have their different uses. For example to estimate the 'chunk' of time left in a lesson, the teacher can gain a quick impression from a glance at the shape between the current time and the end time. However, if s/he is catching a train home from school a digital clock will allow quicker calculation of how many minutes s/he has to reach the station. People brought up mainly with experience of digital displays will perhaps find it easier to relate to them, and the analogue 'supporters' are holding on to an image which they themselves were brought up with. Analogue watches and clocks continue to be produced and so children should be given experience in dealing with them. The reading of dials requires that children have other knowledge such as reading numerals, counting in fives and knowing fractions, such as 'half' and 'quarter'. The reading of the dial may not connect with understanding of times of the day. A child might be able to read *'nine o'clock'* when shown the hands in place or *'nine fifteen'* when looking at a display. While this builds confidence and is a useful skill, the child may not relate the times to when events occur. It is probably best to integrate time telling and estimating into the everyday life of the classroom, beginning with looking at what the clock shows at significant times of the day.

There are children's books, based on stories and games, such as 'What's the Time, Mr. Wolf?', which can be used as a staring point to make class books. One group of Year 2 children, who needed reinforcement on reading hours on the clock, made a book entitled *'What's the Time 3C?'*. By good fortune, times were often 'o'clocks', so each child illustrated a page. Raymond's was *'What's the time, Raymond?' '9 o'clock – Time for Miss to open the door'*. He illustrated the page, and all the children made clock faces with movable hands to stick onto their page. The children in the class could move the hands to the time described.

This activity was started by getting children to imagine a clock they knew and then draw it. The teacher was trying an activity which was described in an article by *Helen Pengelly (1995)*. Figure 3.39 shows some of the clocks they drew. They showed the teacher some of the things children already knew about clocks and telling the time and allowed her to think about what might be appropriate next. For example, Amy knows there are numbers around the clock face and where 12 is, but she continued writing numbers beyond 12. She would benefit perhaps from looking at clocks, drawing them and fitting numerals onto clocks. For the book, the teacher gave the children paper circles, and asked the children to fold the circles into halves and then into quarters. They were then asked to put in 12, 6, 3 and 9, after looking at a clock face, and then fill in the remaining numerals. Raymond, who drew a clock face with only the 12, 3, 9 and 6 and was very confident in reading and drawing times, could be given experience in calculating time intervals, problems from contexts familiar to him, and so on.

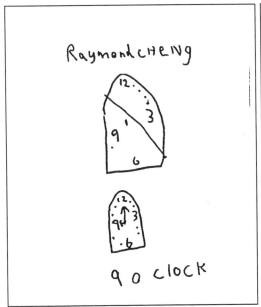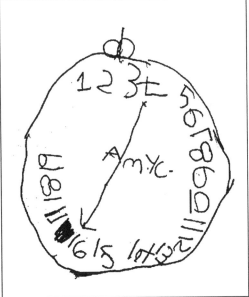

Figure 3.39 Clock faces

The second aspect of time, the concept of time, is about ideas of time passing and the measurement of intervals. For example, how long does it take you to walk to school? One reception child said to his teacher, while experimenting with a set of sand timers, *'I'm going away until the last one's finished'*, showing he has some ideas that time will have passed when the sand has run out. She was surprised to find that his estimation was quite good, and he returned within a few seconds of the sand running out! Making a variety of timers, e.g. water and sand with holes in paper cups, and setting up activities to do alongside can help with these ideas. The children can be asked, *'How many times can you hop before the sand runs out?'* or *'How many times can you write your name before this clockwork toy stops running?'* Sand timers measuring 1 minute, 3 minutes and 5 minutes are useful. Children often respond to tasks such as, *'Who can get changed for PE before the sand runs through'*. (This might require more than one turn, depending on the age and speed of children!)

Case study: Food technology Richard Harrison and Geraldine Wood

The marginal notes show how the children's work links to the using and applying Attainment Targets.

Our case study is from a Year 5 class. The children were asked to design packaging for a selection of goods to be sold. They were working with two teachers, Richard and Geraldine. They introduced the activity by saying *'We are going to sell these things in our delicatessen and we need to design some packaging.'* This was creating a context for learning rather than saying, *'We are going to learn about weight and volume. First of all I want you to weigh these objects and then tomorrow we will find their volume.'*

A table was prepared with bowls containing dried peas, lentils, raisins, oats, rice and demerara sugar. Richard and Geraldine had selected these particular substances because of their differing densities so they had to work these out themselves first! The sugar had the greatest density, and the oats were the lightest for their size. It was important for the children to feel and compare the materials, so the bowls were wide. Scoops were provided so that the children could fill boxes easily later on (Figure 3.40).

Richard showed the children the materials and set the problem, which was to:

- select a standard weight for the packaging
- estimate the size of the box
- make a prototype
- find out 'how far out' the box was (and to be prepared to be wrong!) and work from there to improve the dimensions of the box.

Geraldine identified the different roles which children should take in their groups, and the need to keep a diary which recorded fully what ideas and decisions were made, before, during and after each 'lesson' (Figure 3.41).

There were a number of weights available. Children had to select an appropriate one to be the 'standard' for their delicatessen (Figure 3.42).

Use and apply mathematics in practical tasks, in real-life problems...

Select and use the appropriate mathematics and materials...

...taking increasing responsibility for organising and extending tasks

...devise their own ways of recording

...present information and results clearly and explain the reasons

Figure 3.40 Bowls of dried peas, lentils, raisins, oats, rice and sugar

Jane, William & Clare
1st Box
30th Jan

① Weight – 300 grams – we decided we didn't want it to heavy because we dont like carrying heavy things around supermarkets.

Substances – rice – we thought that rice was small but still heavy, good for what we were doing.

card – we saw how much rice 300 gr was. It was quite alot so we needed alot of card. After talking a but about it we decided it needed to be water proof because rice gets bigger when in contact with rice water.

Figure 3.41 Children's record of their decisions about weight and substance

Figure 3.42 Choosing a standard weight

They were encouraged to take any of the weights (not only the one they had chosen as their standard) to the bowls of substances to make further comparisons (Figure 3.43).

Figure 3.43 Estimating weight

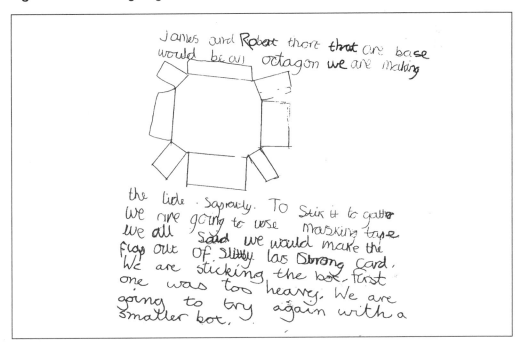

Janes and Robert thort that an base would be an octagon we are making

the litle . Sapratly. To stik it to gather
We are going to use masking tape
We all said we would make the
flap out of slitty las strong card.
We are sticking the box. first
one was too heavy. We are
going to try again with a
smaller box.

Figure 3.44 Design for a box with an octagonal base

The children were given access to commercial packaging to analyse the design and encouraged to make nets of their boxes (Figures 3.44 and 3.45). They had to remember to keep records of the dimensions of the box.

Figure 3.45 Drawing the net

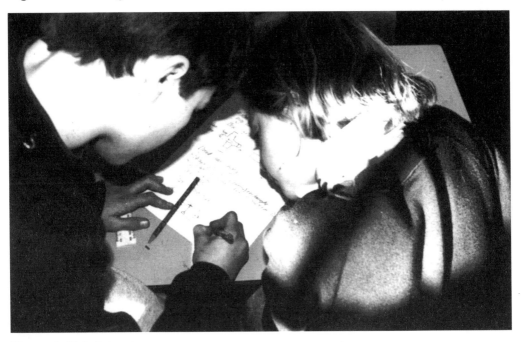

Figure 3.46 Refining the prototype

The nets were then made into boxes. The children were able to establish the 'nearness' of their estimate. The boxes were either too big or too small. How would the prototype aid their refinement (Figures 3.46 and 3.47)?

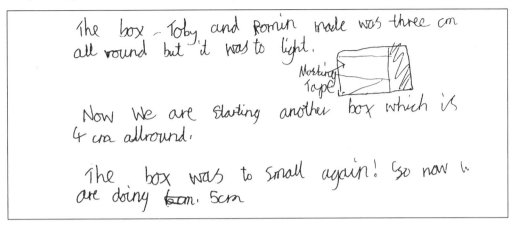

The box - Toby and Romin made was three cm all round but it was to light.

Masking Tape

Now we are starting another box which is 4 cm allround.

The box was to small again! So now we are doing from. 5cm

Figure 3.47 Adjusting the size of the box

Having reached a satisfactorily-sized box which would contain their standard weight, the design and technology aspect emerged, and they used a variety of materials to decorate their boxes (Figures 3.48 and 3.49).

Figure 3.48 Packaging for 300 grams of dried peas

Although the teachers intended that the box of weights should contain only metric weights, some old Imperial weights had survived. In the second lesson they discovered one child, Rheem, trying to balance metric against Imperial weights. Because she couldn't maintain a balance easily, she investigated systematically, balancing a 1-ounce weight against grams, then a 2-ounce weight, and so on. She concluded that the best approximation was '*25 grams is equivalent to three ounces.*'

The teachers were pleased with this because it was a child-initiated investigation and one of the main aims, that of sensible approximation, was being served. Rheem had to make many judgements about how closely the metric and Imperial weights

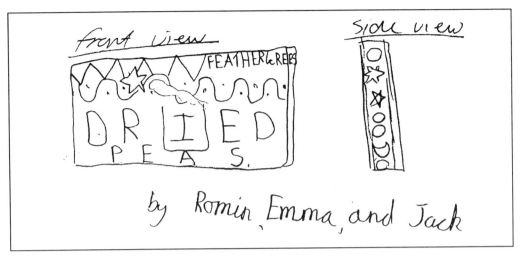

Figure 3.49 Front and side view of packaging

should match and the kind of numbers she wanted in her conclusion.

One of the groups had carefully measured the dimensions of their prototype and found it was too big. The pupils said to the teachers, *'We don't know what to do with the numbers.'*

Here is a flow sequence of what the teacher tried to do:

● Tell me what you've done so far.
● What do you think would happen if you made the numbers smaller?
● How much smaller?
● OK, try it and see what happens.

The questioning was not instructive, but it was 'opening out', or enabling.

Zoe and Charlotte's box was far too big. Before they proceeded to cut it down (a common strategy used to solve this particular problem), Richard suggested that they fill it and weigh it to see what the box would have weighed when full. It weighed 1730 g. This was an opportunity to explore alternative expressions. They had used 1 kilogram weight, seven 100 gram weights and three 10 gram weights, and the following table was compiled:

kilograms	hundred-grams	ten-grams	grams
1	7	3	0

This could then be read out in several different ways, e.g.

'One kilogram, seven hundred and thirty grams'
'One thousand seven hundred and thirty grams'
'One point seven three zero kilograms'

Thus the teacher was able to introduce the decimal point as a marker or unit point (to show which one was being used as a unit). A structured set of measuring units offered by far the most meaningful approach to decimal notation, as mentioned in the National Curriculum at Number Key Stage 2.

The groups quickly discovered they needed to know how heavy the box was and subtract this from the full weight. So it wasn't necessary for the teachers to teach this (i.e. 'gross' weight and 'net' weight). But they had been prepared to!

Alex, Chantelle and Kaya were one group to demonstrate the success of approximation (should it be 'successive approximation'?). This can be shown best like a strip cartoon (Figure 3.51).

Figure 3.50 Weighing on balance scales

So, having observed these children using and applying their skills of approximation, some thoughts occurred to the teachers (with implications for differentiation in future sessions):

- What do they know now?
- Do they know how volume 'behaves' now?
- What work would be suitable next for this this group?
- Could they make a bowl half the size of this one, but still the same shape?

(Not so easy as it seems – halving all the sides does not give half the volume! Figure 3.51)

It was a great joy to the teacher when, in the third or fourth session, Kaya explained that *'a raisin is about five times as heavy as a lentil but a whole lot bigger'* (and of course she hadn't found the weight of a single raisin). Many of the children used phrases like *'heavy for their size'*.

The children were encouraged to record all their hypothesising, ideas, thoughts, plans, decision-making, differences of opinion, discoveries and disappointments as they worked through the investigation (Figure 3.52). In the initial discussion with the children, the teacher talked about the value of each child having a role to play within the group, one of these roles being the *scribe*. The children discussed who would take on the responsibility, and it was understood that the job could be rotated

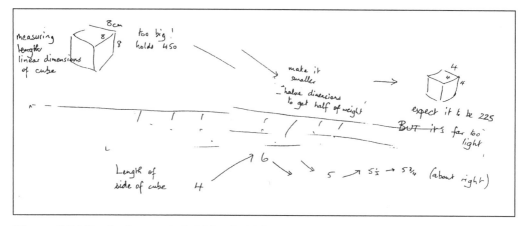

Figure 3.51 Teacher's record of children's thinking

around the group. This aspect of the investigation had to be monitored closely as the children quickly became absorbed in the action and neglected to record events as and when they occurred. With two adults taking the group, an ideal situation, it was possible to circulate the classroom, monitoring the situation closely and questioning the children, reminding them of the importance of keeping a written account (Figure 3.53).

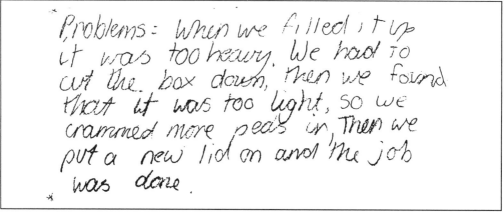

Figure 3.52 Children's recording

With the benefit of hindsight there was a need to reinforce the question, 'What do we need to record?' This could have been built into the beginning of the second session so that the children could establish for themselves the important aspects of their path through the investigation. Useful questions as a result of this discussion, written on a card and centrally placed so that the children could refer to them, would have helped keep the recording relevant to the investigation. Some children became very involved in the aesthetic value of the box, and this detracted from the mathematics of the task. However, the recording enabled the children to maintain interest, understanding and continuity, so that the activity could be picked up at any time and continued over the course of a week (Figure 3.54).

It was also important to make records of the children's work to be aware of necessary teaching points, questions to raise the children's awareness of their discoveries and to enable us to make assessments of the children's learning. Notes were also made on the effects of the organisation on the investigation which would

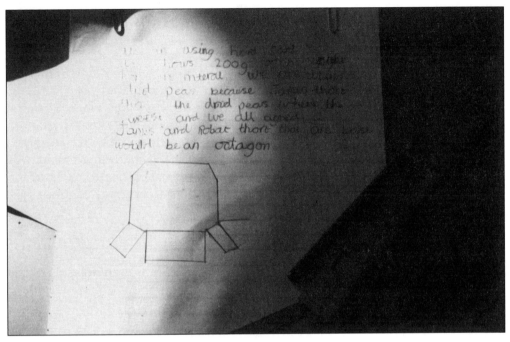

Figure 3.53 Record of children's decisions

1. What are we trying to find out ?

2. What materials are you going to use ?

3. What weight ?

4. Shape of box and dimensions ?—Net ?

5. Granular material ?

6. What happened when you made box and filled it with material ?

7. What have you found out ?

8. What are you going to do next ? Why ?

Could children be encouraged to work in a grid form to cut down on writing, but jog memory for recording?

    Flow diag – decision diag

Figure 3.54 Teacher's notes

help when a similar investigation is introduced in the future.

Organising the classroom and children appropriately

Organisation is important in any lesson. But measurement is a particular case in point because it requires access to materials, tools, and a variety of apparatus. In the case study, the teacher even had to rearrange the furniture so that children had unrestricted access to the six bowls (of raisins, oats, sugar, peas, lentils, and rice), to the consumables with which to construct boxes, and to different kinds of balances, weights, etc. She also had very definite rules about *how* to fill the containers they had made (*over* the bowls), *when* and *where* they were allowed to use the balances (they couldn't, for example, take a balance to the granular substances in order to weigh out as much as they needed). What we are saying here is that the organisation of the classroom and of the children *determined* the level of problem-solving, and, therefore, the mathematical learning. That was why it had to be set up so carefully, and why the teacher had continually to monitor the effectiveness of the rule system.

Using and Applying

In addition to links made between Using and Applying through notes displayed in this case study, it will be useful to make a few points about linking this aspect with work on measures in general:

1. To apply skills of measuring as we have noted earlier there needs to be purpose in the task. Why is it important to know how long, heavy or full, something is?

2. Opportunities for measurement occur in different contexts in school: in play, in other curriculum areas and arising from story or fantasy contexts, for example.

3. Early in Key Stage 1, children's play involves much comparison – choosing particular length bricks to fit a structure, using different sized containers in sand and water, fitting clothes to dolls and dolls to beds. The teacher's role is crucial in developing thinking by talking with children about what they are doing, helping them to predict which brick, container or bed will suit their needs, and developing the language of comparison. At times the teacher will intervene judiciously to challenge thinking: for example, she might place a set of containers in the water which will puzzle children because the shapes appear to hold more or less than they do.

4. Story contexts can lead into fantasy measuring tasks such as making artefacts for the Three Bears, glasses for the giant, or judging which of our possessions would be useful to the *Borrowers* (BBC TV). Reading *Alice in Wonderland* can lead into many speculations about scale and proportion.

5. Many science and technology tasks require measurement, e.g. designing packaging for a particular object, or finding ways to compare the effects on flight of the addition of weights to paper aeroplanes. In the latter example, measure is required in setting up different weights and in comparing distances

flown. Both contexts could use standard or non-standard measures according to the children's understanding.

Section 4: Handling Data

4.1 INTRODUCTION: HANDLING DATA

Handling data is a statutory part of the content of the National Curriculum but it is much more than that. It is a life skill.

We are bombarded by data in the media: what a healthy diet should be, our chances of winning in the National Lottery, who's ahead in the opinion polls. If children are to be educated to become adults who are able to make informed and sensible decisions, they will need to develop understanding of the ways in which data can be used to inform, persuade or even coerce. They will need to question the accuracy of the information, know something about how data was collected, be able to read tables and graphs and be aware of plausible interpretations, explanations and conclusions. Children should be helped to develop a critical, questioning approach, for example through being able to examine claims made by advertisers and particular interest groups.

Questions about the likelihood or probability of events can emerge from the collection of data to answer particular questions, and data will sometimes need to be collected to address questions of probability. Explorations of games, or investigation into the frequency of events relevant to children, can build towards an understanding of the chances of winning (or not winning!) in competitions and towards informed decision making, for example in making choices about insurance or risky enterprises.

National Curriculum

In the current (1995) National Curriculum for Mathematics, relevant sections in the Programmes of Study which addresses the handling of data are as follows:

- *Key Stage 1* Number – Sorting, handling and classifying data
- *Key Stage 2* Handling Data – Collection and representation of data
– Introduction to probability.

If children are to understand the issues in all stages of the data handling process, published mathematics schemes can offer aims and support for the work; but there is no substitute for children addressing questions arising from their own experience and interest.

Handling data in the classroom

Data handling is experienced in many different ways in the classroom and curriculum. Here are some examples:

- *Classroom organisation* – through contexts such as tidying (identifying common attributes in objects which are stored together). For example, children can be involved in addressing *'What is the best way to arrange the books in the Book Corner?'* (arising from a real need to find a particular book or type of story).

- *Issues affecting children out of school* – e.g. *'Is my bedtime reasonable compared with that of other children in my class?'* (from work on time or from ordinary discussions children have in the course of a day).
- *Science* – Children can investigate preferred living conditions for minibeasts and will need to make decisions about what data will need to be collected, how they can represent their data to make interpretation easier and so on.
- *History* – Children might look for differences and similarities between toys past and present. To do this they could display and discuss old photographs or toys and set up questionnaires to investigate the toy preferences for people of different ages to see if choices have changed between generations. This would involve the children in evaluating how the way in which they phrase the questions can affect the answers obtained.
- *In school life* – There are issues that can be investigated with the support of data collected by children, e.g. is it true that the playground is dominated by one type of play? How can data be used to argue for a particular viewpoint?
- *Story/fantasy contexts* – In the Key Stage 1 case study, described later in the chapter children investigate like or dislike of carrots. This arose from the *Three Billy Goats Gruff* story. If work were extended into preferred diet, story or fantasy characters could become an interest as subjects in a database as well as real people. For example, does the *Very Hungry Caterpillar* have a balanced diet?

All of the above examples involve a question or enquiry of potential interest to the children, a set of relevant data to handle, the need to represent findings in a clear way, interpretation of results and the making of deductions from results.

The data handling process

This is often presented as a circular process, as in Figure 4.1.

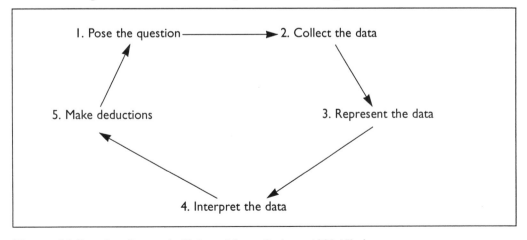

Figure 4.1 Data handling cycle (Adapted from Graham, 1990:15)

The cycle has various points which mark stages in the process. First of these is a starting question. This needs to be framed so that it is clear what data it is appropriate to collect. Secondly, decisions will need to be made about how to collect the data. Next the data must be processed and presented. Finally interpretations can be made and deductions offered. At this point the cycle is completed, but there might be a return to the original question as further questions will emerge which require another turn around the cycle. These questions will arise from new lines of enquiry emerging as work progresses, or because there was a problem with the design of some aspect of the work. The questions asked may not elicit appropriate data, for example.The cycle can appear very neat but the reality is not always as tidy as this!

Here is an example of the data handling cycle in practice. The teacher spots an argument between children about which story she will read next to the class, and she decides to use the context to introduce the idea of making decisions by voting. She asks the children which stories they want, and lists them on a large piece of paper or on the board. She asks them then to indicate preference by putting hands up while she counts and records choices by tallying or noting names. Then children can help to count so that a result can be obtained. There was a question (Which story?), a method of collecting data (hands up to be counted and the teacher might have discussed with the children how to do this), a representation (lists of names or marks against titles) and interpretation (Which story did most people want? How do we know?). In this case, the question arose spontaneously and was dealt with on the spot in a fairly informal way. This work will be approached with differing degrees of formality depending on the context and the process will also be entered at different points. For example, a question can arise from the collection of data stage. Counting how many children have school lunch might give rise to comment – *'When we were in Class 1 nearly everyone had packed lunch'* – and the teacher might take the opportunity to follow up with some kind of investigation, such as comparing different classes. This question is also a good example of how what appears clear initially, can throw up difficulties in investigation. For example, how will we deal with children who vary their lunch, having school dinners sometimes but packed lunch on other days?

The staged model of the data handling process is a useful framework in planning and evaluating the experiences offered to children, but it is a model which is not reproduced in exactly the same way in all such contexts. Enquiry will not always begin neatly at Stage 1. In the lunch example above interest was sparked at Stage 2 as data was collected for school administration purposes. Similarly, a question could arise at Stage 4 as, for instance, in the interpretation stage of data handling in the media. One of the sparks for the Key Stage 2 Case Study, to be described later in this chapter, was the reading of statistics about asthma and increased levels of pollution reported in the press.

What is important to stress here is that the whole cycle is applicable at both Key Stages but there will be differences in emphases on the stages and degrees of sophistication to which they are addressed. For example, there is a difference in the degree to which children bring their own knowledge of data collection to the task and are more independent in designing questions and methods of collecting data. Also, in interpretation of results, the teacher will encourage children to give reasoned judgements but the degree to which this is done and the complexity of the hypotheses and variables involved will increase dramatically between the Key Stages.

To illustrate progression Table 4.1 demonstrates a typical class topic, toys, and shows how it might be developed at Key Stage 1, early Key Stage 2 and later Key Stage 2 , addressing the stages in the data handling cycle above.

The teacher's role in the process

It is important that children have opportunities to explore their own questions and ideas. What, then, is the role of the teacher at different stages in the cycle?

1. Posing the question

If data handling is to be purposeful the teacher needs to be aware of opportunities which might lead to purposeful data handling.

In relation to the Toys, this work will probably be part of a whole class theme or topic (e.g. Play, Childhood or Toys) and the context for investigation here is related to a History strand.

Children will need *help to identify the actual question* to be investigated. The teacher first needs to initiate discussion about toys, so children are encouraged to bring in and/or talk about their toys. There would be a whole class discussion where emerging issues with potential for investigation are picked up by the teacher. For example, a child might say *'My mum had a teddy'* and children will make other points about parents and their toys. The teacher's role here is to support these ideas and to make suggestions, e.g. *'How could we find out about the toys our parents (older siblings, grandparents, etc.) played with?'* Actual toys, photographs, books and talking to individuals are all possible sources of information which can be used in 'sorting and classifying a set of objects according to one, two or more criteria related to their properties.' (National Curriculum Programme of Study for Key Stage 1). Toys, and pictures or photos of them, might be classified by owner (e.g. boy, girl, parent, grandparent), type (e.g. car, doll, board game) or ordered according to age to reinforce the idea of a time line.

The teacher's role so far has been *to identify possible starting points and incorporate them into planning.* She will need to consider the sort of questions which will provide rich starting points for children's learning. Such questions will not always be neat and well focused. Because of this, children's attempts at data collection will not always enable them to answer the original question. We *sometimes want children to learn from mistakes or trial* and to see that the way you frame question influences the kind of data you can collect. With the toys the question might be *'What is your favourite toy?'* This will possibly result in each child in the class responding with a different toy. It might be fruitful then to go on to either narrow the choice or give a the question a sharper focus (e.g. *'Do girls and boys like different toys?'*). Sometimes the teacher will decide to resolve these difficulties at the start. Sometimes she might

	Key Stage 1	Early Key Stage 2	Later Key Stage 2
Posing the question	What is my favourite toy?	What sort of toys did children play with when...(mum, gran, Mr. W.) were children?	How have toys changed through the ages?
	Questions will tend to be personal, related to child's experience / Questions will emerge from discussion	Questions slightly more abstract, looking more at children in general / Questions more topic centred	Questions reflect a broader historical view / Questions will be more carefully refined
Collecting the data	Toys, photos / Talk to adults	Photos, non-fiction books / Interviewing people	Range of source material – books, paintings, photos, writing etc, Museum visits
Representing the data	Mainly tally, tick charts, drawings / Toys displayed in sets	Drawing and producing different graphs, some from databases	Choose/select from different ways to represent data
	These arrangements of pictures/objects can lead into pictorial representations. They will mainly be counts.	Children will begin to learn about axes, meanings of different charts/graphs. Producing representations from databases allows a wider variety to be analysed. e.g. lists, tables	Children will be more selective about appropriate representation. They will begin to learn about how varying aspects such as scale can give different messages.
Interpreting the data	Reading results – 6 children have teddies	8 parents played with dolls / 5 of our class played with dolls	In all our books about toys there were no Gameboys / In our class 10 children have Gameboys
	Deductions – most children in our class like teddies	More people of my mum's age played with dolls than we did	Some toys that children played with in the past are still used now. There are new toys which were not used in the past because they needed microchips.
	Interpretation very close to the data read and still personal	Inference made from comparing data for 2 groups known to the children	More generalised statements made from a wider sample. Discussion can take place about the representativeness of the data.

At all stages children will initially be reading the results of their data and then being encouraged to look for patterns and make deductions. Interpretation involves reading the explicit information and then using this information to make general statements.

Table 4.1 Progression in data handling

decide that these discussions will take thinking forward. She will make judgements about the learning she wishes to promote in particular contexts.

To maintain an environment which encourages positive attitudes and some risk taking, all suggestions should be accepted as genuine questions with the potential for exploration. The children could be asked to brainstorm and pool ideas from which a selection can be made. The teacher can then judge whether the child would benefit from exploring a particular line of enquiry, or whether further discussion might lead to amendment or withdrawal of the line of enquiry.

Progression in helping children to frame questions can be seen as moving children from a close personal view into a broader perspective. So children at Key Stage 1 will pose questions which are personal and immediate ('my toy'). Later children will be able to ask questions about groups to which they can relate ('brothers and sisters', their 'friends', then 'children of my age'). By the end of Key Stage 2 children should generally be encouraged to develop questions about groups more distanced in time and place from themselves ('toys my parents played with' 'my grandparents' then 'toys through the ages').

2. Collecting the data

Children should be given the opportunity to suggest and then to try out ways of collecting data.

The data which they will collect might be obvious in some cases, as in an enquiry centred on the question *'What is your favourite toy?'*, but less so in others. For example, if children want to investigate ways to improve the Lost Property system in school, what will they need to find out? What kinds of information will help? In each case discussion will be necessary, to help children to come up with ideas for themselves in the first instance. Of course, these initial attempts at data collection might result in data which does not answer their question. For example, suppose the question was *'Do you play with roller skates?'*. Left to her/his own devices a child might list the names of children in the class as they are asked whether they play with roller skates or not. S/he might not, without help, see that what is also needed is a system for coding responses such as ticks/crosses or 'yes/no' labels. Just as children need help with the framing of questions, they will need help at this stage in the process. The teacher's role here will be to engage children in discussion about why their method has not worked and about how else they might do it. (*'Have you asked everyone?'* *'How do you know?'* *'Can you see who plays with roller skates and who doesn't?'*)

Another issue to be aware of is whether data would be better grouped or presented discretely. For example, if prices of toys were a factor in the investigation, the data would be better grouped in ranges (0 – 99p, £1.00 – £1.99, £2.00 – £2.99, etc.) to produce a more useful result.

During the discussions about possible methods of collecting data, the teacher's role will be to decide whether the children's proposed strategy will be a fruitful learning experience. Will they simply become disheartened and waste time collecting data which is not very useful, or not recorded in a way which will facilitate interpretation, or can the learning from this experience be built upon in deepening their understanding? It is the teacher's professional judgement which will determine the appropriate point at which to make a suggestion to the children, building on their ideas but also introducing new ones. Among the various ways of collecting data that she could suggest are questionnaires (progressing from one question with a yes or no answer to a schedule of questions around a theme), looking up information in books and taking and tabulating measures of various kinds and making and recording observations.

Progression – At Key Stage 1, it is more likely that childrens will be focusing on a fairly small range of questions, so that the data collection system in the main involves writing names or ticking them off on a list, making a tally chart and the asking of responses to single questions.

At Key Stage 2 the range of approaches should be widened as children progress into thinking about how different questions and ways of framing them might influence the kinds or response obtained. For example, if they want to find out about preferences for toys according to gender, would it be better to offer a list for respondents to select from or should the question be left quite open? They will also be able to consider in more depth the possible variables, e.g. if they hypothesise that the age of a child influences their choice of toy, then age must be incorporated into a questionnaire.

3. Representing the data

Pictorial and graphical representation is a means of mathematical communication, and children will need to explore the various forms in which the information they collect can be expressed visually. The terms used to describe the different types of graphs children are likely to meet in Key Stages 1 and 2, as well as examples of the graphs themselves, can be found in the Glossary.

The data handling computer packages that children use will present information in tabular form or graphically at the touch of a button, but we would argue that children might miss the opportunity to learn the conventions of organising and presenting data if they do not have the opportunity initially to construct their own graphs. Not that these skills are necessarily an end in themselves, nor should children spend a disproportionate amount of time colouring or decorating their graphs; but actually having to label axes, devise keys, and decide on scale might be instrumental in helping children to develop an understanding about and confidence in using and interpreting graphs, charts and diagrams.

The illustration of statistical data is progressive and the teacher's role will be to help move the child from reality to its representation in abstract form. In the early stages graphs should be made from real objects; later, pictures of objects might be used in place of the real things; and finally, symbols can be used to stand for the real objects. The children will need to meet both counting/bar charts and graphs showing relationships such as scatter diagrams.

Counting/bar charts
Key Stage 1 – The earliest graphs may arise from sorting, and/or matching. Toys

might be sorted and classified using criteria related to their properties, e.g. size, material, power, and displayed in set hoops. Children can be grouped themselves to show preferences, for example by standing in lines or sitting in hoops.

Since the above graphs are not necessarily count graphs, they can be attempted with children as pre-counting activities. When graphs based on counting are introduced the teacher will need to introduce the idea of a base line. Initially children should be helped to make a graph with three-dimensional material, such as counting cubes, bricks, or even match boxes, using the table top as a base, as shown in Figure 4.2.

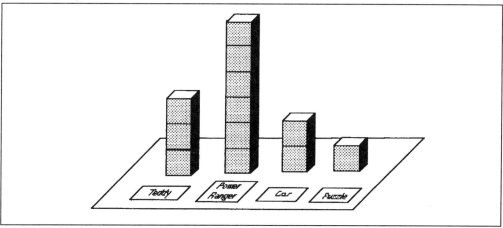

Figure 4.2 Table top display

Progression to the stage of making picture graphs will require the teacher to reinforce the idea of the base line, and help the children realise the need for identical units and the need for those units to be placed edge to edge. The teacher can prompt discussion of the need for this uniformity if different children are given different sized paper on which to draw their favourite toy. The papers can be placed in position to allow discussion. Questions about the numbers of toys represented and whether it is fair if one toy is on a smaller piece of paper than another will help to elicit children's ideas of the need for the conventions to meet the need of accurate communication, as illustrated in Figure 4.3.

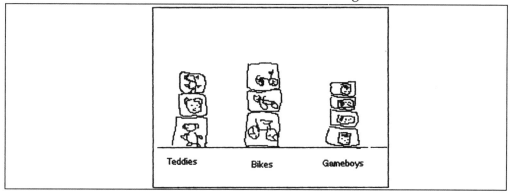

Figure 4.3 Misleading graph with different sizes of paper

In the early stages there is no need for the vertical axis to be drawn or labelled since the pictures or 'units' can be counted where numerical comparison is appropriate. However, as the size of the count increases so will the need to label the vertical axis; and, although it might be acceptable initially to label the spaces, the teacher at Key Stage 2 will need to ensure that children label the lines.

Key Stage 2 – Progression in the representation of count graphs is achieved by using a continuous strip or block to represent the total count or frequency, and by the use of scale in drawing the graph.

One method of introducing children to scale is to build a three-dimensional graph from matchboxes where the matchboxes each contain, for example, 10 counters. Children then get the idea that one unit on a scale (the matchbox) can represent several counts. Similarly children can be encouraged to draw pictures where one drawing representing multiple objects can be made (pictogram; Figure 4.4). If the symbol represents multiples of 10 children will need to discuss how to represent numbers like 87 or 23.

Bus	🚌 🚌	1 bus represents 10 children
Car	🚗 🚗	1 car represents 10 children
Walk	👣 👣 👣	1 pair of feet represents 10 children

Figure 4.4 Pictogram

A parallel development is the representation of data which involves counting rather than measuring. Children might draw around the outline of their feet, cut these out and lay them against a baseline to make comparisons of length. Further degrees of abstraction are achieved by representing the length of their feet by a paper strip. Scale can then be introduced by halving or quartering the length of the strip.

As children's understanding of the measuring units and their interrelationship develops so can the idea that the vertical axis be apportioned to represent these different units. For example, a distance of 2.5 m might be represented by a 25 cm long block on a graph. A series of such blocks would show the distances travelled by a selection of toy cars rolling down a slope.

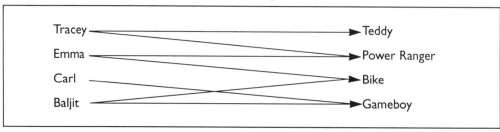

Figure 4.5 Graphs showing a relationship between two sets of data

Early in Key Stage 1 Relationships can be seen by linking data with arrows. Thus, in Figure 4.5, the arrows stand for the relationship 'has'.

Alternatively, such relationships could be represented on a two-way table (Table 4.2).

	Teddy	Power Ranger	Bike	Gameboy
Tracey	✔	✔		
Emma		✔	✔	
Carl				✔
Baljit			✔	✔

Table 4.2

Later in Key Stage 1, or early in Key Stage 2, children can mark points on a grid representing two sets of numerical data (e.g. arm span and height) to see whether there is a relationship between the two. On a floor grid or on paper each child could be represented by a named sticky dot or labelled arrows leading to the points, depending on the size of the graph. This is the beginning of work with scatter diagrams, as shown in Figure 4.6.

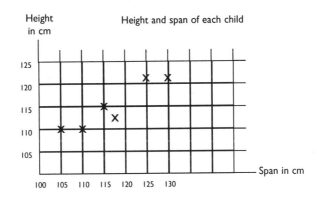

Figure 4.6 Scatter diagram

In investigating the relationship between reach and height, which is supposed to be close, a scatter diagram would show how many people have greater reach than height, how many have greater height than reach and how many have equal measurements. Body shapes can be classified into 'squares' (arm and reach the same) or 'rectangles' (arm and reach significantly different) according to the results! A correlation between the sets of data is shown by the arrangement of the points.

Both count and relationship graphs in the later stages require the children to identify and plot points on a square grid based on two number lines intersecting at right angles. This means that the teacher will need to introduce the children to the use of *ordered pairs*, or *coordinates*. The teacher will need to emphasise the convention that points are located by first finding the distance from the vertical line (i.e. along the horizontal axis) and then the distance from the horizontal line (i.e. up the vertical axis) and give the children opportunities to familiarise themselves with this notation. Of course this work links with the development of mapwork skills; and, for further reinforcement, *'Treasure Island'* maps can be drawn and directions given using co-ordinates.

Further extensions to children's graphing skills will occur when data needs to be grouped in order to show any relationship. This will require the teacher to introduce the children to the convention of describing class intervals. For example, the cost of toys be grouped in intervals £0 – £4.99, £5 – £9.99.

Although children will meet pie charts in their everyday lives and in data handling packages, displaying information in this diagrammatic form is very difficult. Since their construction is based on sectors of a circle which are proportionate to the internal angle of that circle, making pie charts is likely to be too demanding for most children in Key Stage 1 and Key Stage 2; but they are able, by using computer databases, to produce this type of representation and focus on the interpretation of the results. The key aspects of the pie chart is that it is useful in showing proportion and that the pie must make sense as a whole. In the example in Figure 4.7 the pie is a nonsense because the children in this class feature more than once and the pie shows more than 100% of the class. The block graph (Figure 4.8) is more helpful in showing the frequency of ownership of the individual toys and children will need help in deciding which type of graphic display to use for their particular purposes.

4. Interpreting data

The end result of much data handling work is the display of a graph in the classroom. However, the question of interpretation is not always fully addressed, so the teacher will need to include, in planning, time for children to be able to read and interpret their own and other graphs.

Well-drawn graphs can help us to interpret figures, but they can also be used to misrepresent them, so it is important that children learn to interpret data. They must be encouraged to 'read' a graph for the explicit information it presents if they are not to be duped by representation devices which exaggerate trends. Reading graphs can be encouraged by asking closed questions: *'How many children chose teddy as their favourite toy?' 'How many more children chose roller skates as their favourite toy than chose Gameboy?'* Children can also be asked to frame their own questions to ask each other.

When 'reading' graphs with children, the teacher will notice that language structure becomes complex; but it is important for children to hear it and to respond to it so that they develop their skills in identifying and communicating mathematical relationships.

At a deeper level children will also need to be encouraged to seek patterns and relationships which the graph might reveal, remembering, of course, that the lack of a pattern or relationship may in itself be a significant finding. Again the teacher

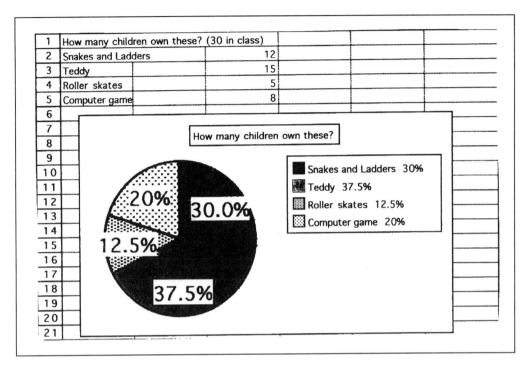

Figure 4.7 A pie chart that makes no sense

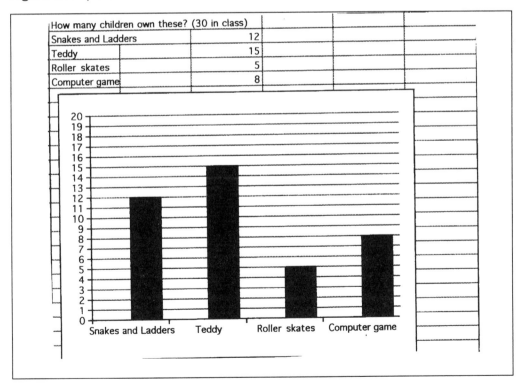

Figure 4.8 A block graph showing the same data

will probably need to lead the questioning. In doing so she will not only be helping the children to find relationships, but will also be providing a model for children to use in future situations. Comments such as, *'The metal cars went fastest down the ramp'* are beginning to lead children into looking for pattern in their findings which can then be followed up with further investigation.

A yet deeper level is achieved when children are encouraged to make deductions from the data they have collected. Deductions can be prompted by open questions from the teacher. For example, *'Why do you think the teddy bear has been a popular toy for such a long time?'* might prompt the children to make the interpretation that children like to cuddle toys.

Since the interpretation of visual representation of data is more important than the actual drawing, the teacher will need to ensure that any display of graphs is accompanied by questions which encourage children to analyse the information.

It is highly likely that in interpreting the data and making deductions more questions will be posed. This might indicate that a new problem has been posed which will require a further run through the data handling cycle, or it might be that the question raises issues about the design of the project itself. Was enough information collected? Was it the right information? Should we have found out...? In effect, the teacher is encouraging the children to evaluate their research design, a skill which will not only eventually permeate all areas of the curriculum but will help children to develop a healthy scepticism with which to interpret the vast amount of information they will receive during their lifetimes.

4.2 CASE STUDIES

In this section we will examine two case studies and show how aspects of the data handling process apply in each case. The Key Stage 1 Case study is from a Reception class and the Key Stage 2 Case Study is from a Year 5 class. The intention is that the reality of the model in action will clarify aspects of the teaching role and show what sort of evidence might support assessment of data handling experience.

Case Study at Key Stage 1

As part of the 'broad-based' topic of 'stories' in the reception class, the children's work had been planned around the story of the *Three Billy Goats Gruff*. The teacher had used the story to develop the following concepts: three, first, second, third, last, under, over. They had constructed the infamous bridge from a variety of boxes which was tall enough for the children to walk under, even if it wasn't strong enough for the children to walk over! Here is what subsequently happened.

At carpet time there was some discussion about what goats might eat. The teacher asked *'I wonder if we eat the same?'* *'Well, we don't eat grass.'* volunteered Natalie. *'Carrots!'* contributed Ade eagerly. *'Yes, I think you are right'*, replied the teacher encouragingly, only to be challenged by those children who thought that carrots were *'Yuk!'*

Pose the question

or a similarly disparaging adjective. The vocal straw poll that followed suggested that more boys than girls liked carrots. Regaining the children's attention she posed the question *'Do you think that more boys than girls like carrots?'* The children were discouraged from calling out their replies and instead were asked to think about how they might find out. Skilfully, the teacher helped the children to formulate a question and then prompted them to think about how they might collect the information to help them find an answer. Her aim was to engage the children in designing a data capture sheet.

She targeted some individuals: *'Dean, how do you think we could find out?'* *'We could ask our friends.'* *'Yes, and how would you remember how many liked or didn't like carrots?'* *'We can write it,'* replied Natalie. *'Show me how on this sheet of paper',* responded the teacher inviting the child to come up to the easel. *'You can write their names and yes and no',* volunteered Petra. The teacher accepted this response but still prompted the children to consider further. *'You could do that but it would take a long time. What if I put a line down my paper like this and put a mark here (in the left hand column) for every one who doesn't like carrots, and a mark here (right hand column) for everyone who does. Let's see if it works.'* The teacher offered the symbols of a smiley and sad face to head the columns and began to collect information from the children marking the appropriate column with a tally (Figure 4.9).

Figure 4.9 Tally chart

The children then counted the tally marks. Four children didn't like carrots and thirteen did. There was a feeling that the task had been successfully completed and indeed some children were ready to move off the carpet when the teacher intervened to prompt them to think further. *'But does this tell us whether more boys than girls like carrots?'* she quizzed.

The children decided that they only needed to find out whether a person was a boy or girl if they liked carrots. *'How can we show this on the data capture sheet?'* asked the teacher. Petra was invited to the easel and given the felt tip. She adjusted the sheet as shown in Figure 4. 10.

'I think that will work very well.' responded the teacher. *'Let's give it a try.'* She

reassured the children that they would all have a turn asking their friends whether they liked carrots, but that it would be much too confusing if they all did it at once, so some of the children would be carrying on with their work and others would come around to ask them whether they liked or disliked carrots. She 'dispatched' from the carpet area those children who were obviously at their limit of concentration. Some were directed to the sand tray, others to the role play area and another group to a construction activity. The remaining group of six children were told to get paper, to make their data capture sheet and then to collect their data. The teacher appealed to children's sense of playing at being market researchers by providing them with clipboards. She then called a group of children to work with her on a language activity whilst the 'data collectors' delighted in asking their colleagues whether they liked carrots and were even amused at asking whether they were a boy or a girl.

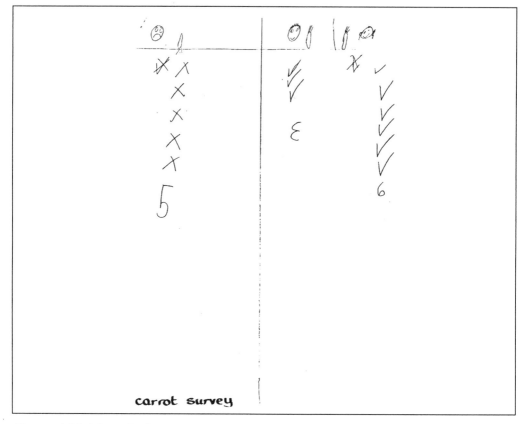

Figure 4.10 Adjusted tally

At the start of the afternoon session, after the register had been taken, the children were asked to share their findings. They brought their clipboards to the front of the group to 'show' what they had found out. The teacher had anticipated that this would give the opportunity for the children to talk to their colleagues for the purpose of describing their findings; but because there was little consensus among the researchers with respect to the number of children who liked or disliked carrots, the carpet session produced much rich discussion among the children as to why the results should be so different. *'Did anyone change their mind about liking carrots?'* asked the teacher. *'Do you think Wesley asked everyone in the class?'* As might be anticipated with such young children it transpired that some children had not been consistent in their answers and not only had Wesley not asked some children about whether they liked or disliked carrots, he had asked some twice!

Through well-constructed questioning the teacher prompted the children to think about how such difficulties might be avoided in future but resisted the temptation to 'sanitise' the children's data. The following day, she told them, they would make a graph.

The teacher chose to help the children make a pictorial representation of their findings by introducing a chart for the children to complete. They were told that in the top row they would put a picture for each child who didn't like carrots. In the next they would put a picture for each boy who liked carrots, and the bottom row a picture for each girl who liked carrots. The children continued with representing like and dislike of carrots by expression and said that they would use a picture of a carrot for children who liked carrots. They then began to translate their information into pictorial form producing graphs like the one shown in Figure 4.11. Once the teacher could see that the children had understood the task she moved her attention to another group of children who had been working on a 'maintenance' activity (working independently of the teacher).

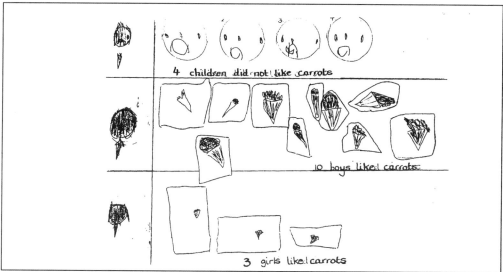

Figure 4.11 Carrot graph

When the graphs were completed the children counted their symbols to find out what their data showed, and the teacher scribed their oral contributions. All agreed that more boys than girls like carrots. *'In this class'*, cautioned the teacher, giving the children the opportunity to suggest that it might be different in another class –

but none of the children suggested testing their findings on a wider population. The teacher had earlier seized the moment and she decided not to follow up further at this point.

Case Study at Key Stage 2

During the Spring term, a Year 5 class had followed the topic of looking after themselves as part of their work in science and their personal and social education curriculum. The plan was for the children to study the Victorians in the summer term.

A spell of warm weather had sparked off debate in the media about the incidence of asthma. Since the debate focused on the issue of pollution, the teacher chose to use this to make links between the two topics.

The children watched recorded clips from regional news and were given newspaper cuttings. Without prompting they began to volunteer their own experiences with asthma. There were graphic tales from children who had asthma and those who had had asthma in the past and clearly some felt left out because they didn't have to go to the office at lunchtimes to use their inhalers!

When the discussion got to the point of sounding like the conversations overheard in the doctor's surgery, the teacher steered its focus to that of the causes of asthma. She then sat with a group to record their ideas.

Fully anticipating that the question was posed and that the children would be happy to collect data on the causes of asthma, she was surprised to find the children becoming much more interested in the question of whether asthma could be cured. Clearly, given the sample of the school population from which the data was to be collected, this investigation would not be likely to result in rich data handling experience for the children. The teacher did, however, pick up on another part of the discussion where the children were quite animated in their views about whether children can grow out of asthma. This then became the 'big' question.

Having posed the question the children needed no prompting to discuss how they would collect information. *'We can ask everyone in the school!'* *'We can do a survey.'* *'Can we do a questionnaire like when people stop you in the street?'* *'We can print out some graphs on the computer.'* The children's suggestions were received enthusiastically by the teacher and they were excited by the idea of writing questionnaire on the computer and *'doing some graphs.'*

The children had jumped straight to the stages of collecting and representing data. They needed help from the teacher to think more deeply about whom they would ask and the specific questions they would need to ask to find the answer to their main question. Suggestions from the teacher referred back to some of the earlier discussion, e.g. is there a link between what causes your asthma and whether or not you grow out of it?

Interestingly enough, several children already has some ideas about this. Jasmin thought that *'You might have asthma from car fumes when you are small because you are near the car fumes.'* Joel took this idea further drawing on some sophisticated thinking. He thought that *'You might grow out of asthma because the amount of pollution in the body is less to the size of body as you get bigger'.*

The children then settled in two groups, by choice one of girls and one of boys, to draft their questionnaires. It can be seen from their questions that the children were keen to follow their own lines of enquiry (Figure 4.12). The questionnaire was then transferred to Junior Pinpoint, a data-handling program which constructs a database from the questions posed in the questionnaire (Figure 4.13). The children were very excited by the sophistication of their published document and couldn't wait to pilot it on the other members of the class.

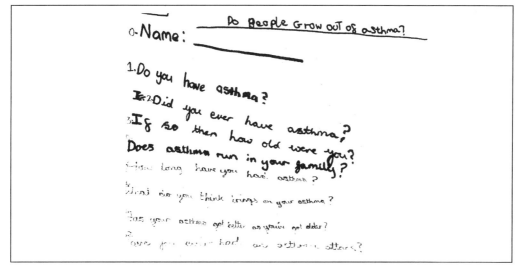

Figure 4.12 Questionnaire in children's writing

Initially, the boys had planned only to survey junior children, but during the pilot Ralph offered the hypothesis: *'If you do grow out of asthma there would be less children in Year 6 with asthma than in Red Class* (reception)'; and so that group decided to include infant children in their survey. They then evaluated their original questions with particular reference to whether they thought the younger children would be able to understand them. Similarly, the evaluation of the girls' pilot focused on whether or not the questions made sense.

Adjustments to the original questionnaire were made and the children then organised themselves to visit the classrooms to collect their data. Anna could collect information from Year 3 and 4, by administering the questionnaire to the class as a group whilst Jasmin and Rosie collected information from the reception children who would have to be interviewed. Hayley would begin work on entering the data as soon as she had a class set of completed sheets.

The children's enthusiasm and pressure of time led to the omission of a vital stage which was regretted by all later in the project. The information from the pilot survey was not entered into the database for interrogation. In other words, the questionnaire was not evaluated with reference to the scope and limitations of the data-handling program. For example, Rosie's insistence on just leaving spaces for people to fill in the causes of their asthma because *'it gives them a chance to answer for themselves'* rather than use the multiple choice option in the questionnaire design meant that this data was not easily processed by the computer.

As the children returned to the computer stations with their completed questionnaires so they began to make their entries. Since the whole school had

What is your name?	
Are you a boy or a girl?	☐ boy ☐ girl
Do you have asthma?	☐ Yes ☐ No
How long have you had asthma?	——————years
Did you ever have asthma?	☐ Yes ☐ No
If so how old were you when it started?	——————
How old were you when it stopped?	——————
Does asthma run in your family?	☐ Yes ☐ No
What do you think brings on your asthma?	———————— ———————— ———————— ————————
Have you ever had an asthma attack?	☐ Yes ☐ No
If so how old were you when you had it?	——————
Has your asthma got better as you have grown older?	☐ Yes ☐ No

Figure 4.13 Questionnaire produced in Junior Pinpoint

been surveyed there was a large number of entries to be made. Although the educational value of working with real data is evident, that of typing in so many entries can be demotivating. A compromise was reached. Each child made 10 entries at convenient times during the day, and the rest were made by the teacher and an assistant. This meant that a system had to be devised so that the children could keep track of the entries. They decided that they would need to keep a note on the hard copy of the number of the corresponding record in the database, and, since there were times when the children needed to refer back to the original documents, this proved to be a very useful precaution.

Excitement levels rose again when the data entries had been completed. The children wanted to play with the program's graphing facility. They were not so interested in the variables as the visual images they could produce! 3D Pie charts were the favourite. They clearly challenged the capabilities of the program and tested its boundaries of graphical representation by asking for a pie chart of all the names of the children in the survey, but for the teacher this was an opportunity to encourage the children to be critical of the graphs they produced (Figure 4.14).

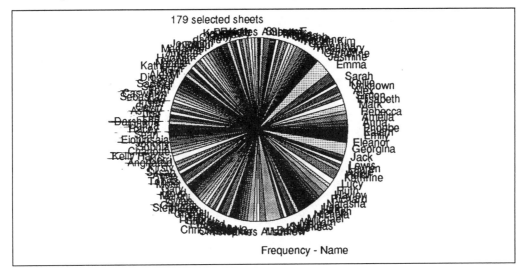

Figure 4.14 The software will produce this chart – but what use is it?

Having given the children the opportunity to explore the program, the teacher refocused the class on the question they were trying to answer. Which graphs would help to show whether children grow out of asthma?

Martin said he wanted to look at a graph of the children in school who had asthma. He produced a pie chart and found that not all children had answered this question. He then went back into the database to find those records, located the hard copy and amended the entries as appropriate. This time he produced a block graph. With the two types of graph to hand (Figure 4.15), the teacher asked which of the graphs was more useful. Martin thought that the block graph was more useful because it gave him the numbers of children with or without asthma. He was challenged by David who thought that the pie chart showed that about an eighth of the children in school have asthma. When the teacher asked whether he thought the actual numbers of people would help find the answer to the question he was adamant that it was the 'amount' not the number. The mathematical term was not readily to hand for David, but clearly he was moving towards grasping the concept of proportion.

'*But does this graph show whether children grow out of asthma?*' prompted the teacher. '*No*', replied Ralph, who was keen to test his hypothesis that if children did grow out of asthma there would be more children in reception with asthma than in Year 6.

The children now needed to interrogate the data further. Using only the records of children with asthma, the computer was asked to draw a graph of comparative ages.

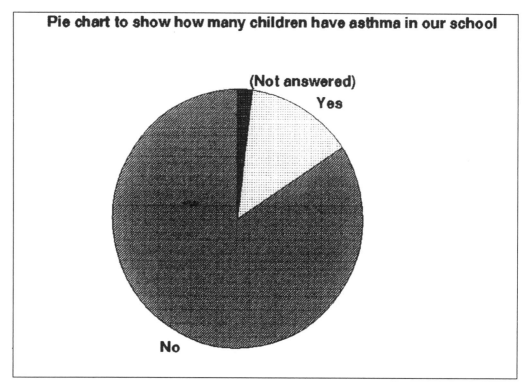

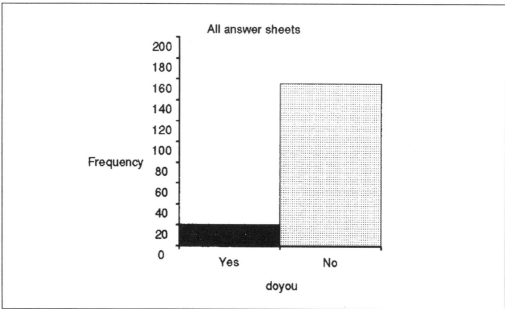

Figure 4.15 Pie (a) and bar (b) charts for interpretation

The graph shown in Figure 4.16 was drawn and gave rise to discussion about the information it gave. The children tended not to read the graph for information, but moved straight to interpretation. *'What does this graph tell me?'* the teacher asked.

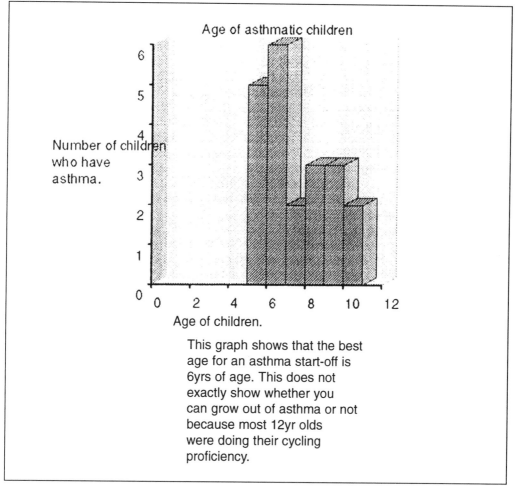

Age of asthmatic children

Number of children who have asthma.

Age of children.

This graph shows that the best age for an asthma start-off is 6yrs of age. This does not exactly show whether you can grow out of asthma or not because most 12yr olds were doing their cycling proficiency.

Figure 4.16 What does this graph show?

Martin ventured *'Six is the best age for asthma.' 'The best age Martin? What do you mean "the best age"?' 'I mean that because there are more children aged six with asthma than aged five, so six is the best start off age for asthma.'* There was some good logic behind Martin's thinking but all that he could tell from the graph was that more children in the group he surveyed had started to have asthma at age 6.

In retrospect maybe slightly more closed questioning might have prompted the children to read more of the information presented by the graph, e.g. *'How many 5 year olds have asthma?'* Further areas discussed were the lack of columns for ages 0 to 4. *'That's because everyone we asked was over five'*, came the confident reply from David. *'So are we able to say that this graph shows that children grow out of asthma?'* asked the teacher. *'Oh no!'* cried Ralph, his head clasped in his hands, *'we didn't survey all the Year 6 children. They were doing their cycling proficiency!'*

Discussion of the graphs generated further lines of enquiry. The girls were interested to know whether the incidence of asthma in a family affected the chances of having and/or growing out of it. The boys were interested to discover whether there was any difference between the number of girls growing out of asthma and the number of boys.

To produce the appropriate graphs the girls had to select the records of those children who were asthma free to discover whether they had incidence of asthma in their families. They were very interested to discover that all the 'asthma free' children came from 'asthma free' families. From this, they deduced that asthma must run in families. *'It might be different in another school'*, suggested Jasmin, obviously appreciating the danger of generalising from a sample.

First, the boys produced a pie chart of the total number of boys and girls in the survey. They then looked at the number of boys and girls who have asthma. Reading the graph posed no problem; clearly more boys than girls had asthma. 'OK' encouraged the teacher, *'but let's look back to the graph showing the number of boys in the school.' 'What conclusions can we draw if we look at the two graphs together?'* The children were being prompted to deal with some complex thinking using their knowledge of ratio and proportion. It was clear that they had the understood the significance of comparing the two graphs and they were able to make the appropriate deduction. Their difficulty was in finding the appropriate words to express their findings. *'Look'* said Joel *'This,* (Figure 4.17(a)) *shows that there are more boys than girls and this* (Figure 4.17(b)) *shows that more boys than girls have asthma so that means more boys than girls have asthma,' 'But do we need the two graphs to show us that more boys than girls have asthma?'* There were sighs of frustration. *'If you are a boy you are more likely to have asthma,'* offered David. Rosie had become interested in the boys problem at this point. *'Putting it all together,'* she ventured, *'it means that the fraction of boys surveyed who had asthma was larger than the fraction of girls that had asthma. So, in our survey, it seems as though boys have more chance of getting asthma'*, Ralph then found the word he was looking for: *'If you are a boy, you are more vulnerable to asthma'*, he concluded with an air of satisfaction.

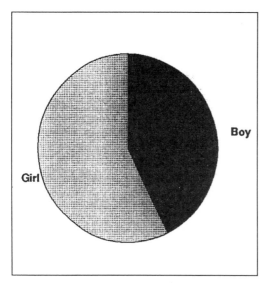 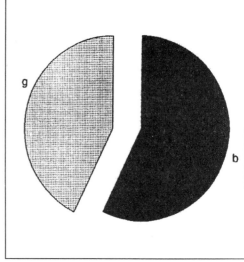

Figure 4.17 What conclusions can be drawn from these graphs?

The children had deviated somewhat from their original question *'Do you grow out of asthma?'*, and yet the questions that were arising in discussion were all legitimately part of the overarching question. When sharing their findings, they were critical of the validity of their method of data collection. *'Really'*, said Martin, *'I would, personally, question children who have asthma now and those who have had it. I would need to find out whether they had had medicines or special diets, for example.'* *'Well, to make it a fair test,'* suggested Rosie, *'you would need to find some young children and ask them about their asthma over several years.'* Both suggestions would clearly help the children to find the answer to their problem but would be impractical in a school.

4.3 USING AND APPLYING IN THE CONTEXT OF DATA HANDLING

The attainment target 'Using and Applying Mathematics' is not a separate area of mathematics but an approach to the teaching of mathematics which is applied in each of the content areas. The Data Handling case studies will now be evaluated to see how they address the criteria of 'Using and Applying'.

The **strands** in Using and Applying Mathematics are:

- making and monitoring decisions to solve problems
- developing mathematical language and communication
- developing mathematical reasoning

(DFE, 1995)

Making and monitoring decisions to solve problems

In the Key Stage 1 case study, the children were asked to think about how they would go about collecting the data and how they would keep track of the information they were gathering. The children *decided* that they needed a data capture sheet which showed whether they liked or disliked carrots and whether they were a boy or a girl.

When they had asked some children they realised that they could not tell how many ticks were boys and how many were girls.They had therefore not identified the key factors they needed to answer their question *(monitoring decisions)*. The teacher talked about this with the children and they adjusted their data capture sheet so that they could find out what they wanted. Because the teacher allowed the children to go with that data sheet they were able to discover the limitations of their initial decision.

In the Key Stage 2 case study the children were encouraged and were able to plan so that they would collect data systematically. They were able to decide at the outset how they would obtain information related to the sex of respondent, for example. They were expected to more readily identify the key factors. This does not mean that everything ran smoothly, and, indeed, there was still a great deal of revision, through *monitoring*, as they proceeded.

Developing mathematical language and communication

In the Key Stage 1 case study the teacher gave the opportunity for children to *explain* to their peers what they had found out and for others to *ask questions*. The presentation of results was a pictorial *representation*, with a written caption (scribed by the teacher, in this case).

Giving children the opportunity to *explain* why they chose a particular way of collecting and representing their data and *sharing their findings* will help develop their mathematical language and skills of communication.

In the Key Stage 2 case study children used a wider range of representations of their findings and were expected to make decisions about presenting information and results in the most appropriate way. They were being taught how to articulate reasons for their choices.

Developing mathematical reasoning

At both the Key Stages mathematical reasoning was developed by asking children to *interpret* their results to search for pattern and relationships and to *make related predictions*.

Some children in the the Key Stage 1 case study *interpreted* their results in the statement *'Lots of boys like carrots'*. The teacher helped them to refine the implicit comparison by asking, *'So, do more boys than girls like carrots?'* Children might be prompted to develop predictions through interest in what other classes might feel about eating carrots, e.g. *'I wonder whether lots of boys like carrots in Miss A's Class?'* This can then be the starting point for the next turn around the data handling cycle.

At Key Stage 2 the children were expected to be more critical and less egocentric in their interpretation of results of data collection. They were expected to be more sophisticated in their analysis and to be able to *make deductions* beyond the immediately obvious. The key to this is in presenting a rich and relevant context in which we know that children will need to learn about and use mathematical knowledge, skills and understanding.There will be possibilities to respond in different ways according to their confidence and competence, and there will be challenge built in to take their thinking further. As teachers we need to consider the type of questions we ask to stimulate thinking or to find out what sense children are making of the task.

We consider next some points in relation to the role of computer databases in children's data handling.

The use of computer databases

Mention is made of the use of databases in the National Curriculum in both Key Stages 1 and 2. In our Key Stage 2 case study, the database played an important part. It should be noted that the Key Stage 1 work could also have incorporated the use of a database, but did not in this instance.

The National Curriculum Programmes of Study state:

At Key Stage1 – Number 'Pupils should be given opportunities to use computer software, including a database.' (1. f.)

At Key Stage 2 – Handling Data 'Pupils should be given opportunities to use computers as a source of interesting data, and as a tool for representing data.' (1. c.)

'Pupils should be taught to collect and represent discrete data...; interpret a wider range of graphs and diagrams that represent data, including pie charts, using a computer where appropriate.' (2. b.)

Databases allow children to handle data efficiently and to have opportunities to interpret a wider range of representations than they could produce themselves. For example, at both Key Stages, children can produce pie charts from data they have put into the database, without having to know how to construct the chart for themselves. They are then freed to concentrate on the more advanced thinking involved in interpretation and deduction.

However, the same key points relate to the use of computer databases as to data handling in general: that is, to what extent do databases help children in posing questions, setting up hypotheses and interpreting results? Databases can be used to allow children access to real data, such as census data, to explore and interrogate. Comparing residents in a local street now with the past can be aided by this, for example. However, because children at the primary stage will in the main be collecting and storing and retrieving their own data, the focus of this section will be on this procedure.

Different types of database

Simple counts, e.g. Counter (Black Cat)

teddies	6
dolls	10
bikes	4
computer game	5
board game	2

Figure 4.18 Toys table

This type allows straightforward inputting of data, such as preferred toy (choice from a list) or likes/dislikes Gameboy (yes/no) (Figure 4.18). Results appear in a simple chart.

Using a database of this type, children can produce various graphs and charts showing their results. They can be encouraged to compare the different representations and write statements about what results show (Figure 4.19).

In this case children were asked to select the toy they liked best (one response only) and the pie, therefore, actually represents the number of children in the class.

Tree/sorting databases, e.g. Idelta (ILECC) or Branch (NCET)

This type depends on the logical asking and answering of questions to sort one item of data from another. In a database for 2D shapes, for example, a question to

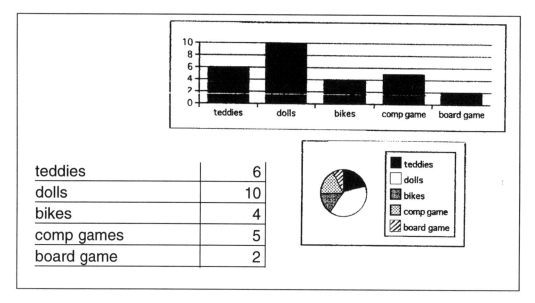

teddies | 6
dolls | 10
bikes | 4
comp games | 5
board game | 2

Figure 4.19 Block and pie charts produced from database

distinguish a triangle from a square might be 'Does it have 4 sides?'. Children need to know about the subject they are addressing in order to frame questions in setting up the database. They will also develop their classification skills as they move from questions which have a range of possible answers (how many sides does it have?) to ones that can be answered 'yes' or 'no' (does it have three sides?). Once a store of shapes has been set up, other children can interrogate the database by answering, in turn, the questions offered in the search for the shape they are thinking of. If that is not found the program requests a new question to distinguish it from the last object offered (see 'Trees' in the Glossary). Children are developing logical thinking here in eliminating other possibilities in the search for a particular shape and experience in defining key discriminatory characteristics.

Through the search and addition of questions children are responding to questions from information they have gathered and are framing new questions based on their research. A development in thinking with this type of database is to refine the sequence of questioning to identify the object in an economical number of moves – can you find your shape with three questions?

The representation of the tree can be reinforced by making a physical representation of a tree using sticks (rulers) to link the objects being sorted on table tops or the floor. Pictorial representation can be made by drawing lines between objects on large sheets of paper. Labels for questions/choices would also be required (Figure 4.20).

Index card types, e.g. Clipboard (Black Cat) or Junior Pinpoint (Longman Logotron) used in our Key Stage 2 case study

This type allows the comparing of data and searches for relationships. Information is put into 'files' which can be thought of as index cards (Figure 4.21).

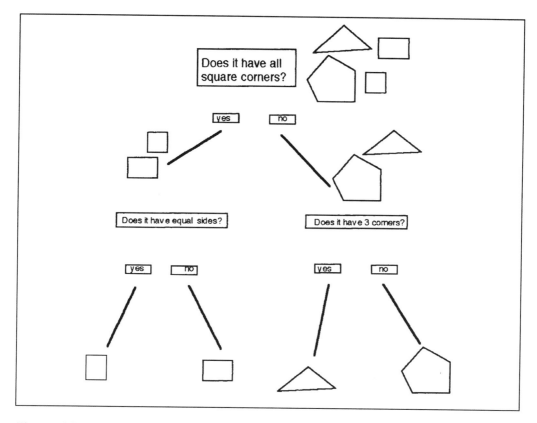

Figure 4.20 Tree diagram of sort shapes

Field names are selected by the user as you set up the database e.g. name, age or other personal details. If a card referred to a toy it could have material, power etc. as fieldnames.

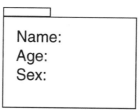

Name:
Age:
Sex:

Figure 4.21

In these programs, children need help to realise when they are operating on a subset of the data. They also need help on how to obtain the data showing the relationship they require, e.g. 'and' and 'or'. The word 'and' is used to narrow the search. This would produce only girls who like bikes for 'girls and bikes'. The 'or' ('girls or bikes') , on the other hand, produces girls who like bikes, girls who don't like bikes *and* boys who like bikes. Children will need to experiment with the data to develop understanding of the structure (Figure 4.22).

Girls OR Bikes

The circle 'girls' represents all the girls who took part in the survey and the circle 'bikes' represents everyone who said 'yes' when they were asked if they liked bikes.

Searching the database for Girls OR Bikes widens the search and gives all the categories shown in the diagram, that is anyone who is a girl OR likes bikes.

To find the answer to the question 'How many girls like bikes?', the search needed is 'Girls AND bikes', to be included in this search you have to be a girl AND like bikes.

Girls AND Bikes

Figure 4.22 OR and AND

Spreadsheets (e.g. EXCEL, Applemac's ClarisWorks)

The Spreadsheet is a datahandling facility which has the benefits of showing all the data at once and performing calculations on it. It can produce a range of graphical representations (e.g. barchart, pie chart) quickly and allows children to make comparisons of the different graphical representations easily. If a number entered in a cell is changed, the graph which is based on the spreadsheet is automatically adjusted (Figure 4.23).

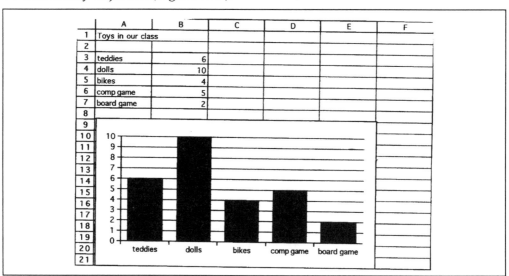

Figure 4.23 Graphical display on a spreadsheet

General points in making up a database

This section has introduced different types of database, though each commercially produced program has its own features. A selection is listed at the end of the chapter. Children at both Key Stages 1 and 2 need the experience of putting data into a database and producing representations of results to interpret. In this way they will become more confident in understanding the structure of the database, for example, whether it is an 'index card' type or tree sorting type. It is also valuable at some point to model these with written and/or physical representations to allow a more considered approach to understanding structures. The speed of the computer allows efficient sorting and the production of graphs and so on, but this very characteristic can mask the process by which these outcomes are achieved, and there are points where children can probably gain from a 'slowing down'.

For example, children can sort real objects on to charts like those produced by the programs by using floor grids. Large grid plastic-coated table-cloth fabric is available from department stores; or the teacher can draw up grids on paper or on the playground depending on what size of square is required. Once the children have placed objects or name cards or number cards to make a chart, the information could be transferred on to the database so that children might have a better understanding of what the computer is doing.

This procedure can also be applied to tree-type databases. Metre rules could be used for the branches on the classroom floor or playground, with objects and cards for questions and 'yes/no' choices, as detailed in the sorting program section above.

Key points to remember when children are using the computer

When it comes to using the computer:

- All children should have a turn at entering data in building up the database. However, it can be extremely time consuming to enter all data in this way. Classroom help (ancillaries or parents) could be brought in here so that children are not demotivated by the size of the task.
- When children are having their turn, they should be encouraged to help each other so that their understanding is reinforced by explaining to someone else.
- The teacher needs to get to know the program well to avoid the frustrations children might have in losing data if they are not confident and the teacher is not aware how to retrieve mistakes.
- The teacher needs to find out how to make alterations or add information once a file is set up.
- Data should be saved at regular intervals onto disk particularly if large quantities of data are involved.
- Inaccurate typing or inconsistent use of headings (e.g. 'dog'/'dogs' used interchangeably) can have unintended results. In the index-type database where children might type in 'dog' for some children and 'dogs' for others, two columns will be produced on a block graph, one labelled 'dog' and the other labelled 'dogs'. This can be a point for discussion, but can be frustrating. The teacher needs to find out about these effects through familiarisation with the program and so pre-empt the problem.

● The manual should be kept near to hand!

Activities

There are many different contexts in which data handling can be used and we can only give a flavour of the kinds of questions which might prove fruitful for investigation. In line with earlier comments, children will gain from handling data close to them, and our experience tells us that motivation is encouraged if children genuinely have an interest or issue to pursue. This means that the teacher's role should be to identify starting points which will stimulate the particular children in the class, and note questions arising from planned work. The examples to follow should give a general guidance for types of question and helpful resources.

Having stressed the need to take starting points close to the children, we feel we need to say something about topics which require sensitivity because they are too personal and might cause upset or embarrassment. You need to consider in advance, where possible, what these might be and how to deal with them. For instance, asking children to compare weight with others might cause more unease than asking them to compare their own height and foot lengths to look for a proportional relationship (Is it true that your feet fit about 6 times into your height?). Differences between children (e.g. cultural background) can be dealt with positively if the climate in the classroom is conducive to open discussion, with the *teacher as chairperson*. An example of this from a Year 5 class was where one child suggested skin colour as a category on the class's 'Ourselves' database. The teacher knew the class well and felt able to open this up for discussion. Some children did not at first agree with its inclusion but the class was encouraged to debate the pros and cons. Eventually they came to an agreement that it would be included but children could decide on their own preferred self-description. Of course, as we have said, data handling can be used to examine issues, which might be controversial, such as a children choosing to investigate dominance of the play-ground by football. In these ways children can begin to see how they can support a particular viewpoint with data and how data can be used (or abused) to show different viewpoints. The teacher's role is to consider issues of sensitivity during planning for work with children and to make professional educational judgements about the best way to handle them in the particular context. One condition, which might have an influence, for example, is how well s/he knows the class.

Examples for Key Stage 1

Starter questions – problems, maths and other curriculum areas

● *Making decisions about classroom issues and areas:*
  – What story shall we read?
  – How shall we organise the books?
  – How can we make using the computer fair?
  – How many children are having dinner/milk today?

- *Maths:*
  - Which number comes up most often when we roll the dice?
  - Which box holds the most?
  - What goes in my set (sorting/logic e.g. with shapes)
- *Science:*
  - Which ball is the bounciest?
  - Which car goes fastest down the ramp
  - Where did we find most minibeasts in the school grounds?

Resources

Apparatus helpful in creating representations:
- Set rings/string/ropes/hoops – table top or children in hoops.
- Abacuses (open at the top) to make physical block graphs.
- Unifix or other cubes.
- Grids of various sizes, some reusable e.g. fabric with squares large enough to contain objects such as fruit. Some will have only two columns.
- Reusable items to use as objects/symbols on graphs:
  - small photos of children
  - name cards
  - matchboxes with children's names.

Examples for Key Stage 2

- *Making decisions about classroom issues and areas:*
  - Lost property.
  - Charts to show use or classroom areas/resources e.g. rota for the computer.
  - What is the probability that the weather will be fine on Sports Day?
- *Issues dear to children's hearts:*
  - What is the average pocket money in this class?
  - Is my bedtime reasonable?
- *Other curriculum areas:*
  - What worked best in attracting particular birds to our bird table?
  - Which is the best waterproofing material?
  - What was the most common occupation of the people living in our street 100 years ago?

4.4 PROBABILITY

Probability is not explicitly required in the National Curriculum at Key Stage 1, but there is much experience at this stage which can be seen as a foundation for later ideas as well as a worthwhile experience in its own right.

Probability in society

Many of the decisions we make in life contain a level of uncertainty. To make informed judgements we need to have some understanding of probability. As adults, our decisions are often informed by our experience and knowledge of a situation. For example, if we are planning a barbecue, we may have a back-up plan for the eventuality of bad weather. Children do not have such a repertoire of knowledge to draw on, and so may make decisions based on intuition. Of course, adults also use intuition, and the problem with this approach is that decisions based on it are often wrong!

Examples of intuitive reasoning are:

'When I go to the supermarket the other queues always move faster than mine.'

'It isn't fair to have to get a six to start a game because it's harder to get a six.'

Young children are also likely to explain events in relation to themselves, for example, *'I like that number'* or *'That number likes me'*.

Early ideas of probability usually centre on discussions about the likelihoods of different events happening in stories or in the child's experience. Here, prediction is involved in thought about appropriate possible outcomes, for example, *'What do you think will happen next in the story?' 'Do you think Jenny will meet a dragon in the street?'*

A simple activity which can be set up to develop these processes (as well as to sharpen observation before an outing) is to ask children about what they expect to see *'on your way home tonight'*, *'when we go to the park tomorrow'*, *'when we visit the farm next week'* or *'on our outing at the end of term'*. What kind of ideas do children have about what they are *likely* to see? (*'What will we definitely see?' 'What won't we see'*, *'What might we see?'*)

Again, in discussion about everyday life, children could be asked what events they see as certain or unlikely? (*'I'll definitely get sweets tonight because we go to Sainsbury's every Thursday' 'I'll never see an elephant in school!'*). Quite a lot of fun and imagination can be had in these discussions as children predict events and discuss possibilities in real life and in fantasy.

Another aspect of prediction is the role of *chance*, as in some games. Dice throwing or card selection, for example, could be the subject of debate. It is interesting to ask whether children (and adults) take losing very much to heart because they do not fully understand the role of chance and feel they have more control over events than they actually do. Games of chance (Snakes and Ladders) can be contrasted with games including an element of decision making (as in Monopoly), and children can design and make games which incorporate chance or strategy aspects. They will be aware of competitions such as at the school fair, raffles or the National Lottery and will be able to discuss their understanding of what you have to do to win.

At Key Stage 2 – Probability is introduced in the Handling Data section of the National Curriculum. Here, further development of ideas of fairness, certainty, likelihood and terms such as 'probable', 'equally likely' will be refined. Children will be introduced to the concept of a 'probability scale' by ordering terms such as 'unlikely', 'possible', 'probable' and 'definite' and thinking of events to match the point on the scale. This experience should help children to move more smoothly on to the numerical scale, where absolute certainty is denoted by 1 (or 100%) and absolute impossibility by 0. In between positions can be labelled as percentages, vulgar fractions or decimal fractions (e.g. 'evens' would be 50% or 5/10 or 0.5).

The other main aspect of prediction is estimation. Activities here could involve conducting experiments to estimate (e.g. rolls of dice) or learning about situations where outcomes are equally likely (e.g. rolling a number 1–6 on a die).

Activities

Key Stage 1

1. Preparing for an outing to the park, ask children to contribute to lists:
- We will see....
- We might see....
- We won't see....

Encourage children to give reasons for their choices and you can make assessments of their reasoning.

On return from the park, compare observations with predictions. Ask questions such as, *'Why didn't we see many leaves?'* or *'How many things did we guess right?'*

2. Discussions about luck and games

(a) Ask children about luck, 'When you play games, are you lucky?' Probe to find out what children think makes them lucky. What do they think it means to be lucky?

(b) Observe children playing games with dice. What sort of comment do they make about the number they want? For example, one 6 year old when asked whether it's hard to get six, said, *'It's not hard for me...well sometimes it's hard. When I get bigger I think I will throw it better...(but it's broken now so I can't play it any more!)'*. Children can develop some ideas of chance by experiencing different types of game, some based on chance and some with strategy.

(c) Stories which can be used to discuss ideas of likelihood, what will happen next:
- *Anno's Hat Tricks*. Mitsumasa Anno, Bodley Head.
- *The Shopping Basket*. John Burningham, Picture Lions.
- *Time to Get Out of the Bath, Shirley*. John Burningham, Picture Lions.
- *The Tiny Seed*. Eric Carle, Hodder & Stoughton.
- *Dear Zoo*. Rod Campbell, Picture Puffin.
- *How Many Bugs in a Box?* David Carter, Orchard Books.
- *Princess Smartypants*. Babette Cole, Picture Lions.
- *Rosie's Walk*. Pat Hutchins, Bodley Head.
- *The Doorbell Rang*. Pat Hutchins, Picture Puffin.

- *Clotilda's Magic*. Jack Kent, Hippo Books.
- *There's No Such Thing as a Dragon*. Jack Kent, Blackie.
- *The Tiger Who Came to Tea*. Judith Kerr, Collins.
- *Not Now Bernard*. David McKee, Sparrow Books.
- *On the Way Home*. Jill Murphy, Macmillan.
- *On Friday Something Funny Happened*. John Prater, Picture Puffin.
- *Alexander and the Terrible, No Good, Very Bad Day*. Judith Viorst, Angus & Robertson.

Key Stage 2

1. Find the Fairer Game (from NCTM, 1981)
There are actually two games, based on scoring odd and even numbers with dice. Both need two people, two dice (numbered 1 to 6), paper and pen for recording and a watch or timer. For each game play three rounds.

One person claims 'odd' results and the other 'even'. Time each round equally, say 2 or 3 minutes.

First game – Roll the dice and find the difference between the two numbers. If the result is odd, the 'odd' person gets a point. If it is even, the 'even' person scores. Continue for the allotted time and compare results (count 0 as even). What do you notice about them?

Second game – Play as the first but this time multiply the two numbers and record as before.

The winner in each game is the person with more points.

Questions – Which is the fairer game and why? Children can be asked to make a table of results to help see what is going on.

2. Ordering events according to likelihood, leading to the idea of a scale
This can be done by suspending cards on a length of string or lining them up across a table top. It is some times helpful to make up some for children to use at first and then get them to make up their own.

It will rain tomorrow	An elephant will walk past the school	I will win the Lottery	I will come to school tomorrow

These cards can be ordered, after discussion between children, by the degree of likelihood. The discussion will encourage children to give reasons for choices and the task requires agreement if done as a group. A scale can be introduced by first using labels such as 'certain', 'possible' and 'impossible'. Refinements can be made and more categories created – 'Highly Likely', 'Likely', 'Unlikely' and 'Highly Unlikely'. Then numerical scales can be introduced – 0 for impossible and 1 for certain. As ideas are refined, subdivisions will be needed and conventions of 'half' or 50% or 0.5 for even chance can be added to 100% or 1 for 'certain'. Further subdivisions will be necessary as children discuss the relative likelihood of various events (see Glossary).

Glossary

This section is intended as a reference for teachers and many of the terms mentioned do not need to be used directly with children. They include terms used in the National Curriculum and are mainly to inform teacher planning.

Attribute (also property): A quality, not numerical, possessed by an object or subject, e.g. soft, battery operated, round, straight.

Average: We use the idea of an average when we present complicated situations in a few words or figures. An average is in some sense typical of the whole set of scores or measurements it represents. At Key Stage 2 children should understand and use the ideas of **mean, median** and **mode** (see under each of these below).

Block graph: There are two types of block graph: one where the columns touch (Figure 4.24, also referred to as a Bar Chart) and the other where there are spaces between the columns (Figure 4.25). Touching columns are used to represent continuous data and separate bars to represent discrete data.

Carroll diagram: A representation using two different criteria (Figure 4.26). This is named after Lewis Carroll.

Charts/tables: Large sets of data can be recorded in a way which makes the data more accessible (Figure 4.27).

Class interval: Often a set of data is too varied for direct tabulation and representation to be useful, so it is more convenient to subdivide the data into classes. The class interval represents the range in any one class.

Cost of toys favourite toys in £	No. of toys	Total
0 – 4.99	////	4
5 – 9.99	///	3
10.00 – 14.99	///	3

Continuous data (and discrete data): Consider a running race. The number of runners taking part is discrete data, expressed in whole numbers (4, 6, 10... contestants). It wouldn't make sense to talk about 1.5 runners. The time in which they complete the race is continuous data, points along a range (47 secs, 47.5 secs, 50.8 secs...). Discrete data should be represented by non-touching bars on a block graph and continuous data should have touching bars. Continuous data is usually grouped e.g. in the race example 45 – 47.59 secs, 48 – 50.59 secs...

Data collection sheet: A table, chart, or even questionnaire, designed for organising the collection of data.

Discrete data: (See Continuous Data above)

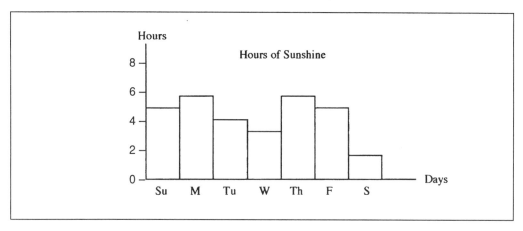

Figure 4.24 Bar chart (From National Curriculum, 1991)

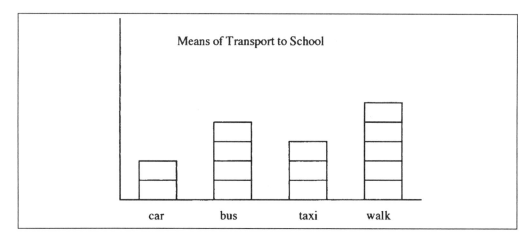

Figure 4.25 Block graph (From National Curriculum)

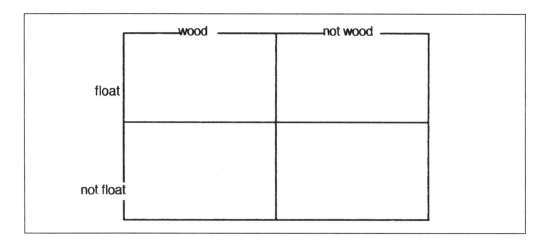

Figure 4.26 Carroll diagram

Darren	bike
Tracey	roller skates
Emma	doll
Carl	Power Ranger
Andrea	Power Ranger
Ali	bike
Satvi	roller skates
Julie	Barbie
David	Gameboy
Rebecca	Gameboy
Sean	Gameboy
Charlotte	bike
Lee	bike
Scott	Power Ranger

Becomes

bikes	dolls	r.skates	g.boy	p.rangers
Darren	Emma	Tracey	David	Carl
Ali	Julie		Rebecca	Andrea
Charlotte		Sean	Scott	
Lee				

Figure 4.27 List/table

Event: A mathematical term to describe a situation which may have more than one outcome, e.g. in rolling a die numbered 1 to 6 there are six possible outcomes of the event of rolling the die.

Experimental probability: The results obtained from an experiment or survey, e.g. there is a theoretical probability of scoring 25 heads and 25 tails from 50 tosses of a coin, but the actual outcomes may be very different, particularly for a small sample.

Frequency diagram: The generic name for pictorial representation of relative frequencies, e.g. on a graph for travel to school data recorded would show how many times children came to school on particular forms of transport.

Frequency table: Large sets of data may be shown more simply in a table recording the number of times (frequency) each value occurs.

Frequency table for heights in a Year 3 class (from NCC, 1992:G2.7)

92	110	87	87	83
87	91	93	89	86
115	90	98	119	108
111	109	81	90	119
100	110	88	106	101

This data could then be grouped, e.g. 81–90 cm and frequency graphed from the figures following.

Class	Frequency
81–90 cm	9
91–100 cm	5
101–110 cm	6

Grouped data: Data which is grouped into **classes**, as in the heights in the **frequency diagram** entry above. The group becomes the **class interval**. This usually applies to continuous data. It may be convenient to group **discrete data**, e.g. 0–4 seeds, 5–9 seeds, 11–14 seeds, 15–19 seeds, etc.

Line graphs: A line graph is used when representing two sets of continuous data. Remember each point on the line/curve must be meaningful, e.g. a graph to convert temperatures from Fahrenheit to Centigrade. Each point is meaningful and the line joining them shows a proportionate increase.

Mean: The mean, sometimes referred to as the arithmetic mean, is found by 'levelling out' the values. For example, the mean value tells us how much time each child would spend playing with their toys if they each played with them for the same amount of time.

Time in minutes: 10,10,10, 15,15,30,30,30,30,30,60,60,60,60,120

$$\text{Arithmetic Mean} = \frac{10+10+10+15+15+30+30+30+30+30+60+60+60+60+120}{15}$$

$$= 38 \text{ minutes}$$

Median: The median is the element which occupies the central position. In a survey to discover how much time children spent playing with their favourite toys, the median would be found by arranging the times in order of magnitude, taking account of each score, and finding the value which occupies the central position.

Time in minutes: 10,10,10, 15,15,30,30,<u>30</u>,30,30,60,60,60,60,120

Median value: 30 minutes

Where there is an even number of values the median value need not be one of the amounts.

Time in minutes: 10,10,10,10, 15,15,30,<u>30,40</u>,40,40,60,60,60,60,120

Median value $\frac{30+40}{2}$ = 35 mins

Mode: The mode is the element that occurs most frequently in a set of data. In a class survey of times children spend playing with their favourite toys which showed the following set of scores:

Time in minutes: 10,10,10, 15,15,<u>30,30,30,30,30</u>,60,60,60,60,120

The modal value is 30 minutes

Although the mode is a useful average it is important to note that it does not take account of the other values and and there may be more than one modal value.

Outcome: The result of an event. There are six possible outcomes to the event of rolling a die numbered 1 to 6.

Pictograms: A graph using repetitions of the same symbol to show the size of the variable (see Figure 4.4, page 138).

Pie chart: This type of graph is particularly useful to show how a whole is made up from its parts. It is probably more difficult to construct than to interpret. Computer database packages can allow young children to produce data in this form without the need to deal with its construction. (See references to pie charts in earlier parts of the chapter, including the Key Stage 2 case study.)

Probability scale: The probability of an event occurring is a measure of how likely it is to occur. Events can be categorised on a continuum between impossible and certain, on a scale from 0 to 1:

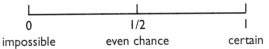

Range: The spread of results between the smallest and the largest value.

Scattergraph: A scattergraph is used to show whether there is any relation between two variables (see Figure 4.6, page 139).

Tallying: A tally is made by recording a series of single strokes. Usually every fifth stroke is a bar to the other four for easy counting.

Theoretical probability: A description of the probability that an event will occur based on a knowledge of *equally likely* outcomes. The theoretical probability of picking an ace from a pack of playing cards is 4/52.

Venn diagram: This is a pictorial representation (Figure 4.28) from the sorting of data using two or more attributes. The attributes represented by the circles are 'triangles' and 'shapes with a right angle'. The section in the overlap between the two sets contains shapes which have both attributes – triangularity and right-angled corners.

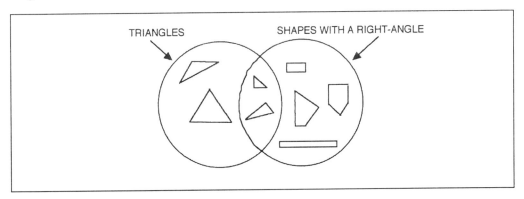

Figure 4.28 Venn diagram

Section 5: Planning, Assessment and Classroom Organisation

5.1 PLANNING AND ASSESSMENT

Time spent on maths in a typical week

The guidance from SCAA (1995b) suggests that the equivalent of 1 hour a day should be spent on mathematics. In formulating their policy for the curriculum, schools will have made decisions as to how this time should be distributed over the week, and over the year. In planning for maths the teacher can make best use of time by identifying all the opportunities for teaching in different contexts, for instance cross-curricular work, maths focused work and short whole-class sessions. Even if the school operates a thematic approach, it is usual for some maths to be taught separately because some aspects, such as mental maths, require frequent practice.

In the preschool context, maths may be planned as an area of experience, mainly addressed in particular aspects of the nursery provision, such as block-play or group singing times. It may also be planned as a result of observation of individual children's needs and interests, such as an interest in big numbers.

In a typical week a teacher could identify several different contexts for maths teaching and we will now look at these.

Cross-curricular work – planned for two or more subject areas

Included in planning for another curriculum area or broad activity can be planning for mathematical work as well. For example, if children are designing and making, comparing and measurement are needed in the process of achieving the design aim and these skills might usefully be anticipated and taught in preparation. Some maths may be taught as a result of a problem arising in the context. For instance, in the case study on packaging in Section 3.4, the teachers made use of the opportunity for children to explore equivalent ways of expressing weights of objects, involving decimals and place value.

Maths focused work – time set aside mainly, but not exclusively, for work on mathematics

These sessions might be regularly timetabled (perhaps at the same time each day) and involve work from a published scheme. Or there might be a maths investigation workshop with all the children working from the same starting point. Different outcomes will be anticipated by the teacher, based on her knowledge and observation of the children, as in the How Many Ways activity (Activity 4) on page 88. Or children might be divided into groups working on different aspects of the same mathematical theme, for example carrying out a variety of activities on reflective symmetry, with some groups using mirrors, some cutting paper and some printing or painting. The advantage in having these types of sessions is that the teacher can focus her attention more effectively on mathematics without having also to address other curriculum areas, and that the class can all be brought together to discuss maths at the end of the session.

Less formal contexts – anticipating opportunities to work on mathematics

Maths can arise unplanned in children's work. If young children are engaged in role play in the Home Corner, for example, counting might be used in laying the table. With older children, work on number might arise in calculating how long ago something happened in history. Sometimes these will be taken up at the time by the teacher and sometimes they will alert her to experiences she needs to plan to address a lack of understanding or to extend thinking. There will also often be short periods of time when the teacher has 5 or 10 minutes to spare when, for instance, short quizzes or guessing games can be used, which will add to the children's experiences of maths, e.g. 'I'm thinking of a number...' Children can ask questions and the teacher will only respond 'yes' or 'no'. Through successive questions children can try to work out the number. For more ideas see 'Maths on the Mat' under Groupings (see page 183)

Nursery/early years

A useful starting point for this stage of education is identifying the mathematical potential in existing provision. One aspect of maths may permeate a range of areas. For instance children might not learn about volume and capacity only at the sand and water trays. There will be other contexts for addressing capacity such as in pouring 'cups of tea' in the Home Corner – *'How many cups can we get from this tea pot?'* – or in real contexts like 'juice time' sharing juice between children. The water tray, in turn, can also be the site of other aspects of maths, e.g. if children are testing how many puffs of breath send boats across the water, counting is involved. The teacher can observe and encourage the child in this context. *'Which one was best?'* *'How many puffs did you do?'*

The teacher's planning and interaction with the children is crucial, for instance a judicious choice of containers, will encourage discussion about the relative capacities because tall, thin containers and wide flat ones can all hold the same.

Counting books and stories such as *The Great Big Enormous Turnip* can encourage children to tackle number in a context. Children can be asked to predict how many people there will be next. Enactment can make this even more memorable. It is important that stories like this are chosen to allow children to encounter numbers beyond three.

Board games with simple tracks and dice are good practice for counting and may have been experienced at home. The Shopping Game described in the case study in Section 2.2 is an example of a different sort of game which also gives opportunities for counting and prediction as well as shopping role play and turn taking.

Everyday contexts in the nursery can be used to give maths a real purpose, e.g. a teacher organising a group of children for cooking might ask: *'Can you get aprons for these children?'* Observing a child's response to this can be informative – does the child grab an armful, match or count to do this? There are also many opportunities in the organisation of the day, such as tidying blocks away and making sure they fit the right way in the box (shape, space and measures), sorting objects into the right places (sorting and classifying). Children can see whether they have all the pieces needed for a game (e.g. for four children to play the Insey Winsey Spider Game (Orchard Toys) there need to be four spiders) or put pieces away in relation to numbers on tins or boxes. Signs such as *'4 children may play with the sand'* are also good reference points for children in learning about number and numerals. The discussion with the teacher in these contexts will help children to articulate their ideas and allow assessment of understanding.

Planning and assessment

It is usually considered that planning and assessment follow the cycle in Figure 5.1. We would suggest, however, that the activities of planning, teaching, assessing and evaluating are not separate and sequential in practice. Assessment needs to be built in at the planning stage, so that the teacher knows what, how and when to assess. For assessment to inform teaching it needs to be ongoing as well as summative, and aid the evaluation of teaching effectiveness. Schools will have different policies with regard to planning, which is often done by teams of teachers, but the following is one model which fits in with different forms of current practice. The key steps are:

- Identify the area of mathematics.
- Read about it.
- Develop a scheme of work.
- Identify assessment points.
- Plan assessment opportunities.
- Refine to weekly or daily plans.

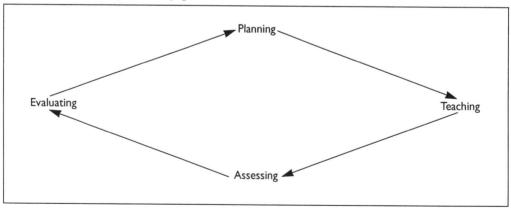

Figure 5.1 Planning the assessment cycle

Identify the area of mathematics to be taught

This will usually be determined by the school's scheme of work. According to SCAA (1995), this might be continuous, blocked or cross-curricular, and will include processes and content of maths (referring to the National Curriculum Programmes of Study for children in Year 1 and above), as well as broader dimensions of learning, such as attitudes and social skills.

Read about it

This involves reading the mathematical background, to get a feel for the key ideas, how children progress to more advanced and abstract notions, and to identify potential areas of difficulty.This may include referring to the sections of this book, a published scheme handbook, or other reference and resource books.

Develop a scheme of work

This allows for a progression of ideas and levels of difficulty with a range of teaching approaches. Some published schemes are better than others at providing this range, and it is useful to check by referring to the National Curriculum on Using and Applying: is there, for instance, a range of contexts, *practical, real problem-solving and within mathematics itself*, and are there opportunities to develop mathematical language, communication and reasoning? The strands *Children should be given opportunities* to at the beginning of the relevant section of the PoS provide a reminder of the range of apparatus and resources required. For instance, for Shape and Space, *children should be given opportunities to ... use computers*. Some published schemes may not provide for this. The important point here is for the teacher to use the scheme as a resource rather than feel driven by it.There are many activity books and resources available which supply a range of activities. Closed activities can be easily adapted to allow a more investigative approach by children, as suggested in the *Non-Statutory Guidance for the National Curriculum* (NCC, 1989:D7).

For example, often schemes include an activity around bonds for a particular number, usually single digit at Key Stage 1. Children may be expected to write answers to number sentences all with the same result, and the intention will be for them to spot patterns because of the order (closed task), e.g.:

$$7 + 1 =$$
$$6 + 2 =$$
$$5 + 3 =$$

etc.

A way to cover this and more is to ask *'How many ways can you make 8?'* (open task). See 'How Many Ways?' in Sections 2.2 and 2.6 of this book.

It may also be necessary to refer to the scheme handbooks for several levels to ensure the full range of expectations for the age range.

Here is an example of a scheme of work for multiplication and division from Section 2.3, showing a balance of activities, contexts and resources:

Key ideas	Activities
Counting groups	talking about pairs
Repeated addition	staircases
Number patterns	counting aloud, number square patterns
Recall of multiplication facts	calculator games and circle games
Division – grouping	PE groups, take a handful of cubes
Division – sharing	teddies and sweets problems, Towers game
Inverse operations	blobs and arrows
Factors	investigating rectangular numbers (pegboards)
	factor trees
Multiply and divide by 10	calculator patterns
Two digit multiplication	Three digits: what is the greatest product?
Larger number problems	value for money for party food
	Euro-corner: currency conversion

Identify assessment points

It is useful to ask at this stage: What might children do or say which would show that they have understood a particular idea? This involves deciding what you are going to look out for in the children's responses and finding out about children's informal knowledge and previous experience they may have had inside and outside school.

Here is an example of a scheme of work for early number from Section 2.2, with assessment points identified:

Key ideas	Assessment points	Activities
Counting	saying numbers in order	counting children, rhymes
	one number for one object	games with objects to collect
		e.g. shopping game
Cardinality	'So how many are there?'	how many in the box? skittles
Counting for a purpose	counting not grabbing	'please fetch me 6 aprons',
	counting to check	sharing 'sweets' with teddies
Comparing	using 'more' or 'less'	sharing fruit and snacks
	using numbers to compare	
Representing numbers	using tallies or numerals	scoring skittles and games
		making labels
		'my numbers' books
Reading numerals	saying the numbers,	rhyme time, calendar, books
		calculators, number walk,
	referring to numeral to check	tidy up labels
	number there should be	
Addition and subtraction	using visualising, fingers	how many's hiding in the box?
	with a range of numbers	
	knowing number bonds	
	'How did you work it out?'	

| Multiplication and division | counting groups as items
sharing equally
knowing facts
e.g. 4 means 2 each | PE – getting dressed (pairs),
sharing problems |

Plan assessment opportunities

Children need to be given the chance early on to show you what they know and can do, as well as what they find difficult. Starting with simple ideas and building up to more complex ones as time goes on may mean that some children never reach challenges that match their capabilities. It is useful to plan an initial activity which gives children the opportunity to show you what they know and to discuss what they mean by using mathematical terms. An example of this is in Section 2.6 (How many ways?) where the teacher was able to assess that some children could confidently add fractions mentally. Other examples are the visualising activity in Section 3.1 and the shopping game in Section 2.2. Planning ongoing assessment means identifying questions you might ask, problems you could pose and choices you might offer, as in the above scheme for early number, for example, or the packaging problem in Section 3.4, where choices of approach were offered to the children.

Refine to weekly and/or daily plans

These could include shorthand reminders of key aims and assessment points. Pinpointing when assessments will take place helps ensure they actually happen! Assessment might take place during an initial discussion, or by targeting groups towards the end of the week. It is also important to plan how children will be focused on in turn. How this is done will vary according to the age of the children and the style of teaching and organisation involved. A group could be selected for assessment in each session. If three children are targeted in a session, over 10 sessions there will be notes on 30 children. If the teacher is working mainly with one group in a particular session anyway, then it makes sense to assess these children. If children are working independently, the teacher may choose a few each session to discuss their work. Even if the whole class is together for a discussion, it is useful to select a few children for focus.

Subsequent short-term plans will then need to be amended in the light of ongoing assessments and evaluations to allow for differentiation and to follow the children's needs and interests.

The key thing is to have a *system for looking*, so that no children are ignored and a breadth of mathematical development is considered. A single sheet which has all the children's names and the different aspects of maths is useful to keep track of who you have made assessments of, and when. This helps you to monitor that all children are receiving your attention. The headings for Key Stage 1 and 2 would be:

Names	Using & Applying	Number	Shape & space	Handling data (KS2)

This allows any gaps to be spotted and children not making progress can be identified, whether high or low attainers in mathematics. The system should also include making adjustments to plans in the light of the children's responses, and provide whatever evidence is needed for reports. (See 'Recording' below.)

Some useful assessment strategies are:

- Asking children to talk through what they have just been doing: this can allow children to spot mistakes for themselves as well as giving insights into their strategies.
- Asking a group of children to solve the same problem, then asking for individuals to explain methods: an example of this is the children explaining methods for working out six nines (page 36).
- Asking a group of children to solve a problem collectively, then listening to the discussion, e.g packaging case study (Section 3.4).
- Asking children to report back to the whole group at the end of the session – this gives them opportunities not only to communicate findings, but to *explain their thinking to support the development of their reasoning*. They can be asked to explain methods used, and to justify choices they have made about methods and apparatus, e.g. Key Stage 1 data handling case study (Section 4.2).
- Giving children a choice of apparatus which includes some unsuitable equipment. For instance, offering children shells of different sizes and multilink for weighing allows the teacher to see if children appreciate the need for equal units. Questioning them will help in ascertaining whether they have chosen the unsuitable materials just on a whim, or because they really do not understand.
- Asking children to record a practical or mental activity in their own way: what they choose to stress or ignore, and the degree of abstract symbols or language used will give useful clues to be followed up by questioning. Examples of this are children's recording on page 27 (Figure 2.9) in Section 2.
- Giving children a range of examples to sort, which includes a variety of non-standard possibilities as well as more common ones, together with 'nearly but not quite examples' will help to show whether they are focusing on significant features. An example of this is discussed in the Introduction to Section 3.2, Shape and Space (page 77).

- Making deliberate mistakes, or examples which follow children's incorrect reasoning, in an atmosphere which invites them to correct the teacher. One example might be cutting unequal 'halves' and seeing if children spot this A useful strategy with very young children is to have a puppet or toy who is not very expert and known to get into muddles, and invite the children to help out, for instance in sorting letters from numbers, or making number sentences
- Asking children to give instructions to someone else, as with the drawing activities in Section 3.2 (Figure 3.7).
- Asking children to use an idea in a different context: care needs to be taken that the context is one in which the child feels confident, and that the level of difficulty is not too high, or the accumulation of unfamiliar challenges may make the problem overwhelmingly difficult. Examples of this are the problems for multiplication and division of converting currencies and scales, or costing drinks for a party in Section 2.3.
- Asking children what they thought about doing an activity: this may range from asking children to select from a smiley face or a frowning face, to choosing statements such as *'I did my best'* or *'I could have tried harder'* or asking children what they found difficult or easy. Older children might keep a maths diary, in which they record activities and reflections on them, and which can form the basis for a written or verbal dialogue with the teacher.

Recording assessments

Some different kinds of recording

Identifying particular needs during a session. The teacher notes these in a daily diary and refers to them when planning the next stage of the work. In the Nursery shopping game case study (Section 2.1) a group of children could already read confidently numerals to six on a dice and the teacher would need to build on this in making future provision with these children in mind.

A child makes a significant breakthrough in understanding – as revealed by a comment. The teacher has a record book with a page per child and, as part of a regular routine, notes this at the end of the day. This is referred to when writing a summative report for parents. If the significant remark was in relation to some work on paper, this (or a photocopy) is put in the child's file, with the context and the remark written on the back. If this is the main mode of record keeping, it is useful for the teacher to keep a review chart at the front of files as mentioned above.

Making observations of very young children – The teacher may spend 10 minutes of each session observing a particular child, as well as noting significant incidents. Usually such observations will cover social, emotional, physical and cognitive aspects of learning, including more than one Area of Experience, such as language and literacy, mathematical, scientific and technological. Sometimes the focus will be more mathematical, perhaps because the child is playing a game, or solving a problem involving mathematics. Where the teacher works as part of a team, the observations are usually shared, before being filed, by placing them in a central location, and implications for planning are identified by the team.

Working with a focus group – The teacher may prepare a sheet to record observations for the group, with headings. This can be photocopied to put in each child's file. At intervals they can be reviewed and patterns of development identified.Here is an example from the packaging case study (Section 3.4). The headings are adapted from the *Primary Learning Record* (Hestler *et al.*, 1993)

CONTEXT	designing packaging for delicatessen items
NAMES	
ATTITUDE & APPROACH	
STRATEGIES estimating measuring	
UNDERSTANDING calculating volume making nets	
CHILD'S COMMENT	
SIGNIFICANCE & PLANNING	

Noting responses of the whole class in a record book with children's names listed down one side of each page. The teacher will record one line of observation and comment against each child's name. This is particularly useful for regular written work from the class which needs to be analysed after each session, noting children with difficulties or needing further challenge. This allows the teacher to modify work in the following session. Developments can then be followed through easily by following an individual child's name across several pages. This type of recording works well for sessions where children work from a published scheme.

Entries might look something like this:

Date 13/11/95 Investigating nets for cubes (page 35, Book 4)
Fadilah A. No problems. Go onto nets of other 3D shapes
Tom C.   Found it difficult to predict which nets would fold into cubes. Use polydrons
Rheem S. Had system for checking all possibilities."you have to have one sticking out on each side"
Tracey W. Found all possibilities but hadn't explained system.Talk to her

Children note their own responses and self-assessments – For older children, written feedback may be part of a written dialogue with the child, which includes their self-assessment or comments, and in some schools children keep notebooks or maths diaries for this purpose. Younger children may be asked to pick smiley or frowning faces to reflect their feelings about an activity.

Keeping a class progress review sheet for a particular topic. This may simply help the teacher to keep track of who has done what, but it may also allow the teacher to summarise progress and note children having problems in coded form such as ticks and stars, plus one-phrase comments where needed. This acts as a reference when planning work and future assessment, and helps to identify groups of children with similar needs in a particular area. This would supplement but not replace evidence of what children say, do and produce. For the multiplication work described earlier the review sheet might have these headings:

NAMES	USE & APPLY	REPTD. ADDN.	RECALL FACTORS	MULT. & DIVN. BY 10	2 DIG. MULT.

Reporting

Reporting methods will depend largely on school policies. Normally schools will summarise children's progress at the end of the year, term or topic and keep samples of work. The assessment system needs to provide enough *evidence* from ongoing records to support a summary of an individual child's progress for parents and future teachers. This needs to reflect a broad spectrum of mathematics and to include Using and Applying Mathematics. The acid test for an assessment and record keeping system is this:

> If at any time of the year a parent asks about a child's progress in mathematics, can the teacher provide a detailed answer, with some examples, relating to different aspects of mathematics, and with indications of the child's mathematical needs?

If a child has particular learning needs, then more detailed evidence of patterns of behaviour will be required.

5.2 CLASSROOM ORGANISATION

Atmosphere

It is essential to consider what kind of messages are transmitted, explicitly or unintentionally, to children about mathematics learning. In our case studies, e.g. on packaging, we have tried to set up situations in which the children were stimulated by the nature of the tasks and experiences and given opportunity to think for themselves. At times the teachers saw the need to impart information or teach skills to move thinking on or to support an observed need. For example, in the Key Stage 1 Handling Data (Section 4.2) children needed help in preparing a data collection sheet . In conversations described, the questioning was significant in the degree to which there was challenge to children but also respect for their developing ideas. There also needs to be concern for the needs of individual children and a consideration of how the teacher can plan to ensure all children have access to the curriculum. For example in Section 2.3, on the Circle card activity, children are given the task of making up their own loops and this allowed individual children to approach the task in different ways. The teacher is planning for differentiation by outcome. One child, a boy with special learning needs, was able to come up with a different idea which was respected by other children. The nature of the task allowed him, with his support teacher, to have access to the work of the class and to respond with his own ideas. The valuing of children's ideas is crucial. Teacher expectation must not limit the possibilities for individuals in individual tasks. In the Nursery Shopping Game context, some children would benefit from the opportunity to work with a dice with numbers 1 to 10.

The teacher would, similarly, need to consider bilingual children at different stages in learning English. For example, would it help to begin with a more practical or body task where children can follow actions, accompanied by appropriate language, before embarking on an oral or written context? (See the comments on 'body activities' later in this section.) Another type of activity supportive of bilingual children is a game with a repetitive structure of moves. This and the accompanying language allows reinforcement and a model for speech.

The case study for Using and Applying (Section 1) explicitly identifies the kind of atmosphere supportive of developing children's mathematical thinking through the encouragement of prediction and conjecture. There is also an element of risk-taking for teachers in the more open-ended work, in that likely outcomes for the children can be identified, but they will need to keep an open mind in looking for particular approaches and strategies which may surprise and require continual reflection on the children's development.

The teacher's role is central, and has been examined in particular contexts in this book. What we wish to address here is how the teacher organises overall for successful mathematics learning. We will look, in particular at:

- Starting work in stimulating ways.
- Various groupings of children to suit different purposes.
- Display ideas to support mathematical learning.
- Using resources, including published schemes.

The intention is to suggest how all of these considerations can be drawn together in providing for a context in which challenging work and confidence building can be developed. There will be descriptions of how two teachers address planning, organisation in their classrooms and a section specifically on mathematics in the Early Years to draw out principles particularly focused on that stage of learning.

Starting an activity in a stimulating way

Engagement with a task

How can we make the experience one which children are able and eager to tackle? The initial presentation and questioning is crucial. If the teacher is introducing a new topic, how can children's current understanding be built on? If fractions were being taught to a class, asking children how they would explain or 'make a picture' to show a half to someone else, what would they do? If the teacher expects and encourages creativity in showing half a shape in many different ways, the activity will begin to develop momentum. In the Measures Section, children working on reading clocks were asked to recall from memory 'a clock you know' and draw it. Their drawings and accompanying discussion involved the children in discussing something familiar to them and allowed the teacher to make informed judgements about how to proceed.

Puzzles or questions

Setting challenges like, *'Who can find the biggest number in the newspaper?'* or *'How many sweets are the jar?'* can encourage thinking about the possible outcomes but also about how to tackle the question. Magic squares is an example of a puzzle *(Can you fit the numbers 1 to 9 in a 3 by 3 square so that each line adds to 15?)* which can again be used to stimulate thinking *(Can it be done? How can we find out?)*

Drama or role play to stimulate mathematical ideas

This is another possible approach. For example, young children might arrive in school one morning to find a pile of boxes in the role play area (set up as a shop) and a letter from the shopkeeper who has been unexpectedly called away and had to leave stock unsorted: *'Can the children, please, sort the shop out and open up until she returns'* (Figure 5.2). This would lead into sorting items on shelves, setting up a till, labelling prices and so on which can support play in the shop.

Enacting number stories or rhymes can be effective in making mathematics more vivid. The rhyme 'Five Currant Buns in the Baker's Shop' where children

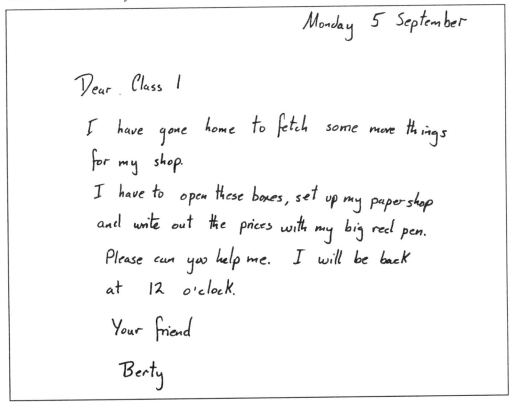

Monday 5 September

Dear Class 1

I have gone home to fetch some more things for my shop.
I have to open these boxes, set up my paper shop and write out the prices with my big red pen.
Please can you help me. I will be back at 12 o'clock.

Your friend

Berty

Figure 5.2 Letter found by children

can 'buy' a bun, pay with a penny and take one away can be experienced by a group of children, and the operations on the small number are supported by the actions in the rhyme.

Whole body activities

These can provide another approach in which children can experience mathematical ideas physically.

Children can be labelled as numbers, for example with hats or numeral cards fixed to jumpers with safety-pins. They can then be asked to make relationships between the various numbers, depending on stage of understanding. For example, children could sort themselves into number order, pairs could get together to make two digit numbers or bonds for 10 or two people could stand on either side of a decimal point person and make numbers with one decimal point. Numbers could relate to the number of children in the class or be varied to suit particular purposes (Figure 5.3).

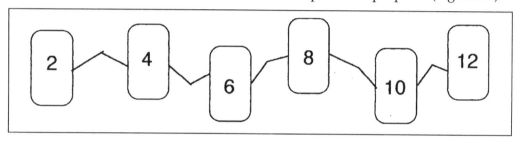

Figure 5.3 Activities for children wearing number cards

Making shapes with the body in PE activities would be one example. In the Corners activity (see Section 2.2) children can stand in groups at the corners of a PE mat and move to the centre to answer *'How many are there altogether?'* (Figure 5.4). This can lead to finding totals by using cubes on paper shapes. At Key Stage 2, numbered children can move across a decimal point when multiplied or divided, as described in Section 2.4. For factors, 24 children from the class can be asked to group themselves in 2s, then move into 3s, 4s, etc., to illustrate which numbers work and which do not. Bilingual children can be helped to see the nature of the mathematical ideas by being involved and work can then move onto arranging objects on table tops. For all children the physical experience can be recalled in assisting the development of mental images.

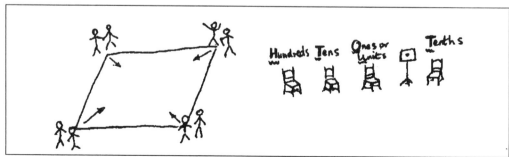

Figure 5.4 Apparatus for whole body activities

Groupings

According to the purpose of the mathematical task or activity, different groupings may be appropriate.

Whole class

This can be used to set the scene for new work, draw points together, ask children to report findings or set up a common starting point. Quick oral games and activities such as Fizz Buzz or rhymes can also be tackled in this context. One concern with a common starting point is that not all children will understand what is aimed at a whole class, but it is possible to plan so that different children will gain different things from the experience. As long as the starting point is initially accessible to all the pupils, particular groups/individuals can respond in different ways (this is known as differentiation by outcome). The teacher needs to be clear what the range of responses might look like and about the kind of support she will offer based on her knowledge of the children. Some examples of activities suitable for the whole class are *'How many ways can you make...'* (choose a number, amount of money, arrangement of squares etc to suit the class or allow children to choose their own – Section 2.6, activity 2). There is also an example of *'How Many Different...'* in Section 3.2 (page 88). Children can respond in different ways through:

- Solutions they suggest e.g. for '10' might be pairs adding to 10, answers involving a wider range of operations or fractions/decimals.
- Approaches they use – do they systematically work through ways of arranging 5 squares?
- Different ways of recording and explaining findings.

Feedback sessions bringing children's ideas together link well with the language and communication strand of Using and Applying (Key Stage 1 'discuss...work, responding to and asking mathematical questions' or Key Stage 2 'present information and results clearly, and explain reasons for their choice of presentation'). If different groups have worked on different aspects of the same theme, reporting back gives opportunity for children to articulate their findings and listen to the ideas of others. The teacher can listen and make assessments as well as participating in pulling out key teaching points. An example of this is in Jon's class description (see page 190).

'Maths on the Mat' times are useful small slots of time where mathematical skills and ideas can be practised and consolidated. Helping the teacher calculate register numbers, add up the dinner money, play games and rhymes, respond to mental challenges in Geometry and Number are all possibilities. Children could be asked to hide behind a screen and hold up hands while others work out how many children are hidden by the number of hands they can see. The teacher (or a child) can hold up a shape, but show only part, such as a corner. Can children guess the shape and say why? Then a bit more can be revealed. Do they want to revise their guess? Why?

Small groups

Children could be organised into groups within the whole class lesson but at times the teacher will need to group children for particular purposes and this will inform the size and composition of the groups. In the case study for packaging in Section 3. 4, children were grouped so that a range of roles could be covered, including the keeping of a diary. For example, the class might be planning an event – a picnic or a party – and groups will address different aspects, identify approaches and gather necessary data. The groups are required to collaborate in solving a problem, using mathematical knowledge, skills and understanding. Other groups may be set up by the teacher, based on observations made of a particular learning need. For example, s/he may observe that some children were having difficulty with using measuring tools in a DT activity and assemble that group to focus specifically on the relevant aspect of maths. Or she may have observed several children who could be taken further in a topic and give them a particular extension task to work on together.

Gender can be an issue in grouping here and needs to be taken into account in planning group composition. In the Key Stage 2 Handling Data case study (Section 4.2), girls and boys chose to work separately and the teacher did not interfere. In some contexts, perhaps where particular girls feel less confident, single sex groups might act as support to the development of expertise free from the pressure of more confident peers. Bennett and Dunne (1992) suggest that the content of the task needs to be taken into account, and that in tasks such as computer work girls may be less confident. The teacher needs to monitor groups to see if all children have equal opportunity for involvement.

For bilingual children the teacher will need to consider how to involve any support teachers in groups and consider different approaches such as pairing children so that a more confident English speaker can support another child who speaks the same mother tongue.

Organising for group work also means planning teacher focus to avoid the pressures of having to respond superficially to the needs of groups. How many groups will there be? When and where will teacher attention need to be greatest?

Which groups can work without teacher help? All the children need to benefit from teacher support at times and so groupings will need to vary to ensure that all attention is not focused on one set of children. In advance the likely times at which teacher support will be needed should be identified. If a group is to be started on a new activity, teacher input may be required at the beginning and other groups will need to be fairly independent to allow this to happen. Similarly, if all groups finish at the same time or need moving on at the same time, the teacher will be unable to give sufficient attention. Groups need to be planned so that while one group is starting on a new activity, other groups are working on tasks they have started previously or on follow-up which they can work on independently.

When children are working in groups the teacher can maximise her teaching by planning her input to different groups. She can have, say, four groups working and plan it so that two are involved in reinforcement work requiring little teacher intervention. Of the remaining two groups one might need attention to start a new activity and the other might need intervention after a beginning task. The main point is that the teacher *plans* her presence with particular groups and sets up other tasks which require less explanation or teacher support. The teacher will need also to anticipate which groups or individuals will need support immediately after a whole class introduction to enable them to engage with the task. A staggered organisation for introducing new work after an explanation to the whole class can allow the teacher to look closely at the extent to which children are engaged and know what to do:

a.m.

Groups A & B finish recording

Groups C & D – introduce new activity

BREAK

Groups A & B introduce new activity

Groups C & D work on activity independently

Individuals

Within whole class and group focuses it is often necessary for the teacher to help an individual child who needs immediate attention to be able to continue with the task. There will also be times when a teacher will plan for children to tackle work individually. This might relate to individuals making records or reports of work undertaken or practice of mathematical knowledge or skills. Some children have particular special needs and may have special teacher support. The class teacher can work with the support teacher to integrate the child into the mainstream work of the class. It is as important to provide special needs support for mathematical work as for literacy. As in group work, although this allows for more focused attention and observation by the teacher, it is essential that others in the class can work independently.

Equipping the learning environment for maths and use of display

We have selected examples of resources we feel would support the tasks described in this book. It is not exhaustive but aimed at exemplifying appropriate material to support our aims.

The range of equipment will be wide in all phases but there are some items which will need to feature particularly at different stages. Messages can unconsciously be communicated if practical equipment is kept mainly in classes of younger children and older children have to go to those classes to fetch equipment. Apparatus such as Polydron may be used more often in a more structured, focused way with older children but it can be extremely helpful in developing spatial ideas, such as nets of 3D shapes.

Nursery/early years

Some preschool learning environments will contain a designated maths area, but this may be more common in later stages of school. Much of the practical equipment suggested for older children is to be encouraged at this stage but it may be integrated into the provision in a variety of areas. For example, in shop role play areas tills with coins, calculators, telephones, tape measures, height charts and scales can all be made available to support the play. At the same time they will stimulate experience with number, measures, money and so on. Just as a note pad by the telephone will encourage young children to engage in early writing, so the recording of mathematical experiences can be stimulated. A carpet square showing all the numbers from 1 to 100 can be obtained for children to walk around. A Number Line for the wall or the floor can be used to stimulate interest in larger numbers.

Sand and water experience, whether in trays or pits outside offer opportunity for exploration with containers but also building, counting (how many bucketfuls of sand did your castle need?). Numerals can be quite naturally displayed and discussed on calendars, clocks and the equipment mentioned above. In addition more structured play equipment can be introduced, for example numeral floor tiles and number rhyme and story books. Large wooden numerals for floor or table top use can encouraging recognition, ordering and so on. Calculators can be incorporated in play but also explored in their own right through questioning, such as what happens if you press this button? Programmable toys, such as Roamer, can also be explored in developing early spatial and measurement ideas through activities such as '*How can you make Roamer come to you?*' Number games and puzzles, such as children experience at home can also be included as table top activities, involving fitting and numerical experience. A variety of construction material, including building blocks, is commonly found in nurseries and building and talking about their constructions will offer contexts for children to physically experience shape and space but also to develop their mathematical language in describing and explaining their building. Sets of shapes or pattern blocks can offer stimulus for pattern making. Cooking and gardening are other contexts which can offer opportunity for number and measures. Equipment which may not at first appear to be 'mathematical' also needs to be considered, e.g. musical instruments in developing patterns of sounds.

Key Stages 1 and 2

Number

- Counting material can include structured as well as more everyday objects. Unifix, Multilink, coloured sticks or rods and teddy counters (they come in different colours and sizes), but there could also counters, acorns, conkers, shells and buttons. It is useful to have quite large collections of objects for 'How many in the jar?' type estimation and counting activities.
- Games could be commercial such as Snakes and Ladders, dominoes or the variety on offer in toy shops, with potential for number, and made (sources like the Bright Ideas Games book are useful).

- A range of dice allows flexibility in game design: commercial with dots, numerals, different number of faces and home made with colours or coin amounts etc. for particular games.
- Number cards (1 to 100) but also playing cards and blank cards for children to make their own games.
- Number lines and squares for reference (0–1,000 or fractions, decimals, negative numbers)
- Calculators. It is useful to have some hand-held and some table-top or OHP versions so that the teacher can focus children's understanding by getting them to instruct on key sequences

Shape and Space

- Puzzles (e.g. tangrams).
- Multilink and mats for building, translating 2D plans into models and representing models as plans.
- Pattern blocks for tessellation, fitting and dissecting shapes.
- Paper, various – squares of different sizes, dotty, 100 square.
- 2D/3D shapes/junk boxes, including Easter egg boxes (make a collection of interesting packets).

Measures

- Rulers and tapes marked in different ways to allow comparisons.
- Real coins as well as 'pretend' so children can feel the weight, see the colour and so on.
- Capacity containers, standardised and containers from home, junk.
- Variety of scales, balance and hanging including some with see-through buckets.
- Spring balances.
- Clocks including real working clocks – analogue and digital timers, tockers, sand and digital/analogue.
- Calendars.

Data handling

- Sorting/venn sets and sorting material – cars, houses.
- Collection of buttons, bought in shop or boot sales (excellent for sorting/classifying).
- Cubes and spike abacus, Unifix and Multilink for 3D graphs.
- Large floor grids for real graphs.

General

- Maths dictionaries, commercial and made by the children.
- Variety of papers for exploring and recording (different sized squares, dotty etc.).

- 'Thinking paper' for children to record in their own ways of draft math ideas.
- Topic collections, e.g. Pattern (wallpaper, wrapping paper, photos from the environment all from a range of cultures).

Display/environment

The learning environment can be set up to encourage mathematical thinking through the organisation of resources as well as displays of children's work or stimulus material.

For example, labels on drawers can be made with pictures from catalogues for young children to match or quantities of objects can be shown to encourage counting and calculation of missing items. Older children can make plans of places of furniture and equipment in the class if rearrangements are a feature, according to type of activity. The purpose of making a range of apparatus accessible to children is also served. Plans for the bases of containers of equipment can be drawn on cupboard surface so that children can match the container to its place by matching shape.

Permanent displays in school can be introduced by the teacher or made by children. Days of the week or months suspended from the ceiling in vertical order are available for use as references by the children. Posters and dictionaries set up by the teacher or made by children provide another source of reference material. Number friezes can again be displayed and varied according to the age of children (e.g. 0–20, 0–100, 0–1000) and very large numbers can be represented by such means as colouring sheets of small squared paper in blocks and displaying the results. Commercial posters help to stimulate ideas or provide reference. Children can write help procedures for other children to use for Logo or the Roamer.

Stimulus collections and interactive displays contribute to the atmosphere of a mathematical learning environment. For example, a collection of patterns from wrapping paper, wallpaper, fabric can act as a focus for children to discuss pattern and then they can add examples to the collection such as beads on thread, records of musical patterns they have made. Children could be asked to match nets to shapes or 'spot the odd one out'.

Other kinds of stimulus might be numerals taped to the backs of chairs. Children will start to talk about them and notice that theirs is 'two more than' their friend's. Questions of the Week can be displayed to initiate discussion, such as 'How many marbles do you think are in this jar?' Children can work at this over a few days and parents and brothers and sisters are likely to get involved when children are collected! Questions can be varied according to the age of children. For older children a challenge might be *'What is the largest number you can make using the digits 1,2,3,4 with multiplication signs? Is it 12 x 34 or perhaps 231 x 4?'*. These challenges can encourage discussion across a number of classes or act as the introduction to developing a new idea or extending an old one.

Case Study: Key Stage 1

In an ordinary week, following from my half termly planning, I plan a range of mathematical experience for the children. I use a range of resources, including a published scheme, HBJ (1992), which starts with themes, and the investigation material (*Miss Polly Investigates*) from Cambridge Maths (1989).

On Monday morning I introduce a variety of work set out on the tables and remind the children of ongoing activities they can pick up if they finish (e.g. number games they know).

The theme from the scheme provides the focus for a half term and I group the children using names relating to the theme. These groups are mainly friendship based but I ensure the mix contains children who can read and write or speak sufficiently confidently to record and communicate group findings.For each half term these groups are changed so that the children have the opportunity to work with all the other children in the class over the year.

I set up challenges for the groups from the HBJ scheme and make sure that only one or two groups start these at once while others work on reinforcement work (maths or work in other curriculum areas). I can then concentrate on the groups with the new work. The next day these groups will follow up with more independent work from the challenge and I can then introduce the new work to the other groups. This does not mean that I have not planned or set up tasks in other areas, but they may be fairly quick prompts to stimulate the work for that day, e.g. when the role play area was a pirate ship I told them that another pirate ship was coming near. What would they do? As work progresses I can break off from the maths groups briefly to visit the role play area at points and ask, *'Has the ship arrived yet?'* Although I am focused mainly on the new work there will be points at which they can continue alone, which means I can still maintain the overview of the whole class. As work progresses on the maths I will set up an investigation which will be done more independently by the groups, and I will also be looking out for particular individuals or groups who need gathering together for some reinforcement or extension work. By Thursday or Friday I will be drawing the work together and noting what needs to be built into the following week.

Each day at the end of mornings and afternoons there is opportunity for groups to feed back findings so far to the class. There are also mat times for short bursts of whole class practice and reinforcement of number e.g. showing a stick of 10 Unifix to the children, breaking some off (without showing them) and then asking them to work out from the remainder I show, how many are missing. Another activity I do regularly with the class is discussing the date with reference to the calendar. There may be birthdays coming up or holidays. Questions such as *'How many days is it until...?'* provide a chance for children to practise mental arithmetic and for me to make informal assessments of individuals.

Case study: Key Stage 2 (Year 6)

I will look at a typical week where I am part the way through my half termly plan. I usually set aside the period after group reading in the morning for Maths or Science work. This means that I can start the whole class off on new work in maths on one day but on the next I can have some science work alongside. The week I am describing is during my block of work on Shape and Space. On Monday I will begin a new investigation with the whole class, in this case based on a page from the pupil book of the scheme (nets). I wanted them to develop Using and Applying skills alongside understanding the construction of 3D shapes. The scheme page gives the children a net and asks them to copy it, cut it out and assemble a cube. I have decided to open this up for investigation by starting to ask children to think about possible arrangements of six squares. Next I will want them to predict which would fold into cubes. They will need to give reasons for this. I will offer plastic squares which fit together, like Polydron, squared paper and scissors. I ask them to try to find 10 different arrangements, thereby giving them a goal, but I anticipate that some children will wish to try to exhaust the possibilities and others will stop at explaining how they know the ones they have found are all different. Some children might pose questions of their own such as *'I wonder what would happen with nets of a pyramid?'* I feel it is important to emphasise that children should be encouraged to do this as their motivation is likely to be increased.

I know the children who will need support to make a start and I know that I will have to adjust my intervention according to individual children as they progress with the investigation which will develop over the next 2 or 3 days. At the end of each morning or day there will be review of their findings so far. This allows me to see how well children can explain and communicate their ideas, to think about the next intervention needed and to suggest ways forward for other children. At the end of the review sessions I will keep any children back who need further help or questioning, such as those who are having difficulties in deciding if they have repeats, and this might require less open questions in some cases such as have you tried cutting out the shapes and comparing them by putting them on top of each other?

By Thursday most of the children will have explored the problem sufficiently and are able to give a group report back to the class. Some children will then go back to the page from the scheme for reinforcement while others will write up their results and think about possible extensions for example: *'Do you get the same number of possibilities with 6 triangles?'*. Some children will become interested in the nets for other 3D shapes (which I plan to move onto next week) and some are investigating whether other 2D shapes can be made into 3D shapes using only six pieces. Polydron is helpful here. All the children can expect to have their contributions valued in these class sessions. Children are encouraged to see that different ends can result from the same starting point and that they need not only value the maths produced by those who are 'good at maths.'

On Friday morning I pick up on the ongoing number work I have identified in my longer term planning. I will group them and give work which is suitable for that group's level of understanding, based on my observations and records of previous work. If I feel I wish to select work from different level books in a scheme I will copy the activities rather than give children books numbered so as to lower self-esteem. I may sometimes convert the scheme page into my own worksheet for the children.

In this way I have selected from my half termly scheme on Shape and Space and continued ongoing work on number. In addition to this, in a typical week, I will use opportunities to set up mental maths challenges. For example, I will ask the children to work out a calculation mentally and explain the steps. We might also as a class play a short game of Fizz-Buzz to practise particular multiples.

Conclusion

Mathematical experience planned within the primary curriculum needs to demonstrate its distinctive nature and also to link with and reflect overall primary practice. There needs to a stimulating environment showing its cross-curricular links but also addressing mathematical tasks for their own sake. A questioning, conjecturing atmosphere can be fostered by encouraging children to see that maths can be presented in different ways and that a variety of methods can be employed in solving problems. There needs to a variety of approaches and teaching strategies according to clear aims and the organisation of the learning environment needs to reflect these aims.

References

Askew, M. and William, D. (1995) *Recent Research in Mathematics Education 5–16*. London: OFSTED.

Atkinson, S. (ed.) (1992) *Mathematics With Reason*. London: Hodder and Stoughton.

Bennett, N. and Dunne, E. (1992) *Managing Classroom Groups*. Hemel Hempstead: Simon & Schuster.

BEAM (1994) *A Feel for Number: Activities for Number Recovery Programmes*. London: BEAM.

Cambridge Maths (1989) *Investigating Miss Polly*. Cambridge:CUP.

Carpenter, T.P. and Moser, J.M. (1982) The development of addition and subtraction problem solving skills. In Carpenter *et al.* (eds) *Addition and Subtraction: A Cognitive Perspective*. New Jersey: Lawrence Erlbaum.

Dickson, L., Brown, M. and Gibson, O. (1984) *Children Learning Mathematics*. London: Cassell.

DfE (1995) *Mathematics in the National Curriculum*. London: HMSO.

Graham, A. (1990) *Supporting Primary Mathematics – Handling Data*. Buckingham: Open University.

Harrison, R. (1987) 'On fullness' *Mathematics Teaching*, **119**.

Hestler, H., Ellis, S. and Barry, M. (1993) *Guide to The Primary Learning Record*. London: Centre for Language and Primary Education.

Hughes, M. (1986) *Children and Number*. Oxford: Blackwell.

Kerslake, D., Burton, L., Harvey, R., Street, L. and Walsh, A. (1992) *HBJ Mathematics*. London: HBJ.

ILEA (1976) *Checkpoints Cards*. London: Harcourt, Brace & Jovanovitch.

NCC (National Curriculum Council) (1989) *Mathematics Non-Statutory Guidance*. London: HMSO.

NCC (National Curriculum Council) (1992) *Mathematics Programmes of Study*. York: NCC.

NCTM National Council of Teachers of Mathematics (1981) *Teaching Statistics and Probability*. London: Jonathan Press.

Nugent, W. (1990) 'Tomorrow I'm going to turn into a giraffe'. *Mathematics in Schools*, **19(1)**, 10–12.

OFSTED (1993) *The Teaching and Learning of Number in Primary Schools*. London: HMSO.

Orton, A. and Wain, G. (1994) *Issues in Teaching Mathematics*. London: Cassell

Pengelly, H. (1985) *Mathematics Making Sense*. Perth: University of Western Australia.

Piaget, J. (1952) *The Child's Conception of Number*. London: Routledge and Kegan Paul.

Pinel, A. (1994) *Loop Cards*, Bognor Regis: J. Pinel.

PRIME (1991) *Calculators, Children and Mathematics*. Hemel Hempstead: Simon & Schuster.

SCAA (1995a) *Exemplification of Standards*. London: SCAA.

SCAA (1995b) *Planning the Curriculum at KS1 and KS2*. London: SCAA.

Schaeffer, B., *et al.* (1974) 'Number development in young children', *Cognitive Psychology*, **6**, 357–79.

Vygotsky, L. (1978) *Mind in Society*. Cambridge, Ma.: MIT

Wigley, A, (1994) *Teaching Number Mathematics Teaching 146*. Association of Teachers of Mathematics.

Young Loveridge, J. (1987) 'Learning mathematics', *British Journal of Developmental Psychology*, **5**, 155–67.

USEFUL RESOURCES

Ball, G. (1990) *Talking and Learning*. Oxford: Blackwell.

Baratta Lorton, M. (1976) *Mathematics Their Way and Workjobs 2*. London: Addison Wesley.

BEAM (1994) *A Feel for Number: Activities for Number Recovery Programmes*. London: BEAM.

BEAM (1995) *Number at Key Stage One*. London: BEAM/King's College London/London Borough of Tower Hamlet.
and other BEAM publications, including *Exploring Place Value, Spot the Pattern,Triangles and Quadrangles, Start from Scratch Series* (e.g. Measures).
BEAM, Barnsbury Complex, Offord Road, London N1 1QH.

Bell, R. and Cornelius, M. (1988) *Board Games From Round the World: A Source Book for Mathematical Investigations*. Cambridge: Cambridge University Press.

Bird, M. (1992) *Mathematics for Young Children*. London: Routledge.

Brewer, C. and Cranmer, M. (1988) *Bright Ideas: Maths Games*. Leamington Spa: Scholastic.

Bloomfield, A. (1990) *People Maths*. Cheltenham: Stanley Thornes.

Burton, L. (1994) *Children Learning Mathematics*. Hemel Hempstead: Simon & Schuster.

Clarke, S. (1995) *Formative Assessment in Mathematics, KS1 & KS2*. London: Hodder & Stoughton.

Griffiths, R. (1988) *Maths Through Play*. Hemel Hempstead: MacDonald Children's Books.

Gura, P. (1992) *Exploring Learning Young Children and Blockplay*. London: Paul Chapman.

Haylock, D. (1995) *Mathematics Explained for Primary Teachers*. London: Paul Chapman Publishing.

Langdon, N. and Snape, C. (1984) *A Way With Maths*. Cambridge: Cambridge University Press.

Lutrario, C. and Mosley, F. (1990) *Count Me In Games*. London: HBJ.

Mathematical Association (1987) *Maths Talk*. Cheltenham: Stanley Thornes.

Matterson, E. (1991) *This Little Puffin*. Harmondsworth: Puffin.

Mosley, F. (1986) *Count Me In*. London: Harper Collins.

Mottershead, L. (1985) *Investigations in Mathematics*. Oxford: Basil Blackwell.

National Council of Teachers of Mathematics (1981) *Teaching Statistics and Probability*. London: Jonathan Press.

Open University (1994) *An ABC of Number*. Milton Keynes: Open University.

Open University (1990) *Supporting Primary Mathematics*. A course for teachers which includes titles on probability, shape and space, data handling and algebra.

Ross, A. (1984) *The Story of Mathematics*. London: A&C Black.

Straker, A. (1993) *Talking Points*. Cambridge: Cambridge University Press.

Strategies (Journal): Maths and Problem Solving Magazine, 27 Frederick Street, Hockley, Birmingham B1 3HH.

Sugarman, I. (1985) *Children Calculating KS1*. Shropshire Education Publications. Tel: 01745 254521.

Walpole, Brenda (1992) *Millipedes Series*, e.g. *Size, Distance*. London: A&C Black.

Walter, M. *Magic Mirror Books*. London: Andre Deutsch.

Wiltshire LEA (1988) *Mathematics For All*. County Hall, Bythesea Road, Trowbridge, Wiltshire.

Robots

Roamer: Valiant Technology, Myrtle House, 69 Salcott Road, London SW11 6DQ. Tel: 0171 924 2366

Pip & Pixie: Swallow Systems, 134 Cock Lane, High Wycombe, Bucks HP13 7EA. Tel: 01494 813471

Software

Association of Teachers of Mathematics, 7 Shaftesbury Street, Derby DE3 8YB. Tel: 01332 46599.

Black Cat, 3 Beacon's View, Mount Street, Brecon, Powys LD3 7LY. Tel: 01874 622641.

ILECC, John Ruskin Street, London SE5 0PG. Tel: 0171 735 9123.

Longman Logotron, 124 Cambridge Science Park, Milton Road, Cambridge CB4 4ZS. Tel: 01223 425558.

NCET, Milburn Hill Road, Science Park, Coventry CV4 7JJ. Tel: 01203 416994.

SMILE Centre, Isaac Newton Centre for Professional Development, 108a Lancaster Road, London W11 1QS. Tel: 0171 221 8966.

Index